HANSARD SOCIETY S
POLITICS AND GOVE

Series Editor
F. F. Ridley

HANSARD SOCIETY SERIES IN POLITICS AND GOVERNMENT

Edited by
F. F. Ridley

1. THE QUANGO DEBATE, edited with David Wilson
2. BRITISH GOVERNMENT AND POLITICS SINCE 1945: CHANGES IN PERSPECTIVES, edited with Michael Rush
3. SLEAZE: POLITICIANS, PRIVATE INTERESTS AND PUBLIC REACTION, edited with Alan Doig
4. WOMEN IN POLITICS, edited with Joni Lovenduski and Pippa Norris
5. UNDER THE SCOTT-LIGHT: BRITISH GOVERNMENT SEEN THROUGH THE SCOTT REPORT, edited with Brian Thompson

The Hansard Society Series in Politics and Government brings to the wider public the debates and analyses of important issues first discussed in the pages of its journal, *Parliamentary Affairs*

Under the Scott-light: British Government Seen Through the Scott Report

Edited by
Brian Thompson and F. F. Ridley

Series Editor
F. F. Ridley

OXFORD UNIVERSITY PRESS
in association with
THE HANSARD SOCIETY FOR
PARLIAMENTARY GOVERNMENT

Oxford University Press, Walton Street, Oxford OX2 6DP
Oxford New York
Athens Auckland Bangkok Bombay
Calcutta Cape Town Dar es Salaam Delhi
Florence Hong Kong Istanbul Karachi
Kuala Lumpur Madras Madrid Melbourne
Mexico City Nairobi Paris Singapore
Taipei Tokyo Toronto
and associated companies in
Berlin Ibadan

Oxford is a trade mark of Oxford University Press

Published in the United States
by Oxford University Press Inc., New York

© Oxford University Press, 1997

First published in Parliamentary Affairs, 1997
New as paperback, 1997

A catalogue for this book is available from the British Library

Library of Congress Cataloging in Publication Data
(Data available)

ISBN 0–19–922278–9

Printed in Great Britain
by Headley Brothers Limited, The Invicta Press,
Ashford, Kent and London

CONTENTS

CONTRIBUTORS TO THIS VOLUME

Anthony Barker is a Reader in Government, University of Essex

Patrick Birkinshaw is Professor of Law, University of Hull

Vernon Bogdanor is Professor of Government and Fellow of Brasenose College, University of Oxford

Alan Doig is Professor of Public Sector Management, Liverpool Business School, Liverpool John Moores University

Philip Giddings is a Lecturer in Politics, Universityof Reading

Ian Leigh is a Reader in Public Law, University of Newcastle-upon-Tyne

Ralph Negrine is a Senior Lecturer in Mass Communications, University of Leicester

Barry O'Toole is a Senior Lecturer in Politics, University of Glasgow

Mark Phythian is a Lecturer in Politics, University of Wolverhampton

Brian Thompson is a Senior Lecturer in Law, University of Liverpool

Adam Tomkins is a Lecturer in Law, Kings College, London

Diana Woodhouse is a Principal Lecturer in Law, Oxford Brookes University

Preface

In the foreword to his report Sir Richard Scott commented, 'I am sure that this material will provide the public with a valuable insight into the ways in which the government has conducted itself.' But not just the Conservative government of the time : as a newspaper heading said the day after its publication, 'Scott reveals unique insight into Whitehall'— the ways of the civil service also therefore. The Scott report is thus more than an investigation of past behaviour and misbehaviour in a notorious affair, though the inquiry was set up for that purpose; it can be read as a case study of widerspread politico-administrative styles, a rare searchlight on parts of the British system of government otherwise hidden by a cult of secrecy unusual in western democracies. But Scott looks forward as well as back, raising important questions of practice and principle, thus contributing to the broad debate about reform. The light it throws and the issues it raises made the Scott report an inevitable choice for this fifth volume in the Hansard Society Series in Politics and Government.

Of course, the public debate about the way in which the government conducted itself in the Arms for Iraq affair died down quite soon. As a chattering Conservative minister is reported to have said some time before the report's publication, 'This is a rather esoteric issue which excites only the media and the chattering classes.' Interest might have faded even quicker if the Conservative government had not gone to extraordinary and extraordinarily incompetent lengths to manipulate publication and spin the news. After all, as Harold Wilson remarked way back, a week is a long time in politics. Few of 'the public' (meaning ordinary people, voters, not professional players and commentators of the game of politics) could have explained much of the affair while the report was in the news, even fewer now. To write off the news stories and TV coverage during the inquiry and after the Commons debate is mistaken nevertheless.

As Shirley Williams, Harvard Professor of Politics as well as British politician, said in her address to the September 1996 Liberal Democrat conference, the steady drip of negative campaigning and spin doctoring (Conservative and Labour) threatens to erode trust in democratic as well as other politicians and perhaps even in democracy itself. At much the same time, Joe Haines (Harold Wilson's media man) wrote in the new *Punch* that this has been a Parliament of perks, privilege and peccadilloes, presided over by Conservative ministers who know only one answer to the old political conundrum—should we put principles before power or power before principles? — and act accordingly (adding that Tony Blair is thought to have reached the same conclusion by some in the Labour Party). In a prepublication editorial, the *Sunday Times* said, 'For Mr Major to turn his back on the judge's findings as they relate to ministers, for reasons of political expediency, would be to sully his record and demean the standards of public life he is pledged to support.' Turn his back he did, power before principle — though probably misjudging the longer-than-a-week effect.

This is in a sense a wider question than the particular issues discussed in the present volume, but the evidence in the Scott report, the ministerial and ex-ministerial attempts to discredit it before publication, the government's blatant bias in access to the report before the Commons debate and the disgraceful opening speech of its spokesman (Peter Riddell's description of it as an occasion for propaganda hit the mark if one refers back to the world's best known minister in that field) — all will have left a taste in public memory. In a year's time, the public may not be able to give chapter and verse, holding in mind a feeling rather than a fact, but that makes little difference. The distrust of politicians and, by extension, the political institutions they inhabit, builds up over time, drip by drip. An institutional reckoning may come; meanwhile, opinion polls show politicians less respected than even estate agents, previously bottom of the list.

That said, for those professionally interested in the study of British government and politics, for politicians with a disinterested interest in reform and for the politically active citizen, the Scott report remains a unique source of information and a starting point for debates. A lot has been published, of course, about the Arms for Iraq affair — the export of war-related material to a bloodthirsty dictator with whom our own forces were to be at war, about the Matrix Churchill trial in which British businessmen serving British intelligence were prosecuted without a sleepless night by ministers involved, about deliberately misleading ministerial answers to MP's questions on such matters for reasons of expediency (party politics confused with raison d'état). A lot has also been published about the Scott Inquiry itself, occasionally theatre, making the headlines, painstaking work most of the time, reported more soberly, seriously covered in the broadsheet ('quality') press by a band of established political commentators of which we can be proud, always telling us more than politicians and generally better than political scientists. Nevertheless, such articles tend to become 'ephemera' in that they are not readily available afterwards for those who want an overview. Nor, of course, are they intended to give the specialist in-depth cover that professional journals do. But such articles, too, are dispersed, not just over time but over journals of seemingly different disciplines, where practitioners of one may not be familiar with what is available in another even when their interest overlap. The issues investigated by Scott, on the other hand, clearly form a 'crossroads' situation, involving politics, law, public administration and media studies, for example.

The purpose of this book is to look at British government and politics in the light of the Scott report, different aspects, different approaches, in one volume. We have brought together a good range of specialists with established reputations in their fields. All speak in their own name: the book as a whole does not present a particular view or recommend particular reforms, though views and recommendations will be found in its chapters (it would be dull reading without). That does not mean there is no unity to the work. In this, as in other volumes in the Hansard Series, we seek a coherent framework of chapters as well as a coherence in style. This is not an ad hoc collection of 'papers', united solely by a common reference, in this case to Scott, as so many barely edited collections on one subject or another tend to be. In deciding on chapters, we tried to make the book as comprehensive as possible; and we have tried to ensure that chapters are written in a way that makes them all understandable, relevant, we think interesting, to academic readers in the disciplines mentioned above as well as others with an interest as noted earlier.

As editor of *Parliamentary Affairs* and of the Hansard Series I maintain a strict neutrality in editorial work. That does not prelude the expression of my own views in what I write myself, even in a preface such as this. In that respect, I hope this series will have no cause for a volume on the conduct of government in some other affair in the near future, but it is not a hope based on the government I have seen over recent years. A *Guardian* headline the morning after writing this preface, referring to allegations about the still simmering cash-for-questions scandal, seems to confirm that view: 'pattern of corruption and deceit.' Governments come and eventually go but the system of government remains. This book is about that system as well as a government and its ministers. Scott cast light on it; we hope our book does this in turn.

F.F. Ridley

Introduction

BY BRIAN THOMPSON*

REPORT *of the Inquiry into the Export of Defence Equipment and Dual-Use Goods to Iraq and Related Prosecutions* (HC 115, 1995–6) is not exactly a snappy title but it does have the virtue of stating the scope of the inquiry conducted by Sir Richard Scott. Indeed, the title encapsulates the report, foreshadowing both the painstaking investigatory technique and voluminous writing style of its author.

Publication of the report had been eagerly anticipated. It was thought that it might lead to ministerial resignation(s) or even the fall of the government. This speculation had been aroused because of the evidence elicited at the days of public hearings, and of the leaking of a draft section of the report to the media. Scott had adopted the procedure of sending drafts to people for their corrections, comments and clarification of any uncertainties. Some journalists received a draft in which the minister William Waldegrave was accused of misleading Parliament over the policy on the export of defence equipment to Iraq. The mood of expectancy had been further whetted because publication had been postponed on several occasions. Accordingly, the report caused some excitement when it was published on Thursday, 15 February 1996. The report was lengthy but it did not appear to identify unambiguously culprits who had no option but resignation. The report was the focus of intense attention until it was the subject of an adjournment debate on 26 February. As the government won this by a single vote and there were no ministerial casualties, the report slipped out of sight.

If public interest, measured by press column inches and broadcasters' tapes, decrees that Scott and his report is an old story, is there a case for the proposition that the report is an important episode in British constitutional history? My answer is unhesitatingly yes because the report, in the fashion of the advertised claims for a certain Dutch lager, reached the parts of government that other inquiries failed to reach. Unusually the amount of ground covered by the inquiry dealt with all three of the classic branches of government: executive, legislative and judicial. For good measure we also have that most exotic of governmental activities — the intelligence services. These are the ingredients of a good popular drama, spies, criminal trials and internecine squabbling amongst ministers and officials. Indeed it did make good drama as the *Guardian* journalist Richard Norton-Taylor turned the hearings of the

* Senior Lecturer in Law, University of Liverpool.

inquiry into a play performed on both the stage and television. For the scholar, the concerned citizen and the political and administrative classes, the Scott report provides a painstaking examination of our governmental institutions, processes and players, finding them to fall considerably short of the performance predicated by the theories of a liberal democracy.

Setting the scene

The immediate cause for the commissioning of Scott to conduct an inquiry was the ignominious collapse of the trial of directors of the firm Matrix Churchill for breaches of export controls. The company had been exporting machine tools to Iraq which were dual-purpose, in other words the equipment had a military potential. Britain has a successful arms industry, however, Iraq was not supposed to be able to acquire such equipment from British companies according to the policy which was enforced by the apparatus of export controls. Yet there was a tension between the commercial interests of Britain plc and the geopolitical concerns of the British government. For one important player in the drama, Alan Clark, who had been a junior Defence and Trade minister, this tension was resolved in favour of fuller company order books. It was Clark's evidence at the trial which led to its collapse. Under cross-examination by defence counsel, Clark's oral testimony was inconsistent with his earlier written witness statement and it exposed the discrepancy between the public version of policy on exports to Iraq, the so-called 'Howe guidelines' and the policy's implementation. The prosecution case was that export licence applications were deceitful. This could not be maintained after Clark's evidence in which he admitted that discussions he had had with the Machine Tool Technologies Association could be regarded as advising companies to stress the civil applications of their equipment even though they knew that it would be put to a military use. This information was not news to the prosecuting authority, HM Customs, as stories to this effect had been reported in the press on two occasions but the enquiries made of Clark on the subject were inadequate having been conducted over the telephone rather than in a face to face interview.

On 23 November 1992, the day after the trial collapsed and the scenes of the Matrix Churchill defendants celebrating with champagne, Prime Minister John Major announced that an inquiry would be held. The terms of reference subsequently agreed with Scott, then a member of the Court of Appeal, were: 'Having examined the facts in relation to the export from the United Kingdom of defence equipment and dual use goods to Iraq between December 1984 and August 1990 and the decisions reached on the export licence applications for such goods and the basis for them, to report on whether the relevant departments, agencies and responsible ministers operated in accordance with the policies of Her Majesty's government; to examine and report on decisions taken by the prosecuting authority and by those signing public interest immunity certificates in *R v Henderson* [the Matrix Churchill case] and any other similar cases that he considers relevant to the issues of the inquiry; and to make recommendations' (A2.2).

The inquiry was not established under the Tribunals of Inquiry (Evidence) Act 1921, which has been used for the investigation of political scandals. In the absence of a statutory basis for the inquiry, Scott was promised that he would have full compliance with any requests for cooperation, whether it be for the provision of papers or assistance from ministers and officials. He was also given the right to determine the date of publication, although as we shall see the arrangements for publication were part of a carefully planned public relations operation by the government.

The report and its reception

The first thing one has to say about the report is its size. It weighed in at just under 8 kilograms or 17 pounds, comprised four volumes totalling just over 1800 pages, plus a fifth volume containing appendices, and a separate index. Given this bulk, it is not surprising that readers wanted a summary but Scott did not provide one. When asked about this during questioning by the Public Service Committee, he claimed that a summary would have run the risk of distorting the report, which had been carefully written.

The government had agreed with Scott that they would receive the report some eight days before its formal publication. This was sought on the basis that the government, or more particularly, the President of the Board of Trade who was the primary recipient of the report, would be expected to make some comment about it in the Commons, and also it was argued that those who might be the subject of criticism should have the opportunity to study it in order to prepare a defence. These eight days were put to great use as the report was filleted for quotations which were presented in a comprehensive press pack from the Department of Trade and Industry, HM Customs, the Office of Public Service, the Attorney General's Office and the Treasury. In addition to providing a paper version of this press pack, it was also published electronically on the Internet.

The opposition parties were given the opportunity for their leaders and their chief spokespersons on Trade and Industry to see a copy of the report in rooms at the Department of Trade and Industry where they would be relieved of their portable telephones and thus cut off from outside communication. The leaders of the Labour and Liberal Democrat parties declined this preview and so their front bench colleagues set off to their temporary reading rooms at the head of a media circus.

The statement by Ian Lang, the President of the Board of Trade, was in terms that the charges made by the opposition, and by Robin Cook in particular, that the government had conspired to arm Iraq; and had sought the conviction of innocent men, through the signing of Public Interest Immunity certificates by ministers, had been refuted by the report. Selective quotations were then made to show that William Waldegrave had been 'acquitted' of misleading Parliament, and that the Attorney General who had advised that ministers had a duty to claim PII by signing certificates, had done so in the knowledge that the certificates were not conclusive, as the court would make the final decision as to whether or not the documents referred to in the certificates would be withheld from the defence.

The findings and recommendations

At the risk of distorting the report, its principal findings may be summarised as follows:

(1) The policy on exports to Iran and Iraq dictated even-handedness between them, however, the policy was found to have been changed with a 'tilt' towards Iraq and this was not announced to Parliament and answers to parliamentary questions and correspondence failed to give an accurate account on the issue;

(2) The Matrix Churchill prosecution was stated to be one which, with the benefit of hindsight, should not have been brought. Various inadequacies were found in the preparations for the trial, including coordination between departments and HM Customs, the alteration of witness statements, the poor questioning of Alan Clark in order to determine exactly what he had said to the Machine Tool Technologies Association, the routine and overly extensive claiming of PII, and the failure of the Attorney General to ensure that the trial judge was informed of Michael Heseltine's views on the PII certificate which he signed reluctantly.

The recommendations covered inquiry procedures, governmental powers to control exports including licensing procedures and the role of HM Customs, prosecution procedures, use of intelligence by government, PII in criminal cases, and ministerial accountability. The section on PII is technical and the longest, as one might expect from a judge. The section which is probably the most important constitutionally, is that dealing with ministerial accountability. Here, Scott stressed the importance of a full account being given to Parliament and suggested that there be a review of the practice of ministerial refusal to answer parliamentary questions on arms sales.

The issues

The report is significant because the exhaustive investigation of the recondite topic of export of defence equipment does touch on important matters of general concern. The primary point which one may draw is that Parliament has been weak in its scrutinising and legislative roles.

So far as ministerial accountability and responsibility is concerned, Scott was very critical of the way in which some members of the executive discharged this constitutional duty. Ministers, and in particular William Waldegrave, were found to be less than truthful in the information they provided when answering parliamentary questions and correspondence, or making statements in the Commons. Scott agreed with the somewhat controversial view of the Cabinet Secretary Sir Robin Butler, that one could draw a distinction between ministerial accountability and responsibility. The former could not be delegated but the latter could be shuffled off onto officials. This being so it was all the more important for a full account to be made. He was clear that ministers and officials had failed to do this and that this was deliberate not inadvertent. Yet he accepted the assertion of William Waldegrave who claimed that the Howe guidelines had not been changed and therefore he had not intended to mislead when he answered questions to that effect.

The effectiveness of parliamentary scrutiny other than by way of parliamentary questions is also queried. Select committees are thought to be one of the stronger tools for calling the government to account but when Scott considered the 'Supergun' affair and its investigation by the Trade and Industry select committee, it is clear that the committee was denied cooperation, indeed blatantly obstructed. The 'Supergun' was a project in which the Iraqi government sought to construct a massive shell firing gun whose barrel would be assembled by joining together lengths of pipe which had been manufactured to exacting specifications. This became public knowledge following the seizure of supposedly innocent pipes in Teesport in April 1990. For most people this was the first indication that Iraq was very serious about building up its military capabilities and doing it in a coordinated and stealthy fashion. Unlike Scott, the select committee did not obtain access to important documents and personnel. In addition to those particular disadvantages, the committee suffered from the general defects shared with all committees of having to be able to agree a report in a body which has a majority of members drawn from the party of government. It also had a problem of timing, as its report, if it was to appear at all, had to be published just before the general election and this also affected the agreement of a final version.

Scott was very critical of the arrangements for the control of these exports. The relevant statute was the Import, Export and Customs Powers (Defence) Act 1939, a piece of emergency legislation. While it had been recognised for some time that this legislation should have been replaced with a permanent measure, it had been administratively convenient to continue under the status quo, however, the possibility that there could be a successful challenge to the legal basis for export controls, led the government to produce a strategy for a new statute. The relevant opposition front-bencher (Gordon Brown) should be approached in confidence and advised that it was in the national interest to have new legislation and for it be passed as quickly as possible. Briefings for ministers proposed that the line to take was that, if possible, agreement should be secured to the making of export control orders without parliamentary supervision. If necessary it could be conceded that the negative resolution procedure would be applied to those orders. This procedure allows for an order to be annulled if a prayer is moved. The opposition agreed to the government's proposal and so the Import and Export Control Act 1990 was enacted. Scott took the view that it was wrong not to have required the negative resolution procedure, as it was possible for new prohibitions to be imposed on the export and import of goods, to create new offences to enforce these controls and to prescribe penalties for these offences, all without the involvement of Parliament (C1.108). Scott noted that from the minutes of meetings and the recollections of the opposition front-benchers, it was unclear if they fully appreciated the situation so that criticism of them for not insisting upon the negative resolution procedure may not be justified (C1.111).

Parliament also failed in its consideration of the report. Our procedures vest so much initiative in an executive which has a majority in the Commons. First, there was the publication arrangements for the report. Having obtained a valuable eight days in which to prepare its case before the rest of the world saw the report, the government was able to mount a massive coordinated news management exercise which attempted to set the agenda of the early coverage of the report. Then the particular procedure chosen by the government was an adjournment debate, the least threatening to it. By this time the government's Whips had identified the possible rebels within its own ranks so that negotiations could be entered into. The crucial vote seemed to be that of Rupert Allason, who under the pen name of Nigel West has written several books about intelligence matters. In the debate he raised concerns about PII and hoped that class claims would not be used in future criminal prosecutions. Assurances were given in the speech of Roger Freeman, the minister who wound up the debate for the government and so Allason voted for the government, giving it a majority of one. It is not entirely clear that the government conceded anything in the assurances which apparently swayed Allason, as most of what he seemed to be seeking on PII was reflected in the current state of the law as decided by the House of Lords in 1994.

The second major theme is that of public interest. This theme, like the notion of public interest itself has several strands. First there is the downward trend of Parliament which seems to have lost a sense of itself as the representative of the nation to which it is responsible. With many institutions it is a commonplace to observe that they have departed from a golden age, however, as the Scott report follows on from the Nolan report on standards in public life which was prompted by the 'cash for questions' affair, it seems Parliament cannot be trusted to regulate itself and is thus feeding a damaging discontent amongst the public with politicians and the political process.

The government is expected to act in the public interest but it increasingly seems that for members of the executive, the public interest is the interest of the government. Scott found that some government actions were guided by convenience, and that some failures to render full accounts were dictated by a desire to avoid political embarrassment. It is true that governing is not easy, but it seems that within Whitehall the view is that 'the government knows best', which covers governmental actions and provision of information.

One member of the government who is charged with extensive responsibilities to be exercised in the public interest, is the Attorney General. The report brought the senior Law Officer from the legal wings to political centre stage. Sir Nicholas Lyell was subjected to strong criticism by Scott for his interpretation of the law on Public Interest Immunity and the advice to ministers derived from it, and secondly for his administrative responsibilities in failing to honour an undertaking to convey Michael Heseltine's reservations about the PII certificate which he had reluctantly signed.

Another aspect of the executive's faulty assessment of the public interest derived from the poor coordination within the governmental machine. Information is not shared. It is perhaps understandable that the intelligence agencies may prefer courses of action which safeguard their informants but it does seem that pettiness, and overdeveloped senses of institutional autonomy led to the mounting of the Matrix Churchill prosecution. HM Customs failed to take hints that were being dropped by other departments, The case would not have proceeded if prosecuting counsel had been in possession of more information, some of which the Attorney General should have provided.

Plan of the volume

The order of the subsequent chapters and their topics is now outlined. Anthony Barker deals with the inquiry's procedure. This was subjected to a strong critique by the former Foreign Secretary Lord Howe, which Scott not only defended in the report itself, but also before its publication in public lectures given by himself and the secretary to the inquiry. Ralph Negrine deals with the media's coverage of the inquiry and the report, noting the differences between the broadsheets and the tabloids and the difficulties caused for them by Scott not playing the game of political communication as it is currently practised. The arms trade is the subject of Mark Phythian's chapter in which he concludes that the inquiry was a lost opportunity for an examination of this complex field of commerce. It would appear that, for Scott, this trade was little more than the context for a study of government and its oversight. Ian Leigh takes us through the intricacies of the law on Public Interest Immunity, explaining its current state and how this evolved. He also considers some of its constitutional implications. Vernon Bogdanor, who was a specialist adviser to the Commons Public Service committee during its investigation of ministerial responsibility and accountability, analyses Scott's critique of accountability in the report and also his subsequent proposals made in evidence to the select committee and a public lecture. Philip Giddings deals with the relationship between the executive and Parliament, and draws attention to the partisan nature of Parliament and how that affects relations between the two. Diana Woodhouse explains the office and role of the Attorney General, which embodies a tension between being a member of the government and a responsibility to take certain action in the public interest. Adam Tomkins explores the secret world of the intelligence agencies, reflecting upon its role in government decision-making. Barry O'Toole considers ethics in government and focuses upon the relationship between ministers and officials, including the civil service code of conduct. Alan Doig suggests that the Scott episode is one in which we can see that the actions of those in power are guided by pragmatism. Patrick Birkinshaw discusses freedom of information, looking at the recent developments of domestic and European Union codes of access to information and considers the future prospects. We conclude with a look at what Scott's inquiry and report can tell us about the use of the judiciary as trouble-shooters.

The Inquiry's Procedures

BY ANTHONY BARKER*

THE SCOTT inquiry was procedurally extraordinary, from start to finish, and unprecedently controversial. It has provided future official inquiries with a cornucopia of precedents. But most of its extraordinary character and controversial status was thrust upon it by the government and its public critics, led by the former Foreign Secretary, Lord Howe. Scott's own basic procedural decision to proceed mainly with the private analysis of official papers and written evidence was entirely conventional (in line with Lord Franks' committee on the Falklands War and Sir Thomas Bingham on the collapse of the Bank of Credit and Commerce International). His elaborate arrangements for allowing witnesses to submit additional text in response to the evidence, particularly criticisms, of others (or of Scott's own draft comments about them) was unconventional but reasonable and even generous. His decision that there must be some public hearings (unlike Franks and Bingham) was obviously correct and attracted no criticism. The controversy concerned the fairness of the procedure for oral evidence, notably the alleged role of the inquiry's counsel, Presiley Baxendale QC.

The Scott inquiry's cornucopia of procedural precedents is obviously best reviewed chronologically, from pre-inquiry through to post-reporting stages. As with all good dramas, the climax was delayed to the end when the Commons was suspended for just ten minutes to allow MPs and journalists to collect and assess a five-volume report (which lacked an overall summary) before listening to a wholly self-serving political response to its contents from the government front bench.

The pre-inquiry stage

Here there were three unprecedented features. First, the government promised in advance that if Scott simply called its attention to difficulties in getting witnesses to offer truthful and otherwise adequate evidence, it would ask Parliament to create a tribunal with High Court powers under the Tribunals of Inquiry (Evidence) Act 1921 to compel witnesses to attend and give evidence on oath, or face charges of contempt of court (HC Debs, 23 November 1992). Scott would then conduct this judicial tribunal in place of the non-statutory administrative inquiry he was about to begin. No newly-appointed administrative 'inquirer' had ever been given such a public promise.

* Reader in Government, University of Essex.

Secondly, Scott used the week following the announcement of his appointment to obtain an unconditional promise of control over what he would publish, whether in his report as findings, recommendations or cited items of evidence, or in any appendices of supporting or illustrative government papers. This decision contrasted with the Attorney General's opening position when announcing the inquiry. He had said, 'His report and evidence will be published except insofar as, in the light of his advice, publication is contrary to the public interest' and confirmed the point in answer to a question when Scott 'gives his advice as to what should be published' (HC Debs, 10 November 1992). This was an unsurprising attempt to repeat the Franks committee's position on publishing sensitive material: Lady Thatcher had promised that ministers would be most careful to restrict any cuts in their report before publication to essential points of national security and international relations and would consult Lord Franks (not the full committee) before finally deciding. All members of that committee were privy counsellors (as was Scott, ex officio as a Lord Justice), and both that committee inquiry and Scott's individual exercise had no restrictions placed on what official papers, including Secret Intelligence Service reports, they could see. Scott wanted unlimited access to papers and personal control of his report, including supporting appendices. The Prime Minister duly confirmed, when announcing formal terms of reference, that 'All papers that the inquiry calls for will be made available [and] Lord Justice Scott will be entirely free to decide on the publication of his report and of the evidence he takes' (HC Debs, 16 November 1992). Giving a single investigator albeit a senior judge within the Privy Council engaged on an administrative inquiry (rather than a 1921 Act tribunal) the freedom to see everything and then decide what to publish was the second unprecedented feature of the pre-inquiry stage.

At least this was so in principle, at the high political level of a Prime Minister giving a general assurance to the House. In practical detail, Scott's secretariat would require almost as much vigilance and persistence in settling with departments, particularly the Cabinet Office, which confidential papers could be published or quoted as had been needed at an earlier stage in extracting materials from them. At the public and political level, a government which was itself the subject of an investigation for alleged political scandal could not afford criticisms (least of all from an apparently quite outspoken investigating judge) that it was censoring his report and other published output. At the detailed level, official Whitehall resisted the force of the unprecedented 'Scott' phenomenon and the Prime Minister's public 'cartes blanches' both on what the inquiry could see and what it could incorporate or refer to in its report or appendices were turned into a series of greys. There was, not surprisingly, more difficulty over the precise form in which secret official papers could or should be seen in public, in whole or part, than over the choice of such papers. Scott and his office were not disposed to publish true state secrets which deserve to be kept hidden. But where such restrictions did not apply, they had the government's promise of control over their report and so regarded the choice of papers as a matter for them. As coordinator of Whitehall's response to this sharp and novel challenge and, of course, as guardians of both Cabinet papers as one class of secret materials and secret intelligence material as another class, the Cabinet Office under Sir Robin Butler undertook to control as much as possible of the form of publication.

There was an element of genuine outsider incredulity in this working relationship based upon the investigator having come in to one professional world's innermost practices from another, without prior experience or background advice. Scott happened to be a barrister-judge but would have been almost as baffled by some of Whitehall's attitudes to the precise published form of hitherto secret papers if he had been a product of medicine, academic life, high finance or industry. He would probably cheerfully admit that Sir Robin Butler could have remained as unconvinced by many ideas and practices which the Bar in general, the bench of judges or (particularly) those last remaining medieval craft guilds, the barristers' Inns of Court, regard as essential if he had been investigating and publicising Scott's professional world. Scott's office was staffed by civil servants on loan from various departments and led by a senior (Grade 5) government legal adviser with experience of private practice at the Bar, the Attorney General's office and the Treasury Solicitor's Department, Christopher Muttukumaru. They would have confirmed to Scott that Cabinet papers and secret intelligence reports (and their appraisals) have always been the subject of special rules about their circulation and protection within Whitehall but that it did not follow from their classification that all of them were either very confidential or very important. Not even all actual Cabinet minutes (covering the full Cabinet and its range of official committees and any other offshoots) could make any such claim. Items from both Cabinet and intelligence classes would need to be judged on their merits. For his own part, Scott has commented since his inquiry that he simply could not see why, for example, an extract from a Cabinet or Cabinet committee meeting's minute needed to be redesigned or rewritten to conceal its original form (while conveying the same information) before it could appear in his report or its appendices. This original form seemed to be a mystical craft secret whereas his interest was in reproducing parts, at least, of official papers relevant to his purpose in their original form to help convey the authenticity of his sources. A special version of the same information could give the impression that the content as well as the form might have been censored. The same argument did not normally arise with 'raw' secret intelligence reports: the point was taken that foreign intelligence services might gather too much simply from seeing the normal form of British reports appearing in public. For all other government material to be published with cuts, however, one view in Scott's office maintained that publishing these actual documents, with any blacking out of parts of the information in each case (known to lawyers and Whitehall as redaction) was necessary for the proper authority of the report and its appendices.

The third procedural precedent was Scott's apparent assertion of his control of what would take place in the public hearings of oral evidence which (unlike the Franks committee on the Falklands) he believed would be an essential aspect of a publicly acceptable report. This was seen at the time as a further victory for openness because Sir Robin Butler had told Scott that the Prime Minister had 'endorsed' the proposal that Scott should exclude press and public when, in his view, 'disclosure in public would be damaging to the public interest'. In addition, any current minister or civil servant should be instructed by the government to ask Scott to exclude press and public when 'in their view, the disclosure of information in public might be damaging'. The implication was that, of course, Scott would decide on these requests so that these government witnesses' view of what 'might' be too sensitive would be only the starting point. He would act upon his own view. Even so, this formula looked remarkably loose for an inquiry centrally concerned with alleged ministerial deceit and official connivance, where the deliberate confusion of the national or public interest with the current government's political interest is a principal technique (as the jury which acquitted Clive Ponting for his criminal breach of the Official Secrets Act had noted). On this proposed basis it was no surprise that Scott responded, with some vigour, at his press conference on procedures of 31 March 1993. As the *Guardian's* specialist 'Scott' correspondent, Richard Norton-Taylor, was to describe the point in his early book on the inquiry, 'Scott said he expected testimony of ministers, former ministers and civil servants to be given in public unless there was an overriding reason of national security why it should not'.[1] Scott published Sir Robin's letter together with his reply to it. He had told Sir Robin that his test for closed sessions would be 'serious injury to the interests of the nation', which he intended to be narrower than Sir Robin's 'damage to the public interest'. He confirmed that he would consider any government requests to exclude press and public in other and wider circumstances but said that he would weigh the public interest in having the material covered in open session with the public interest in not doing so. In other words, an assertion of one side of the issue would not be enough.

Whether Norton-Taylor was right to interpret this episode as what he called Scott, rather than Whitehall, laying down the ground rules for the inquiry, as opposed to agreeing with Sir Robin's actual proposal, is doubtful. Rather strangely, Sir Robin's letter immediately qualified its loose formula that government witnesses should request a closed session when disclosure of material 'might be damaging' by adding that in practice, they would generally envisage such requests only to avoid 'serious injury to the interests of the nation'. This precise phrase was taken up by Scott in his reply as his own formula for judging the exclusion of press and public both on his own initiative and in response to government witnesses' requests. Later in his letter, Sir Robin had applied virtually the same phrase when telling Scott that the government 'would expect' him to move into closed session on very sensitive material held by non-government witnesses. The test would be Scott's own view that public disclosure would cause serious injury to the national interest.

Scott's acceptance and repetition (in his letter of reply of 22 March) of Butler's subsidiary phrase 'serious injury to the interests of the nation' no longer seemed to satisfy him on 31 March at his press conference. His oral formulation was now stronger: the argument for hearing secret evidence in closed session should not simply outweigh the argument for a public hearing but be 'overriding'; and the reason must be specifically 'national security', not the more general 'national interest. Sir Robin could reasonably have concluded that Scott had moved to increase, at least a little, the government's already extraordinary potential exposure, including on the core subjects of secret intelligence and international relations. However, the practical difference between them seemed almost nominal and it proved to be no surprise that Scott's actual decisions on closed sessions produced no controversy. Sixty hours out of some 500 were on this basis and 20 out of 81 oral witnesses were so treated. It is wise to put these figures into the context of what was a largely private inquiry, with a total of 81 oral evidence witnesses and 197 written evidence witnesses. The inquiry studied official documents and exchanged extensive questionnaires, written evidence, further questions, draft reports and witnesses' comments thereon, all entirely unknown to the public until the report was published, some considerable time later, or until the appendices were released (on CD-ROM only) five months later still.

Whereas the public promise to Scott to relaunch him as a 1921 Act tribunal if necessary, the grant (in principle) of control over what government papers would be published and his public assertion of his strict criteria for turning public hearings into secret ones were three dramatic political precedents for investigations of government, other features of the pre-inquiry stage were more familiar. His assumption of control over his inquiry's procedures was entirely normal and his exchanges with Sir Robin Butler about closed sessions should be seen in that context, despite their being unprecedented in themselves. On behalf of the government, Sir Robin was coping with the contrast between the Scott inquiry's relative openness and the Franks committee's fully secret operation when both had been offered complete access to official materials. He sought to guide Scott only on secret hearings, not his procedure in general. His right to run his non-statutory administrative inquiry as he thought best was not criticised, although his actual arrangements were. If Lord Howe or other critics had sought a judicial review of his actual procedures, as was certainly open to them, they would have been playing uphill because the courts have a long and clear tradition of leaving official investigators, e.g. government inspectors and others to make their own procedures to fit their needs and even to depart from familiar forms if they have arguable reasons. It was normal routine for the Attorney General to have told the House at the outset that the inquiry's form and procedure would be, 'to a considerable extent a matter for the learned judge' (HC Debs, 10 November 1992).

It was equally usual for the government to have noted that precise terms of reference for Scott would be discussed with him and announced later. The final version fell into two parts: firstly, the casework decisions and policy on the export of defence and dual-use (military/civil) goods to Iraq between December 1984 and the Iraqi invasion of Kuwait in August 1990; and secondly, decisions taken by the prosecuting authority (Customs and Excise) and by those ministers signing Public Interest Immunity certificates in the Matrix Churchill and any other similar cases which Scott considers relevant to the issues of the inquiry. On Iraq exports, Scott agreed to investigate and report on whether the relevant departments, agencies and responsible ministers operated in accordance with the policies of the government. One criticism of this form was that the loose and general American word 'agencies' was used to offer only minimal formal reference to the sections of government outside White-hall departments which may well have proved central to the Iraq exports story: MI6, possibly MI5 and GCHQ. The more important oddity, given the political reasons for launching this inquiry, was the attempt to confine it to the question of whether officials and ministers stuck to government policy or ran wild in some way, perhaps in modest imitation of Oliver North and the American Iran–Contra scandal. Governments do not usually invite outside inquiries to report on the merits of their policies, even in the exceptional circumstances of the inquiry with its atmosphere of alleged official wrongdoing. But the begging of the question by this formula of what government policy on Iraq exports actually was (could it have been a conscious policy of deception wrapped in flexibility and sophistry?) is quite remarkable.[2] Perhaps its best explanation is that Scott, of all investigators, knew that he carried the public's trust, that ministers were in the dock and that, in any case, it is very hard for any government actually to prevent an inquiry exceeding its terms of reference if it is so minded.

Moving on from pre-inquiry to inquiry stage

The main point to note is that the procedural controversy arose from only a limited base: the pattern of oral questioning of the witnesses invited to attend and the absence of questioning by witnesses' own lawyers of other witnesses (loosely termed 'cross examination'). Scott's broad answer to criticisms of this was that witnesses' opportunities for written exchanges with him were so full as to more than offset any conceivable shortfall in the hearings. These opportunities were indeed unusually full: compared to the Bingham and other less usual types of inquiry, Scott's witnesses enjoyed an unprecedented chance to go on arguing their corner in private, long after giving their oral evidence; they would have been envied by witnesses at every other established type of public or private inquiry (e.g. planning) who hear no more until the publication of a report which may very considerably affect their interests.

Scott announced his plan at his sole press conference during the inquiry period (31 March 1993). All invitations to be a witness would include a questionnaire on the matters in question. Having read their responses, he would ask only some to give oral evidence (possibly with the press and public excluded). A lawyer or other adviser could accompany them and give them private advice before they responded to a question, but no statements or questioning of their own or other witnesses by an adviser were anticipated (which term allowed for an exception in some special circumstances). Questions to witnesses would mainly come from the inquiry's counsel (Presiley Baxendale) and occasionally from Scott himself or the inquiry's secretary, Christopher Muttukumaru. Oral witnesses would be free to study the transcript of their answers and write to Scott not only offering corrections, interpretations or amplifications but also any further points they wished to make. At Scott's invitation, one witness could be sent the transcript of another's oral evidence, and invited to comment in writing. (In practice any witness, or even anyone else, could not be prevented from writing to Scott about the public evidence received and might make significant points to be considered.) A further opportunity to influence the findings would come to witnesses whom he proposed to criticise in his report. He promised to give them an opportunity to make in writing any comment on the proposed criticism. He also announced the government's pledge not to use in specified subsequent criminal trials, a witness's written or oral evidence to the inquiry or the contents of any document which the inquiry had required him to produce. (The possible trials were those under relevant Customs or export control laws; magistrates courts and perjury laws; and the Official Secrets Acts.) Finally, he confirmed that government witnesses' legal costs would be met by departments while other witnesses could apply to him for theirs, in addition to their other reasonable costs.

The critical response to witness procedures from Lord Howe and others had their stated foundation in the tradition of a 1921 Act tribunal as the proper device for investigating alleged government wrongdoing, including crimes. Both the Labour leader, John Smith QC, and the Liberal Democrat spokesman, Menzies Campbell QC, had reacted to John Major's announcement of the Scott inquiry with the view that it should be such a tribunal perhaps because they feared guilty ministers or officials might slip off the hook unless placed on oath and under the tribunal's powers to punish contempt. Howe also urged a more judicial procedure, presumably for the opposite reason that it would better defend ministers and officials who had worked normally on arms-to-Iraq (mainly under his authority as Foreign Secretary) and had done nothing to justify even the risk of a political (let alone a legal) pillory. The true intellectual and emotional foundation of this reaction to the collapse of the Matrix Churchill trial and the appointment of Scott may well have been a protest against any type of inquiry. A public investigation would crudely reveal the intricate and intimate processes of government especially those at its most secret heart concerned with diplomatic relations, military strategy and secret intelligence. On this view of foreign and defence policy-making, much of government activity must remain secret in the nation's true interest. Keeping something secret in the face of public questioning, whether from Parliament, the mass media or anyone else, must involve giving vague, incomplete or even deceptive responses. The fear was that a non-judicial inquiry, without each government witness being fully represented by a lawyer able to question others, would offer insufficient protection. And, if there had been errors or impropriety within government, ordinary justice required similar rights to anyone accused.

In addition to his criticisms offered directly to Scott, Howe also appealed to the public through the press. He cited the six 'principles' of procedural fairness laid out by Lord Salmon's Royal Commission on Tribunals of Inquiry of 1966 some 28 years before. He recalled his own appearance as counsel for coal industry managers accused of gross negligence at the 1921 Act tribunal which investigated the Aberfan disaster in 1967. He suggested that every inquiry of this kind (meaning, perhaps, those where blame may be allotted following major accidents or alleged public scandals) since the Salmon report had tried to follow these principles, although pragmatically, and that Scott's procedures were very seriously adrift from them. The six points are: (i) a person investigated must be material to the inquiry's decided purpose; (ii) he must know in advance of giving evidence of any allegations against him and their substance; (iii) he should be able to prepare, assisted by lawyers, and have these costs paid by the government; (iv) as a witness, he should be able to answer questions from his own lawyer (in addition to those put by anyone else) and state his case in public to the inquiry; (v) any relevant extra witness he proposes 'should, if reasonably practicable, be heard'; (vi) his lawyer should be allowed to cross-examine any other witness whose evidence may affect him.

Principles (i) and (iii) were met. Scott also met (v), although in the form of written rather than oral evidence. Principle (ii) could not be met by any investigation which begins work with only allegations rather than a (possibly dramatic) event as its starting point: telling all witnesses in advance of any allegations against them and outline supporting evidence was not appropriate here. By contrast, the allegations about ministers misleading Parliament on changes in arms-to-Iraq policy or signing PII certificates either carelessly or for political advantage needed to be investigated from scratch. But once Scott's work started the hares of allegations and ripostes running between witnesses, his procedure did address this principle: he promised to send any transcript containing allegations or even criticisms of another witness to that person for a written response of their own devising. As regards Principles (iv) and (vi) Scott's oral evidence procedures would not have prevented a witness from stating a general personal case or point of view at a suitable stage (in fact six witnesses did read out opening statements) but would not normally allow these other proceedings. (One ministerial witness, Lord Trefgarne, was granted the closing speech on his position from his counsel which he had requested.) As to 'cross-examination' (an inaccurate term for a non-adversarial, investigative inquiry, although used by Scott himself) the procedure did not close the door on it but postponed the prospect until every witness criticised by another had read the relevant transcript and been invited to respond to the inquiry in writing. Within this novel context, no witnesses took up Scott's offer to consider requests to arrange for their lawyer to question the other witness any further (B2.21–2).

In noting the conduct and apparent opinions on the Scott inquiry of the 278 witnesses (81 of whom also gave oral evidence), it is necessary to put Lord Howe in a class of his own. Claiming throughout to be speaking up for the ordinary civil servants approached by Scott to be witnesses, he mounted a quite remarkably sustained individual campaign, partly in public but mostly in detailed correspondence with Christopher Muttukumaru, the head of Scott's office. It stressed Scott's virtual abandonment of the Salmon principles of fair inquiry procedure, notably the denial of a witness's lawyer's right to cross-examine other witness's possibly damaging evidence and of opening or closing statements ('submissions') by lawyers so that witnesses could not put their responses into a properly explained background or generally set out their evidence in their own way. The other main attack was on Scott's failure to sit with expert assessors as at public inquiries into technical fields: maintaining that government policy and operations on arms-to-Iraq was just as technical a matter as a collapsed insurance company, a Monopoly Commission inquiry or an Aberfan disaster. Retired senior civil servants and former senior ministers now out of politics were suggested as suitable assessors. Howe made a link between the two lines of criticism. He asserted that Scott's fragmented approach to what his witnesses could offer him put him at real risk of misunderstanding his material. Since he had no personal experience of Whitehall at all, to adopt this risky witness procedure with no support or advice from expert assessors was doubly dangerous and the risk of ill-founded conclusions damaging witnesses' reputations even greater. In Summer 1995 when he had read the sections of Scott's proposed draft report, Howe wrote back saying that it contained errors of exactly the type which he had feared. He insisted that Scott's draft criticisms of himself were so awry that his only proper defence would be to address Scott in public through counsel at a reconvened public hearing followed up by what he called an 'oral exchange' between him (with his fully active counsel) and the inquiry duo of Scott plus Presiley Baxendale.

At the level of form, Scott accepted this protracted and inevitably rather repetitious private debate with Howe, using Muttukumaru's very long and painstakingly elaborate letters as a buffer. He had shown some irritation when Howe had prefaced his public oral evidence in response to Scott's standard initial questionnaire with a headline-catching attack on the procedure as unfair to witnesses. He had pointedly asked Howe for whom he claimed to be speaking, trying to identify any concerted attempt, perhaps among Foreign Office interests, to denigrate this public inquiry as they had the official study of their departmental work by the Cabinet's Central Policy Review Staff in 1976–77.[3] Scott was faced by a central figure of his inquiry, the responsible Cabinet minister for one of the most involved Departments and the author of the disputed 'Howe guidelines' on arms sales to Iraq, continuing periodically to protest throughout almost the whole length of the inquiry. This protestor claimed that it was an unfair and unauthoritative proceeding and openly expressed doubts about its ultimate public acceptability if its procedures were not sharply shifted towards the more adversarial model of a 1921 Act tribunal, a large-scale planning inquiry or a court case where lawyers (usually counsel) are fully active and even dominant. This major potential subject of Scott's investigation was also a persistently dissatisfied witness and (having quit the Thatcher government with devastating effect) now a very senior ex-minister in the Lords. Scott's strategy was to give Howe almost all the rope he wanted to continue his arguments: it is only towards the end that he authorised Muttukumaru to offer Howe's solicitor his conclusion that Howe's doggedly repeated procedural claims were a cover for his real objection, namely, to the proposed substantive conclusions in the draft Report, that is, Scott's proposed criticisms of him and others at the Foreign Office. Scott's entire procedural case had been that fairness had been offered to witnesses, particularly in the possibly unprecedented opportunities for them to add what they wished to their responses to Scott's particular questions; to see and make any comment on criticisms of them by other witnesses; and similarly to rebut or otherwise comment on the extracts from the draft report which concerned their evidence. Through Muttukumaru's letters to Howe and his own (unprecedented) public lecture on his procedures given during the inquiry he had stated or implied that criticisms such as Howe's were misunderstandings or even mis-statements of actual inquiry arrangements. Some cross-purposes arose at the outset when Scott had confirmed and commended the obvious fact that this was to be an 'inquisitorial' (not a more formally adversarial) inquiry when Howe had seemed to attack it for being 'inquisitorial' when he seemed to mean aggressive: a form was confused with a characteristic or atmosphere.

Similarly, it is now clear from their private exchanges (not published until the report appeared in February 1996) that Howe's background at the Bar had given him a different idea of witnesses being legally represented from Scott's view based on his own, exactly similar, background. For Howe, proper representation required addressing the court or inquiry ('submissions'); examining the client ('in chief'); 're-examining' him following possibly hostile questions from other counsel; and, crucially, cross-examining other witnesses on behalf of the client's interests. With his rather fundamentalist view of the Salmon Commission's cardinal principles for fair procedure of 1966 (although agreeing that they had been and should be applied pragmatically since then) Howe also gave an impression of having forgotten nothing and learned nothing since Salmon had reported in 1966; only one year later he had played a major role as counsel to the very seriously exposed Coal Board managers at the 1921 Act tribunal on the Aberfan disaster; only two years after that he had himself conducted a statutory inquiry into serious allegations against the Ely Hospital (Cardiff) in 1969, with similarly judicial procedures; and had been re-elected to the House to become Solicitor General during 1970–72. As Ian Leigh[4] has commented, the dramatic advance of public law standards since the Sixties in court, tribunal and inquiry procedures in general has diffused the rather formal and rigid rules laid down by Salmon into a much richer expectation of more developed means to ensure fairness. With his own formative experience tied back to Aberfan and Ely and with his fully preserved former professional advocate's belief in the skills and legitimacy of legal advocacy, he seemed to approach the Scott inquiry from a particular angle and did not shift it despite receiving little public support, notably from his own party in government. (One notable exception is the academic, Vernon Bogdanor who has strongly agreed with Howe on both main counts: witness procedures and Scott's need for assessors.)[5]

Other academic and journalist observers have broadly seemed to accept Scott's claims that his procedures were fair and even generous to witnesses; that his departures from Salmon's model were only limited and, in any case, not the main test; and that a series of virtually untrammelled written responses and wider comments is a more efficient process than the traditional routines of more adversarial, advocacy-based methods. Scott has received less support, however, in his rejection of assessors with Whitehall experience or knowledge. Muttukumaru told Howe's solicitor that any useful assessor would probably have required current or past senior responsibility as a civil servant or minister and this would have blemished Scott's independence when 'the government is itself under scrutiny' (Appendix A, D2 (xii)). He added that Scott had received extensive evidence on how government works and expert interpretation would serve no clear need. (Howe specifically rejected this latter point, claiming that Scott's draft report showed errors based on his early misunderstandings about arms exports which a suitable assessor would have prevented.) Other observers, including academics, have wondered why the expertise of an independent academic expert in British government should not have been recognised in exactly the same way as any other type of inquiry's technical assessors: such knowledge and understanding certainly exists, even in the dark and deep waters of strategic diplomacy and the arms trade.

Having permitted this very important and eminent witness to proliferate and repeat his criticisms over many months in detailed correspondence, Scott decided not to allow Howe's counsel a 'half-day' of general critical oral review of both Scott's procedural record and his relevant draft report. He confirmed the obvious point that a public hearing of this event would allow other witnesses to claim the same. Apart from the extra delay, this process would have destroyed Scott's attempt to keep his draft criticisms of certain witnesses confidential to them. Any witnesses' counsel addressing Scott in public on less panoramic lines than Howe had demanded would have been obliged to refer to the draft criticisms made of his client, in order to rebut or offset them. There had recently been an embarrassing leak to the press of draft report text concerning the three junior ministers operating the Howe guidelines on arms to Iraq and Iran (William Waldegrave, Alan Clark and Lord Trefgarne) apparently by certain witnesses themselves and probably intended to damage Waldegrave. Scott's strategy of putting out draft criticisms hoping to receive useful, frank responses to strengthen his inquiry depended on secrecy. Even private oral submissions by witnesses' counsel (which Howe had reluctantly accepted as a second best demand for himself) would risk this arrangement. Howe was therefore in the end told to put his comments on Scott's draft criticisms of him or the Foreign Office in writing like all other witnesses.

Whatever may be thought of the merits of Howe's procedural arguments or may be surmised about their roots in his professional background and perspective on Scott's less judicial yet generously cut procedural cloth, all of the above assumes that Howe was offering sincere criticism based on genuine concerns. It is possible that his procedural criticism was a cover for his real aim of weakening the authority of an inquiry which he resented on principle (because Whitehall had, as he often said, done no demonstrable harm, at least on the Howe guidelines issue which most concerned him). Alternatively, he, with others, may have recognised the threat to the Foreign Office or to Whitehall at large posed by the first public inquiry to combine full access to secret papers and fully independent control over what it would publish. A campaign to damage the standing of the chosen investigator by calling him both unfair and inexperienced (innocent) would have had a precedent in the Foreign Office's web of criticism and rumour spun in 1976–77 around the Central Policy Review Staff's critical review of the Foreign Office's overall work. Howe himself had gained experience of boot tactics when dismissing the politically embarrassing inquiry report on the making of the TV film 'Death on the Rock' (which claimed to show that army killings in Gibraltar had been criminal acts). He had called the inquiry 'by television' itself, and so not independent, when Howe's fellow QC who joined Lord Windlesham to produce this report (Anthony Rampton) in fact had no prior contact with television clients. On the Scott inquiry it is possible that Howe played a spoiling game, aided by the customary ability of London lawyers to think of and sustain a remarkable range of arguments on almost any subject. Whatever his true motive, there is no doubt that this critical campaign by one of the main subjects of an official inquiry, who had also since become a senior former Cabinet minister, was unprecedented.

The Scott inquiry's cornucopia of procedural precedents also contains the dramatic leakage of draft report text in early Summer 1995, mentioned above. Intended to damage Waldegrave, the leak also weakened Scott when his final report appeared in February 1996 because he seemed to have pulled back from finding Waldegrave dishonest in intention as well as deceiving in actions. The final published phrases about Waldegrave's intentions when deceiving MPs and the public about actual arms-to-Iraq policy have brought some derision on to Scott.

The post-inquiry stage

The dramatic climax to this remarkable inquiry's innovations and alarms came at the post-inquiry stage of its reporting arrangements. Having given Scott control of the contents of his report, ministers decided to manipulate its presentation to Parliament and public and to achieve more favourable initial publicity: this might reduce the chance of any current minister having to resign to assuage hostile public opinion or serious doubts among government MPs. The inquiry had been appointed by the government even though the government itself was the subject of serious allegations, including those against some seven current Cabinet ministers. It is part of the poverty of British scrutiny of the government that Parliament has no investigatory device except a select committee of MPs or peers themselves: no outside resources can be commissioned in its name. An official inquiry report is normally received by the government in private and then considered in private within Whitehall for weeks or even months before it is published together with the government's official reactions. The Scott inquiry was established by the President of the Board of Trade (albeit through the Prime Minister because of the political context) and had to report to him. But because this was an investigation of, not merely for, the government, Scott was as keen to maintain his public image of independence by being seen to control the publication process just as he had controlled his access to government papers and the contents of his report. He made a good try, but failed. The obvious form of publication applied to most departmental inquiries was a Command paper but that seemed to Scott to be too routinely close to the government. Making the report a 'Return to an Address' would require the President of the Board of Trade, Ian Lang, to move a formal motion on publication day, whereupon the report would be formally published and copies distributed immediately to MPs and the press. The minister would then make a government statement, followed by the customary comments and questions from other parties and MPs. This unusual procedure attracted Scott because it would look more parliamentary than governmental. (He therefore asked Lang to arrange for at least one Labour and one Liberal Democrat MP to sign the formal motion calling for the report to be published but as soon became clear ministers were not in a bipartisan mood and the idea was rejected.)

An incidental technical advantage of this method of publication was the statutory protection against libel proceedings (which, remarkably, a Command paper status does not offer), but even then a litigant must show malice, which would be very hard to do, so Scott was uninfluenced by this formal point. He thought it much more important to prevent the government from sitting on his report until it suited them to publish it with their well-prepared defence, which would both damage Scott's independent status and risk more leaks from the ministers and officials poring over the text in six or more relevant departments. This normal delay was naturally what the government wanted, whereas Scott's initial preference was for publication with no prior study period, even for the government. The government persuaded him that ministers must be able to give at least some official reaction straight after publication. Seven days was the agreed compromise period for the government's advance study (Scott wanted less, Lang a lot more). His office also tried to limit Whitehall's prior access to the report, as well as chances of leaks during the agreed seven-day period. Six ministers, two Permanent Secretaries and some 16 further officials with responsibility for briefing their superiors on parts of the report were designated, and departments were asked not to copy extracts to other people without returning names and details to the office. Scott told HMSO that he, not the minister, was their client on this printing job and orders to release any extra pre-publication copies could come only from his office. (When the DTI in due course asked HMSO for 800 copies to be delivered to MPs and the press, the reply was that Scott's office must approve).

It is notorious that ministers used their seven days of privileged access to the report to plan an aggressive defence on the matters inquired into and to project it to the mass media in a package of press releases which distorted Scott's actual findings. Their view was to be presented in Lang's own initial statement to the House: Conservative ministers had not been found guilty of deceit but their Labour and Liberal Democrat accusers had. It was immediately clear why ministers had wanted the other parties to be kept back from the Scott's report until the last moment.

The opposition parties sought the normal informal opportunity (which is shared by the press) to see official reports in advance of publication and under embargo in order to prepare their comments following the minister's statement. Labour's spokesman, Robin Cook, had asked Scott for prior access which Scott certainly favoured, as also for Menzies Campbell (Liberal Democrat) and other spokesmen. Scott wrote to the Speaker about the timing of the motion and prior access by other parties, which normal process she endorsed. She did so again in the House when a Labour frontbencher, Ann Taylor, asked for her help, when it was becoming clear that normal access would be denied by the government. Lang had refused Scott's suggestion of a 55-minute period for MPs and journalists to read the report before his statement at 3.30pm. He insisted that the motion should not pass and the report not be distributed until he rose at 3.30pm confident that only his frontbench colleagues would know what Scott had written. Under the Speaker's influence, the outcome was for Cook and Campbell to be allowed into the Department of Trade and Industry under the surveillance of security guards to look at the report volumes, but not photocopy or remove them, for a maximum of three hours. A car and sandwiches would be provided. The Leader of the Opposition, Tony Blair, had also requested prior access but rejected these janitorial conditions as insulting. As to other MPs, the Speaker's comment that she favoured an informed reaction to ministers' statements when a major report was being published produced the absurd idea of a ten minute delay between Lang's motion coming into effect at 3.30pm and beginning his statement at 3.40pm allowing hundreds of MPs to mob the distribution office, carry five volumes back into the chamber and peruse their conclusions in time to offer this 'informed reaction'. During this demeaning farce, the House seemed even more than usually to be run like a somewhat chaotic, highly authoritarian preparatory school of sixty years ago.

The contrast between the Commons vaunted claims to legal sovereignty or ancient authority and its incapacity to sponsor a major inquiry into alleged wrongdoing within an executive which it is supposed to hold politically accountable, could not be greater. Parliament's standing was damaged by the government's domineering procedures but buoyed up by Robin Cook's remarkable skills in reading the report's key sections so quickly and rebutting Lang's claims on Scott's findings. His speech and questions clearly stand as one of the most formidable Commons performances of the post-war years. On a different scale, the government's press release also counted as a record of some kind. Its errors and selectivity contributed to publication day of an always dramatic and controversial inquiry becoming a memorable political day mainly for the worse.

Following publication and the Lang–Cook contest, Scott gave his second press conference and had to defend the form as well as the substance of his work. Journalists were dismayed by the unenlightening bulk of the report and its general lack of ingress: they felt prevented from doing their democratic job. The absence of a summary baffled them and other people: Scott said he wanted his findings and recommendations to be read as a connected whole and in the round. This negative approach to the effective presentation of three years of toil on matters widely thought to be of great public importance seemed counter-productive. In fact, it helped to downplay findings which had already been amended since the draft report stage. The almost self-strangulating terms chosen to report a minister's 'designedly duplicitous' actions (which, however, he denies and so may not have recognised at the time) fit well within such a generally inaccessible report. There has been considerable academic comment on its nature as well as its content. Sir Christopher Foster suggests that it can only be waded into, like *War and Peace*, and not dipped into because Scott has avoided the kind of concise but careful summaries of witnesses' evidence (which planning inspectors and DTI company inspectors, for example, routinely produce) for fear of a judicial review of his findings succeeding on the grounds of an inaccurate rendering of very complex material. It is, of course, possible that this explanation is correct.

Scott's final travail was to help his office organise the equivalent of some 17,611 pages of official and other papers into fifteen further volumes for deposit in the Commons library and for publication (only) on two CD-ROM discs in July 1996: the first such venture on an official report (and yet another Scott inquiry precedent). This collection was criticised for omitting the draft report's criticisms of witnesses such as Waldegrave and their rebuttals. However, Scott had promised them confidentiality (and, indeed, tried to enforce it on them), perhaps reckoning that he would extract fuller and more accurate information by this private, written method than public, oral questioning. He was certainly not free to publish the exchanges.

Scott made radical innovations in the personal public conduct of those conducting official inquiries into events or policy issues. He gave an extended defence of his inquiry procedures in a public lecture to the Chancery Bar Association in the middle of the inquiry period, as a direct answer to Howe and his few public supporters.[6] He permitted Muttukumaru to follow suit, with at least two similarly public lectures at Jesus College, Oxford and Nottingham Trent University Law School.[7] This publicly controversial role on procedural issues was amazing enough compared to the strict purdah into which all other public (or private) sector investigators retreat as soon as their appointment is announced. This is certainly maintained until they have submitted their report and the government or other commissioning organisation has published it. Scott's unprecedented public defence of his procedures was in response to unprecedented public attacks on them. Like any other investigator, he did not discuss in public the substance of his inquiry until he had reported in February 1996.

Thereafter, he undertook a remarkable sequence of public lectures attacking the legislative basis of arms export controls and the practices surrounding ministers signing Public Interest Immunity certificates to keep government papers and information from the courts (the two major themes of his inquiry), while continuing to defend his view of fair inquiry procedures. He did not rehearse the report's evidence or findings on alleged ministerial or official ministerial wrongdoing but rather continued to appear to let others draw the conclusions which he had indicated in his text, as finally amended. Most chairmen and members of inquiries continue their public silence on the subject after their report is published. One or two rather unusual characters such as the late Lord (Victor) Rothschild (commission on gambling), Professor Sir Alan Peacock (broadcasting), Lord Scarman (urban and social conditions) and Lord Woolf (prison policy) have contributed to debate on their respective reports, and Scott has followed their suit strongly. He also addressed or joined in at least two of the half-dozen academic and specialist seminars or conferences held in the six months following his report. Perhaps he has been seen as being most in the mould of the 'Mr Smith Goes to Washington' folk-mythical American story during his doggedly earnest public lecture on the dry-as-dust technicalities of the British legislative control of arms exports since 1939 (compared with which the finer points of PII certificates, with their dramatic element of 'innocent men going to prison' if the certificates are abused, seem almost racy). Taking his own lectures and the seminar meetings together, he was unprecedently activist. His example may well (and certainly should) be followed in the future by other investigators. For such well-informed but carefully controlled comment and opinion to be fed back into the public record so promptly after a major report has been published can only be in the general interest.

Conclusion

Which of the many unprecedented procedural aspects of Scott's remarkable inquiry into government operations will be copied or developed — and which will remain as somewhat singular historical exceptions — will become clear only over many years of future official inquiries. The future leadership of the civil service may look back on Scott as an acutely uncomfortable experience or claim it to have been a second-rate inquiry with serious flaws (following Lord Howe and the limited group which has agreed with him). Some future government may agree, so that no individual not even (or particularly not?) a senior judge, sitting alone may ever be asked to follow in his footsteps on an expedition into the heart of Whitehall. If this broad sentiment of 'Never Again' prevails, a future government faced with allegations of scandalous or criminal conduct among ministers or officials would face the old choice of other methods of inquiry: the 1921 Act tribunal, the committee of Privy Counsellors or a select committee of Privy Counsellor MPs. One untried device would be a committee of (say three) senior serving (or retired) Appeal Court or House of Lords judges all automatically Privy Counsellors who would combine judicial independence with security clearance.

It will also be some time, at least, before academic or other analysts have concluded on the merits of Scott's procedures and Howe's attacks on them.[8] Certainly, without these attacks and Scott's unprecedented public self-defence, this inquiry would offer many fewer precedents in the investigator's chosen methods and personal conduct. Scott had a lot of his inquiry's novelty thrust upon him and would no doubt have welcomed a much quieter life, allowing his onerous investigations to proceed more smoothly. He had quite enough public prominence and pressure to be the public's explorer into the darkest corners of the state, without needing to joust repeatedly with a prominent political figure such as Howe on procedures throughout most his quest.

1   R. Norton-Taylor, *Truth is a Difficult Concept: Inside the Scott Inquiry*, (Fourth Estate, 1995), p. 38–9; see also *Knee-Deep in Dishonour: the Scott Report and its Aftermath*, (Gollancz, 1996).

2   A. Barker, 'Practising to Deceive: Whitehall, Arms Exports and the Scott Inquiry', *Political Quarterly*, Winter 1996/7.

3   T. Blackstone and W. Plowden, *Inside the Think Tank: Advising the Cabinet, 1971–83*, (Heinemann, 1988), p. 162.

4   Speaking at a Public Administration Committee and Political Studies Association conference on the Scott report, June 1996.

5   Speaking at conferences on the Scott report organised by the Hansard Society, April 1996, and the Public Administration Committee and Political Studies Association, June 1996.

6   Published as 'Procedures at Inquiries: The Duty to be Fair', *Law Quarterly Review*, 1995, 596.

7   'Fair or Foul: Aspects of the Scott Inquiry's Procedures', Jesus College, Oxford, 4 June 1995 (printed in the Report at Appendix A D2(xvi)); and 'The Quality of Fairness Is Not Constrained: The Procedures of the Scott Inquiry', Nottingham Trent University Law School, 5 March 1996; published in *Nottingham Law Journal*, (Summer 1996).

8   The Council on Tribunals, officially responding in July 1996, recommended that principal investigators being assisted by inquiry counsel should normally stand back from that counsel's interrogation of witnesses. This endorsed Lord Howe's criticism of the 'Baxendale-Scott double act'.

The Inquiry's Media Coverage

BY RALPH NEGRINE*

THE Scott inquiry presents scholars with a wealth of information about the process of government and it will be many years before all five volumes of the report have been fully exhausted. Whether interest in political communication with respect to the Scott inquiry—or Scott and the media, for short—will prove to be an area with rich pickings is difficult to determine. There certainly is much in the report which is of interest, but perhaps even more significant are the circumstances surrounding the setting-up of the inquiry and the publication of the report. It is here that students of political communication would be wise to concentrate for it is here that one can begin to understand the true meaning of 'news management'.

Whilst the practice of news management was much in evidence in the period leading up to and immediately after the publication of the report, there are two other points about this period which deserve some comment. The first relates to the nature of the report itself and the second relates to the power of the mass media to put pressure on a government, any government, to act. It may be useful to signal these two points at this stage since they frame much of what is said below.

The report itself is long and complex. Although it is not written in a difficult style, it is not always easy to follow Scott as he weaves his way through the evidence which was presented to him. The index makes it easy to pursue specific leads but the absence of an easy-to-read, easy-to-digest and easy-to-publish conclusion must have been an enormous problem for the media. Scott's motives in not submitting a conclusion can easily be inferred from the general objectives of the inquiry: it set out to examine the facts, to set them out as Scott saw them, and to establish the 'truth' in this very complex area of investigation. It did not necessarily set out to pass summary judgements on policies or on individuals or even establish 'which side has won'.[1]

Nevertheless, the absence of a clear cut conclusion, and one which could be seen either to point the finger at individuals or to completely exonerate them, played right into the hands of the government and government ministers. Few who watched Ian Lang's performance/presentation at the despatch box would not have been taken aback when they heard him call for the Labour MP, Robin Cook to resign! One had to remind oneself periodically that the inquiry had originally

---

* Senior Lecturer in Mass Communications, University of Leicester.

been set up to look at alleged government impropriety, and not the actions of the opposition. If Scott had believed that the government would not seek to defend itself in whatever way it could — as it has done over many years — then its actions in handling the release of the report and in the conduct of the debates soon dispelled all his illusions.

The government's handling of the release of the report — more of which below — made it even more apparent that there needed to be a forum, a 'public sphere', in which one could discuss a controversial report such as this without its substance being inflected by interested parties. Unfortunately such a forum does not exist, and so it was left to the print and broadcast media not only to make sense of the report in very difficult circumstances but also to intervene in the process of governmental news management practices in order to distinguish between what interested parties were saying was in the report and what was actually in it.

This brings us to the point that the handling of the report by the media may have played a part in the government's ability to withstand the criticisms which flowed from it. In the period immediately after its publication, the media gave considerable space to the criticisms made by Scott. They kept up the pressure on the government and in particular on William Waldegrave and Sir Nicholas Lyell. However, Scott's unwillingness to intervene in the general debates about governmental responsibilities and improprieties, and the stand-off between the two major political parties, created a difficult situation for the media. Could they continue to put pressure on the government after the Opposition had failed to move the government or after Conservative MPs had closed ranks? What other examples could they dredge from the report if the most prominent ones had failed to pierce the government's defences? What could they do if the one key critic, Scott himself, remained silent? And as so often happens, the media moved on to other fields, leaving many to wonder if more could have been done to unravel the extent of government complicity in the sale of arms to Iraq. As Martin Kettle acknowledged in the *Guardian*, 'Collectively we stand accused of laziness, treating it as a one-day wonder and not burrowing more assiduously into the mass of lies documented in the report' (24 February 1996). Though there were certainly few references to the inquiry in the two months after the publication of the report — e.g. only six in the *Financial Times* and eight in each of the *Independent* and *Guardian*, compared to the extensive coverage in previous years — Kettle may be too self-critical: the press had found out that its power, like that of the opposition, has real limits when faced with a government determined to defend itself at all costs.

There are many issues, then, in a discussion of Scott and the media. In order to explore some of these, we will look at the different aspects of the inquiry in order to show how the media may have played different roles in each of them. The phases are the setting up of the inquiry, the inquiry itself, the publication and presentation of the report, and the report itself.

The setting up of the inquiry

In the first five pages of the report, Scott makes no less than 15 references to separate newspaper articles—curiously none from the *Guardian*—in order to provide the background to the setting up of the inquiry. Here one can begin to appreciate the significance of the press within the realm of British politics and as an institution which helps to define and determine the state of health of the nation and of governments. In these stories, all published in 1989 or 1990, allegations were made about the nature and extent of the arms trade with Iraq and the government's role in that trade. Some, like the story by the *Sunday Times* Insight team, provoked a ministerial reply in the Commons (HC Debs, 3 December 1990) though the majority did not. They did, however, continue to raise difficult questions for the government. Scott goes on to observe how interest in this topic did not subside. 'Ever since the charges had been laid (in the Matrix Churchill case) in February 1991 the case had been sub judice and press and other public comment on the issues raised by the case had not been possible. Nonetheless press interest had continued unabated. The nature of the defence, the degree of ministerial involvement in the prosecution and, the circumstances in which the prosecution in the end collapsed, all combined to produce, after the acquittal, a flood of press and media coverage and of political attacks on the government within and outside Parliament' (A1.13).

Two later statements by Scott establish his views on the importance of the press in politics and as a vehicle for channelling public concern. They are important because they set out a particular perspective on some important relationships in any democratic political system. Explaining why he decided to hold the oral hearings in public, Scott wrote: 'The public, on whose behalf and for whose benefit government is conducted, is entitled, in my opinion, to expect that an inquiry into the propriety of acts of government will be open to the public save to the extent that some overriding public interest requires the contrary' (B2.7).

The inquiry was set up as a response to public disquiet, strongly expressed through the media, about the events that had led to the collapse of the Matrix Churchill prosecution. Widespread cynicism towards and suspicion of government when official denials or explanations of alleged government misdemeanour are put forward has become a current feature of public attitudes to government. .... It was, in my opinion, desirable that the oral hearings and ... the examination of the important witnesses should be held in public so that ... the public scrutiny of the process by which the inquiry's conclusions had been reached should enable public disquiet to be set at rest. (B2.8).

This may not be the place to unpack these statements, but even a cursory glance reveals certain assumptions about how parts of the

political system are linked together: governments act on behalf of the
public; the public needs to be kept informed about governmental
actions; the media channel ('express') the views of the public; the media
throw light on governmental activity and in so doing enable the process
of public scrutiny. All of these statements uphold the traditional view
of the duties and responsibilities of government, media and public, but
they perhaps only have a purchase on 'reality' if these institutions
unquestioningly accept their duties and responsibilities. Yet as Scott
himself documents, and the treatment of his report confirms, this is far
from the case: political interests very often override other things.

Nevertheless, the press is given considerable credit for helping to
bring about the inquiry and for helping to determine the way it was to
proceed. A more dispassionate assessment of the press in this affair
would probably tarnish its image in significant ways. Whilst Scott is
probably correct in valuing it at a particular point in time and once
certain key events had taken place (from about 1989 onwards in
relation to Matrix Churchill case and from about 1990 onwards in
relation to the Supergun affair), the role of the press in alerting the
wider public to the nature of the arms trade prior to these events is
much less complimentary. Put simply, it failed to report those statements
which were later to form such a central part of the inquiry itself. For
instance, some key statements which came to represent government
policy towards arms sales to Iraq and Iran were not covered by such
newspapers of record as the *Times* and *Financial Times*. These include
statements made by Richard Luce in the House of Commons in July
1984, by Tim Renton in the House in 1987, and, finally, Geoffrey
Howe's guidelines which were contained in a written answer on 29
October 1985.[2] Similarly, in 1989 members of the government denied
the existence of the arms trade to Iraq on at least seven occasions[3] yet
none of these were referred to in either the *Times* or *Financial Times*.
There are occasions when the arms trade is mentioned and is part of a
debate about Britain's relationship to Iraq and Iran, but this is in the
context of more general parliamentary debates. It is not surprising then
to find certain commentators arguing that 'with one or two exceptions
... the mainstream media did not see Iraq's clandestine military-
procurement activities in Britain as a story worth reporting' and that
consequently 'the media was as culpable as Whitehall in keeping the
facts from the public'.[4]

One can only speculate as to why this should be so, though two sets
of reasons stand out. The first is that in more 'normal' circumstances
the arms trade is probably not particularly 'newsworthy' and is not of
'interest' to the media.[5] Anthony Sampson has added his own reasons:
the general cross-party concern to retain jobs in the arms industries;
defence correspondents' reluctance to offend the services which provide
so many of their indispensable sources; defence journalism dominated
by men; editors inclined to regard protests against the arms trade as

part of women's subjects; and the fact that there have been very few whistle-blowers from within the arms sales business. Without the continuous monitoring of the arms trade, much happens which might otherwise not happen if it took place in the full blaze of publicity.[6]

As one broadsheet journalist explained in a personal interview when asked why the media had been so slow to report the implications of the supergun: 'There was no immediate specialist who would pick it up. The initial specialist would be the defence specialist but they get too close to the Ministry of Defence. The Ministry of Defence had an interest in smothering this sort of thing. That was a problem. So you had to go to almost free-wheeling people. People had to be put onto that sort of story; it would involve a conscious decision by an editor to say to a reporter to keep an open brief on it or to take time off to do that and only that. But that does not happen very often in British journalism.'

If the organisation of journalism may have inhibited the collection and dissemination of information, further obstacles were erected on the government side by individuals who did not always care to involve the public or the media. Norton-Taylor records exchanges during the inquiry which illustrates this.[7] 'Did a decision (to change the guidelines dealing with arms sales) depend on the public not being told?' asked Scott. Blackley replied, 'If there had been an outcry, I am not sure it would necessarily have reflected the view of the country, only of people prepared to comment'. Scott, at one point, suggested to Howe that (he) was adopting 'a sort of government-knows-best approach'? Howe replied, 'It is partly that. But it is partly, if we were to lay specifically our thought processes before you, they are laid before a world-wide range of uncomprehending or malicious commentators. This is the point. You cannot choose a well-balanced presentation to an elite parliamentary audience.' Scott: 'You can, can you not, expose your hand to people of this country?' Howe: 'There are reasons for caution. Justice is exposed to emotional misunderstandings in this country.'

Similar caution could be found elsewhere. Initially, it had been intended that the guidelines drawn up in 1984 'would be announced publicly, to Parliament or to the media or to both', although Richard Luce 'referred to the need for careful presentation . . . in Parliament accompanied by detailed confidential briefing for selected Parliamentarians and *trusted representatives of the media*' (D1.63 emphasis added). In such circumstances, it is hardly surprising that the media may not have been as watchful as they ought to have been, and it set the pattern for a typical form of coverage, that is, little or scant coverage of an issue followed by a veritable flood of stories, culminating with the disappearance of the issue as others move centre stage.

The inquiry and the media

Once the inquiry was announced in the House of Commons on 16 November 1992, the media as a whole were provided with an easy point of focus. How well they fared during the life of the inquiry itself is difficult to say. A search through the *Guardian* on CD-ROM identified 108 individual newspaper items which contained references to the Scott inquiry in 1993 and 177 references in 1994. If references to the inquiry in sketches, letters and diary pieces are excluded, these figures come down to about 90 newspaper stories in 1993 and 134 in 1994. A search through the electronic data base FT-Profile for references to the inquiry in other newspapers also proved remarkably fruitful: between November 1992 and end July 1994, 839 items were found in the *Financial Times, Telegraph* and *Sunday Telegraph, Independent* and *Independent on Sunday, Today, Daily Mail* and *Mail on Sunday*. (Unfortunately, the FT-Profile database does not cover the tabloid press so there is no easy way of determining how it treated the inquiry.) Admittedly, these figures are fairly crude and would need to be tidied up before any conclusions about the coverage are drawn but they are nevertheless useful because they give us an overview of its extent. A more detailed examination of the coverage given to three hearings (see below) suggests that in the tabloids it was very restricted. As for television, again, there is no easy way of gaining information about the coverage of the inquiry but, apart from *Channel Four News*, on the main channels it is likely to be less fulsome than the continuous stream of stories in the broadsheets.

There is another perhaps more significant reason why it would be difficult to pass judgement on the media's performance. Although they provided a window onto the inquiry and the many public hearings which took place, these hearings were only a small part of a much larger and less visible whole. Indeed, the inquiry was in reality not public in the sense that Scott and his team spent a considerable part of their time reading documents which were not publicly available and which would lay the foundations for questioning and analysis of the events. In fact, by the time the first public hearings took place in May 1993, the team had read 70,000 pages of official documents; by the end it was claimed that it had collected and presumably read 200,000 pages of documents. The public side of the inquiry consisted only of 87 public hearings, where individuals could supplement their written evidence by oral evidence. Needless to say, the press covering these hearings would select only those extracts deemed interesting and newsworthy; the full transcripts were, and remain, available only to a few.

If the press offered only a glimpse on to a much more complex and hidden process of decision-making, television was even more restricted in what it could do. Early on, Scott had decided to exclude the television cameras from the hearings on the grounds that it would make a spectacle of them in the same way as it had done in the O.J. Simpson trial in the US. This was not, according to Scott, the occasion in which 'to experiment' with television (B2.37). Had television been allowed into the hearings, its coverage would probably have been more fulsome because it would have had access to pictures rather than rely on the chalk drawings which livened up their journalists' pieces to camera. In that way, a wider public might have been exposed to the inquiry and, as important, there would have been some visual record of the hearings themselves. Although Scott may have been correct to question whether television by its very presence would have unintentionally altered the balance of importance of the hearings as opposed to the reading of documents, its total exclusion could only be regretted. As it is, in an age when whole encyclopaedias are available on a single CD-ROM, we have no cheap and easily available audio-visual record of one of the key inquiries of the 1990s.

That said, are there other ways of assessing the performance of the media? One way is to examine how that coverage was spread across the newspapers and television; another is to look at specific moments when the inquiry was considered particularly newsworthy. One of the major differences between newspapers is the intensity of the coverage. The mid-market newspapers such as (the now defunct) *Today* and the *Daily Mail* covered the inquiry in a consistent but less intensive way than the up-market broadsheets. For example, in the months of April to July 1994 there were 17 separate references to it in the *Financial Times*, 22 in the *Independent*, but 11 in the *Mail*; in March 1994 there were 38 references to it in the *Financial Times*, 45 in the *Independent*, but 23 in the *Mail*. A verdict of less than adequate coverage in the *Mail* would be as unjust as one of overkill in the broadsheets. As for the tabloids, in that same month the *Sun* carried 11 stories and one cartoon.

As before, looking at such crude figures only gives us a sense of just how much coverage there was rather than an indication of its quality. Yet even these crude figures are interesting because they provide a rough guide as to which news organisations accorded the inquiry an important status by allocating a reporter to follow it on a full-time basis. By and large, the up-market newspapers did, whilst the others relied on correspondents visiting the hearings when key, and newsworthy, witnesses were giving evidence. The former, having allocated extensive resources to the inquiry, would then be more likely to provide column space for its journalists. We can see this if we compare the coverage (number of newspaper stories) given to three oral hearings when the following were giving evidence: Margaret Thatcher (8 December 1993), Alan Clark (13–15 December 1993) and (almost at random) Ian McDonald (7 October 1993).

1. Stories devoted to hearings involving three politicians

	Margaret Thatcher	Alan Clark	Ian McDonald
Guardian	4	4	1
Financial Times	2	3	2
Independent	5	6	1
Times	4	5	1
Mail	3	2	–
Mirror	3	2	–
Sun	1	1	–

What was being written during the period of the inquiry, and how were the witnesses' statements seen by the press? The overall impression which a scan of the headlines during this phase reveals is of individuals attempting to conceal acts of negligence, incompetence and deceit. Even the tabloids were quick to point this out. 'Law boss faces axe over arms to Iraq fiasco' and 'Waldegrave suicide statement. It's right to tell porkies to Parliament', wrote the *Sun* , and an editorial declared that the 'Rt Hon Wally was guilty of crass stupidity and should go'. The other papers had their own way of highlighting the manner in which the government acted: 'Scott Inquiry is told of evidence altered by prosecution counsel'; 'Scott probe hears of "shambles" at DTI'; 'I know nuffink guv. honest: John Major'; 'Clark admits "sleight of hand" in statements'; '"I saw nothing!" Baroness Thatcher'; 'Parliamentary answers likened to "art form"'.[8]

If one adds to this some of the phrases which have since become well-known—'truth is a difficult concept' (Ian McDonald); 'I quite simply misled myself on what I thought the situation was' (Eric Beeston, DTI); 'Half the picture can be true' (Sir Robin Butler, head of the civil service); 'Something that I was not aware had happened suddenly turned out not to have happened' (John Major); and references to Public Interest Immunity certificates as 'gagging orders'—one can see why Sir Robin Butler felt aggrieved about the 'wild allegations and pre-judging of issues in media reports'. And his complaint was made before Waldegrave 'defended the right to tell House (of Commons) lies'. Butler may have had a reason to feel concerned about the 'tone of coverage', but it was odd to find those in power—and those who hide behind many veils of secrecy—pleading for protection. Had they not benefited from publicly funded legal advice? Had they not been forewarned? Were their actions so misunderstood as to require special pleading? Were they not being judged on the basis of what they had actually said to the inquiry and done in their day-to-day work?

The evidence from the hearings had certainly shown up inefficiencies, lack of coordination in government departments, disregard for parliamentary procedures and many other things, but what did all this amount to? Would Scott's report blame individuals or the process of government itself? Would it be so critical as to lead to resignations? Would William Waldegrave and Sir Nicholas Lyell be able to retain their positions, given the evidence which was piling up against them? Sections of the press were unsure about how much the inquiry would achieve. Jimmy Burns, who followed the inquiry for the *Financial Times*, concluded a review piece in January 1994 with a statement which was echoed in the *Guardian* several months later: will the inquiry 'focus more on political responsibility or opt for a broad critique of government and the shortcomings of legislation'? Interestingly, the piece was headed 'Scott inquiry teeters between dynamite and damp squib' (10 January 1994).

Such questions are important because they begin to reveal the complex relationship between an inquiry, the government, the press/media, and the opposition political parties as each attempts to court public opinion and/or inflict damage on the other. If the report opted for a critique of government, the opposition would find it more difficult to force resignations; resignations would be more likely, however, if individuals were to be singled out for particular criticisms. But, as we shall see, the Scott report was not written in such a way that it could be used easily by the opposition against the government or ministers, nor for that matter was it particularly helpful for the public at large. By contrast, the government was able to take advantage of its contents, partly because it was in control of the process of its dissemination to the outside world.

The publication and presentation of the report

The report generated considerable interest even well before its publication on 15 February 1996. Again, without a full and detailed analysis of each and every news story written about it in the period leading up to February 1996, it would be risky to provide anything more than a sketch of this period; however, one became aware of the government's counter-offensive in the making.

Scott had adopted the practice of letting those he had questioned and commented on have sight of the relevant draft sections of his report. Although commendable, and sound in theory, in practice it gave those in his sights the opportunity to defend themselves — often at great public cost — and to anticipate the sorts of criticisms which would be made in the final report. In these ways, and slowly but surely, the defensive walls were being erected and the answers to accusations being prepared. The public was being alerted to the length the government and its ministers would go to try to pull the sting out of the report. But the government's counter-attack also took other forms. Two are noteworthy as examples of the attempted management of public opinion. The first, and most consistent, was Sir Geoffrey Howe's attacks on the inquiry on the grounds that it did not offer witnesses the chance to defend themselves as they would have done in a court of law (i.e. through cross-examination of other witnesses through counsel of their own). Such comments were seen by many as a pre-emptive strike, and as an opportunity to cast doubts on the value of the inquiry and the report even before it had come to any conclusions. It was also an indication of how its conclusions would be treated once published. The second example, more interesting and complex, focuses on the statements made by Sir Robin Butler about the conduct of the inquiry and its coverage. As we have seen Butler accused the media of pre-judging matters which, by implication, might look different when the full context, and the nature of governance itself, were taken into account. Here one can begin to detect a different strand of the counter-offensive which was based on the idea that those outside government were bound to fail to understand how government really worked and would thus misunderstand what went on.

If one combines these two elements, a strong sense of injustice amongst those in power comes through; a resentment of being judged, of being assessed by outsiders and an implicit belief that only they understand government and the practice of government and only they can fully comprehend—and so judge—what had been going on. One could take all this as evidence that the report would not be given an easy ride but, more to the point, that it would become embroiled in politics and not remain above politics. Very early on in its life, the inquiry had become part of the to-and-fro of politics, but it may have been an error of judgement on the part of Scott and his advisers to believe that his perspective on the report and its significance would dominate proceedings. As we shall see, it was hijacked by the government in its efforts to muffle it.

Yet it is curious that the government's intentions were so transparent: the report was officially released to Parliament at 3.30 pm on 15 February, at which point Ian Lang, the President of the Board of Trade, delivered the government's views. The problem was that the government seemed to go out of its way to make it difficult for others to intervene in the debate:

It had taken great care to manage and lead press opinion. It had insisted that those criticised should have access to the report a full week prior to its official release date. In theory, only those directly concerned should have had access to it', but as one senior correspondent reported, 'the first of the hefty batch of self-serving Whitehall press releases (began) to land on my desk before the report itself came from the Cabinet Office.⁹

Each of these releases repeated the same lines about there having been 'no conspiracy . . . and no cover-up'. The government also prevented the opposition from having access to the report. When protests—and a certain amount of disquiet on the part of Scott himself—built up, it relented and allowed Robin Cook (Labour) and Menzies Campbell (Lib. Dem.) to have sight of the report about four hours prior to publication, in total secrecy and in a closed room supervised by guards. In such circumstances, the task of the opposition was made almost impossible.

It led the debate with Ian Lang who had had the benefit of a close examination of the report. His statement in the House emphasised themes common in all the press releases, namely, that the report 'completely exonerates all ministers and civil servants from any sort of conspiracy or cover-up' and that the whole thing was really cooked up by the Labour Party and Robin Cook in particular, and that they should be the ones to resign. It was an admirable performance but a performance which benefited greatly from the fact that he was the only one who had had sight of the script. Others, who were in the dark, could not contradict him. He had, in effect, managed to set the scene and to force others onto his own territory. Those who wanted to find out what Scott had really said had a double task: first, to unravel Lang's words, then to make sense of Scott. The government had made it difficult to do either.

Although Lang did succeed in obscuring the nature of the report and its contents, his triumph was not complete. Comments on his speech in the press on the following day made much of the cynical way he had filleted it to his advantage. Philip Stephens in the *Financial Times* wrote of 'half-truths' running 'through every sentence' and that 'cynical sophistry infused his version of the report'. In the *Times*, Peter Riddell wrote that 'the more time people had to read the report, the more partial the version presented by Ian Lang looked'. Simon Jenkins, also in the *Times*, described his statement as being 'woefully partial'.[10] Scott did not help matters in this respect: when questioned about his views on Ian Lang's statement, he replied 'I think it is a fair summary. Any sound bite answer, any summary one-line answer is bound to be a distortion of what I have taken care to express in my report'.

Irrespective of these critical jabs, one could argue that Lang's performance achieved the desired effect in setting the tone of the debate and of creating even more obstacles in the way of true knowledge about the report. Paradoxically, if Scott had intended to change the public's perception of government, Lang's performance merely further justified the public's contempt for government and politicians! His performance may have been no more than a direct consequence of the way the government attempted to manage the debate. This is clear from the circumstances surrounding the release of the report, yet it is worth bearing in mind that perhaps Scott made it easier for the government to adopt that strategy than he should have done. This point reflects back on the report itself and on Scott's almost naive belief that his report would live and die above politics.

The report

Journalists and columnists gave their own accounts of the report, but through their comments one could begin to identify not one, but two, reports. One contained the 'verdict' on the charges laid against the government, ministers and the rest of the stock of characters; the other was about the nature of government itself. Though more attention was given to the first of these in general efforts to pin the blame on individuals. Peter Riddell in the *Times* identified a report which went 'to the heart of ministers' relations with Parliament'. It was a point picked up by Norton-Taylor in the *Guardian* when he described the report as providing 'an unprecedented insight into Whitehall culture . . . Sir Richard Scott said yesterday, that he hoped they would be the subject of 'serious and informed debate' (16 February 1996). In very many ways, we can see how Scott attempted to change the nature of the debate surrounding the report, away from a report which had become about politics and government into one which was above politics. This emerges very clearly in the way he handled journalists in his press conference in the early evening of 15 February 1996. As this event demonstrates, he was not 'helpful' to journalists, he adopted a way of communicating which was alien to the ways of modern political communication, and he delivered a report which was not easy to pin down.

In more normal circumstances, authors of reports go out of their way to include executive summaries and/or press releases, so as to enable journalists to write their copy speedily and in a way which draws on the key points of any document. Scott did not oblige. His report was not only very long at five volumes and over 1,800 pages, but it lacked the sorts of signposts which would allow journalists—who had not had sight of it anyway—to identify key phrases, characters or statements. When pressed to comment on this or that aspect of government or ministerial behaviour, he was equally unhelpful. Some instances from this press conference also go to show that Scott appeared to be operating in a different culture when it came to issues of modern political communication. For example, Scott was asked: 'Is it correct to say Mr Waldegrave misled the House of Commons?' and replied, 'Some of the letters he wrote and some of the answers he gave were in my opinion misleading'. Or again: 'Did the government behave honestly and in good faith?', Scott replied, 'The answer is in my report.' As Johnston commented in the *Telegraph*, throughout 'the news conference, Sir Richard gave the impression that he would like his interrogators to draw conclusions that he was unable or unwilling to give. The strong impression that Parliament has been misled, gleaned.. from the report, was not dispelled despite his refusal to confirm it' (16 February 1996).

But why was there no summary? Why was Scott reluctant to make any comments? His words are interesting. 'A summary would risk distortion.' 'I have prepared my conclusions very carefully ... I have expressed in the report in a considered way my view of that topic. Any sound-bite answer is bound to be a distortion of what I have taken care to express in the report.' Though admirable, his position was clearly not helpful to journalists—or the public—and a godsend for the government. As John Kampfer put it in the *Financial Times*, Scott 'leaves it to readers to draw their own conclusions on individual culpability' (16 February 1996). Yet, as we have seen, the way the government handled the publication of the report, the way Scott himself refused to give guidance, and his production of a very lengthy—not to say expensive—report ensured precisely the opposite of what he had intended: the debate was hijacked, and those who would have helped the public to make sense of the report were left to trawl through many pages, to wade through statements and qualifications, to ponder 'whether it had all been a waste of time' in spite of the clear instances of behaviour which were heavily criticised.

It was perhaps not odd then to find newspapers juxtaposing statements which seemed to contradict each other. In the *Times*, 'The government has a case to answer which goes well beyond the personal honour of Mr Waldegrave and Sir Nicholas', next to 'Sir Richard set out to build a mountain over a molehill'; in the *Telegraph*, 'Amid the noise, Scott chooses his right to remain silent', next to 'Ministers misled MPs with inaccuracies'. The one example which best illustrates all this was the verdict on William Waldegrave: 'Waldegrave made "untrue statements" in 27 letters', Parliament was deliberately misled but Waldegrave 'did not intend his letters to be misleading and did not so regard them'; furthermore, although Waldegrave had no 'duplicitous intention' with respect to the change of guidelines on arms sales, the changes were duplicitous in themselves. For many, the obvious conclusion was that Scott had pulled his punches and let many off 'Scott free'. Accusing Scott of ducking the final challenge, the *Sun*'s political commentator, Trevor Kavanagh, delivered his own version of what the report should have said, 'Politicians are just slippery, power-hungry opportunists who will use any legitimate device to save their necks' (17 February 1996).

The handling of the report by the government, and the way its conclusions were phrased perhaps ensured that there would be no real conclusion to the affair. Revelations continued to seep out in the days after the report came out, but by the time the adjournment debate took place on 26 February, it was clear that no minister would be forced to resign and that there was no real ammunition to knock them down with. Charges of wrong-doing, of incompetence, of misleading Parliament did not have sufficient power to force resignations, something which had been ruled out anyway on the day of publication when the Prime Minister said as much. The government had shown itself able to resist the pressure which the report had begun to build up.

Could it have been otherwise? Had the report been more strongly or clearly worded, with sufficient guidance for the media to pursue leads, then it is possible that more continuous pressure could have been applied on those at the heart of the affair. But even these things would have had to contend with two other factors which often have a more powerful effect than media coverage alone. The first is the extent to which the political party in difficulties is able or willing to withstand criticism. As Peter Riddell wrote in the *Times*, 'the key will be whether senior Tory MPs . . . break ranks, and on the extent of media criticism. If the Tories remain united, the two ministers should remain safe'. The second factor is similar in some respects. A political party can better withstand criticism if the furore 'remains an issue for the metropolitan political classes'. However, if it moves out of this arena and 'begins to play also in Portsmouth and Preston', then it becomes much more difficult to pretend that it is only of concern to the chattering classes. In this respect, if the press can show that 'the public' is truly concerned about an issue, it can create a body of pressure which could force governments to reconsider their stated positions.

But fortunately for the government, the public remained bemused by the whole affair. Two surveys carried out within a week of the report's release and extensively quoted in the *Guardian* suggested that about one-third of the sample had no opinion on the report. This is hardly surprising given the nature of the report itself, the media coverage and the various government efforts to manage opinion. Although those surveyed did call for resignations, that was not as strongly expressed as it might have been. Nevertheless, some 86% of one sample felt that the government had misled Parliament. Such views were also expressed by *Sun* readers by a majority of two-and-a-half to one through the *Sun's* Hotline two days after the publication of the report. Despite these public verdicts, there was no real sense of a public ready to march in support of Scott. Did the *Sun* capture a prominent public mood when it wrote that 'We all know that politicians lie and lie. That's how they become MPs in the first place' (9 March 1994). In which case, the public silence was not unexpected. It could also simply be that the public was just happy to wait and pass its judgment at the next general election.

1   C. Muttukumara, *Aspects of the Scott Inquiry's Procedures*. Lecture given at Jesus College, Oxford, 4 June 1995. Published in the report as Appendix A Part D2 (xvi).

2   F.M. Watson, *The Scott Inquiry: Approaching Publication*, (House of Commons Library, UK/Hou., Research Paper 1996/16), pp. 6–7.

3   R. Norton-Taylor, *Truth is a Difficult Concept: Inside the Scott Inquiry*, (Fourth Estate, 1995), p. 84.

4   A. George, 'Missiles and the Media', *Guardian*, 9 June 1995.

5   H. Young, 'Of mires and Ministers', *Guardian*, 24 November 1992.

6   A. Sampson, 'Missile-bound Media', *Guardian*, 15 November 1991, p. 23.

7   Norton-Taylor, op. cit., p. 96.

8   'It's Right to Tell Porkies in Parliament', *Sun*, 9 March 1996; 'Scott Inquiry is Told of Evidence Altered by Prosecution Counsel', *Independent*, 2 April 1994; 'I Know Nuffink Guv. Honest', *Today*, 18 January 1994; 'Clark Admits "Sleight of Hand" in Statements', *Daily Telegraph*, 16 December 1993; '"I Saw Nothing!" Baroness Thatcher', *Today*, 9 December 1993; 'Waldegrave Defends the Right to Tell House Lies . . .', *Independent*, 9 March 1994.

9   P. Stephens, 'An Obsession with Secrecy', *Financial Times*, 16 February 1996.

10 P. Riddell, 'A Blind Eye to Blame', *Times*, 16 February 1996; S. Jenkins, 'Mountain Over Molehill', *Times*, 16 February 1996.

The Arms Trade

BY MARK PHYTHIAN*

FOLLOWING the publication of the Scott report in February 1996, much attention focused on the way in which Scott opened up the workings of Whitehall, his criticisms of the government, and the party political battle over ministerial responsibility and whether William Waldegrave and Sir Nicholas Lyell should resign. With regard to the arms trade, however, Scott has left a whole range of questions unanswered. Rather than represent the subject of the inquiry, 'arms to Iraq' has emerged more as the context within which an inquiry into ministerial and Whitehall conduct was undertaken. This is not to say that Scott has not shed some light on a too murky area of governmental activity. Yet it seems clear that while his procedures served him well in dealing with issues such as ministerial accountability or public interest immunity, they did not lend themselves as well to an examination of the international arms trade.

Essentially, there are two reasons for this. The first relates to Scott's terms of reference, drafted by the government and agreed by him after minor amendments. The key element was that the inquiry was required, 'to report on whether the relevant departments, agencies, and responsible ministers operated in accordance with the policies of Her Majesty's Government'(A2.2), over the export to Iraq of military goods and related technology between December 1984 and August 1990. The natural corollary of this was that the inquiry's focus came to lie in examining 'allegations regarding the part played by government officials and ministers in the decisions that led to the export of defence-related equipment to Iraq' (A3.6). Hence, as he says in his report, Scott consistently declined to pursue allegations of illegal arms-related exports to Iraq which he felt fell outside this remit—that is, unless there were grounds to suspect that some part in enabling the export to take place may have been played by government officials or ministers. It was not the purpose of the inquiry to investigate or expose smuggling operations. This approach obviously limited his need to investigate the arms trade, and where he does he is often required to consider what were in effect de facto smuggling operations—for example, the use of conduits like Jordan to beat the restrictions in place and get lethal equipment to Iraq.

The second reason lies in the limited investigative reach of the inquiry.

* Lecturer in Politics, University of Wolverhampton.

Thorough investigation of a contemporary arms market where, the evidence from the Iran–Iraq War suggests, the international system of end-use certification is frequently abused would have required a much wider reach. In practice, the inquiry's investigative efforts were very limited. In part, this seems to have been a consequence of Scott's belief that involvement could be divined from documents—that a paper trail would always exist. As the report says, the work of the inquiry was based almost entirely on the collection and examination of documents supplied by government departments following requests from the inquiry team. As it also notes, departments were generally reactive rather than proactive in their supply of documents. Cross-referencing at times revealed that some had been withheld, while other important documents were only disgorged slowly and were still arriving as late as October 1995.[1] Can Scott be certain that he finally got to see all of the relevant documents? For example, a former official of International Military Services—a defence sales quango which operated at arms-length from the Ministry of Defence—told the inquiry of how, in the mid-1980s, he was instructed to weed the IMS project file of all papers referring directly to Iraq in order that they could be shredded (D2.220). Was this an isolated operation? In an era that gave us Iran–Contra and various other arms-related scandals, and over a case where Scott heard evidence of the unreliability of the system of end-use certification, how realistic is the expectation of a paper trail? The inquiry's further investigative efforts involved writing to private individuals to ask questions about their alleged involvements. Even here, lines of inquiry were not followed up as thoroughly as they could have been. In practice, documentary evidence seems to have been given precedence at all times over eyewitness testimony, often at the expense of the observations of businessmen and industrialists involved in 'Iraqgate'.

One consistent theme of government statements and protestations when it came to the arming of Iraq was that, unlike other countries, Britain had not in fact sold lethal weapons to that country. Indeed, so persuasive was this line—misleadingly restated in the government press pack distributed alongside the Scott report—that it was even accepted by some commentators as being true.[2] It was a claim similar to that deployed by the Bush administration in the US. While both were superficially true, neither claim stood up to any kind of scrutiny. In the UK case, there are two explanations of how the government armed Iraq without appearing to do so. The first lies in the fact that the trade was in machine tools—that is, exporting the means to produce weapons indigenously—the decisions surrounding the export of which and their compatibility with the government's guidelines are exhaustively followed in the report. The second lies in the diversion of arms through conduit countries, chief among which stood Jordan.

With regard to machine tools for military production, the inquiry's attention focused on Matrix Churchill, the Coventry-based company formerly known as TI Machine Tools Ltd and sold by TI to the Iraqis in 1987. A testimony to the quality of British engineering, Matrix Churchill machine tools were subsequently found in all of the more important Iraqi weapons programmes—from the production of conventional armaments to missile programmes (including the Scud) and to gas centrifuges for the nuclear weapons programme. Although the British government had clear intelligence throughout the 1987–1990 period that the machine tools were going to make armaments, its natural inclination towards sale rather than restraint led it to maintain the fiction that, because they were destined for Iraqi plants which combined military with a modest amount of civilian production, export licences should be approved as there was no 'incontrovertible evidence' that the machines may not be put to a civilian use. Furthermore, because they were believed to be intended for use solely in the more pedestrian technology of conventional arms (a false assumption as it turns out) their export would not represent a serious breach of the government's guidelines. Scott is critical of this myopia—which could have had far more serious consequences if Iraq had not invaded Kuwait when it did. Rather than require 'incontrovertible' evidence of military end-use, he argues that, 'it should have been sufficient to identify evidence which established the intention on a clear balance of probabilities' (D6.254). That is, where serious doubts arose, the government should have erred on the side of caution and refused an export licence. At the same time, Scott is also critical of the machine tool companies themselves. They used imprecise terms such as 'general engineering' in their licence applications to conceal the end-use of what they knew or suspected to be machines destined for a military application. In the cases where the exporters knew that the machines had a military end-use, he says this, 'constituted a deliberate concealment of the known end-use' (D8.9).

Initially, the inquiry team had not anticipated having to look at the role of conduits in any particular depth. It was first alerted to the important role played by conduits, and by Jordan in particular, through the written statements of Chris Cowley who, as project manager for Project Babylon (the Iraqi Supergun project), had spent a year in Baghdad during 1988 and 1989, and Gerald James, former chairman of UK munitions manufacturer Astra Holdings, rather than by the government. Brief questioning of early witnesses towards the ends of their sessions at the inquiry confirmed that Jordan had been widely used. The Ministry of Defence's Lt. Col. Glazebrook, who had already given evidence over two days, was even recalled for a further two days' questioning specifically on Jordan. As the inquiry progressed, it became clear that the lead which Cowley and James had given on Jordan had emerged as a central area of the investigation. In addition to their evidence, James Edmiston, a British businessman who had visited the Jordanian port of Aqaba, told of seeing boxes of arms and ammunition from the UK, US, Germany, Spain, Italy, the Netherlands, Belgium,

Switzerland and Austria stacked up there (*The Economist*, 7 May 1994).

The inquiry was told that Britain's historic relationship with Jordan, its contemporary geopolitical significance, and the importance of not undermining King Hussein's position were all important factors in the turning of a blind eye to Jordan's conduit role and the muting of any criticism of it. During the Iran–Iraq war, the port of Aqaba was a favoured route from which goods Iraq was otherwise prohibited from acquiring could be re-routed. So extensive was this trade that Iraq had a whole section of the port to itself, fenced off from the rest and known as the Iraq Ports Authority. The inquiry heard from Sir David Miers that 'in general, in the Foreign Office, we were quite, how shall I say, concerned, alert, or aware of the possibility that other countries, particularly Jordan, might be used as a diversionary destination', and that the Foreign Office was aware of what Presily Baxendale called 'problems with Jordan' even prior to 1983.

Even so, the British Embassy in Jordan was not instructed to investigate the use of Jordan as a diversionary route. Ian Blackley said that the Foreign Office, 'were aware that Jordan, Kuwait and Saudi Arabia were being used as transhipment ports for goods destined for Iraq'. The Foreign Office's Simon Fuller, in his written statement to the inquiry, said that there was 'a general knowledge that Aqaba was a major route for the supply of military equipment' and that 'Jordan was a strong and consistent supporter of the Iraqi war effort against Iran'. This even extended to the upgrading of the road from Aqaba into the equivalent of a dual carriageway in order to cope with the volume of traffic coming from Iraq to pick up military and other supplies. The inquiry was also given MI6 reports which indicated clear knowledge of Jordan's role. A Jordanian perspective on its involvement was provided by its Ambassador to the UK, Fouad Ayoub, in a radio interview cited by Scott in his report. Ayoub explained that: 'Really, it's no secret that during the years of the Iran–Iraq war, many countries, including Western countries and Arab countries, were keen to see that the Iraqi military capabilities then remained undiminished. Jordan operated within this context and as such we helped to purchase and send some arms and equipment to Iraq. And, in point of fact, those arms and equipments were financed by other Arab countries as well as they were done with the full approval of Western powers and other Arab countries too' (E2.2).

Former Foreign Office official Mark Higson told the inquiry that 'it was long suspected amongst FCO officials that Jordan was being used as an arms conduit. Indeed, even during my time in the British Embassy in Kuwait [March 1983–July 1986] we knew Jordan through Aqaba was being used for imports of hardware from the UK, which was then going on to Iraq.' The jovial David Mellor told the inquiry how he 'knew that all the rest of the Arabs wanted Saddam to win [the war with Iran], and of course knew that he was being provisionally supplied through contiguous countries, Kuwait and Jordan.' In his statement to the inquiry, former Trade and Defence minister Alan Clark conceded that it was 'certainly true that a lot of illicit traffic was going through Jordan at this time'. Despite this high level of informed suspicion, the battle within Whitehall between those eager to promote arms or not damage bilateral relations and those arguing that evidence existed which should be met by refusal to sell was a very uneven one.

One of those who performed the latter role in an environment relatively unsympathetic to notions of export restraint was Lt. Col. Glazebrook. His job was to argue for restraint on the Ministry of Defence Working Group on Iran and Iraq. Counter-arguments would come from the Ministry of Defence's Defence Exports Services Organisation and the outcome would be passed up as the official Ministry of Defence view on each case presented to it. During the Iran–Iraq War, however, it was made clear to Glazebrook that there was no prospect of the government's guidelines being extended to cover known diversionary routes like Jordan—they were only to be applied to Iran and Iraq.

In view of this kind of evidence, what does the Scott report say about the use of Jordan as a conduit? Scott traced British government knowledge of the use of Jordan as a conduit back to 1983. As early as 1983, he cites an MI5 note which observed that 'in view of the restrictions imposed on the sale of war material to Iraq and Iran, Iraq has been using Jordan as an intermediary.' (E2.5). He goes on to record a series of instances, stretching across six pages, indicating ever-growing government awareness of Jordan's conduit role. However, there is no evidence that this awareness translated into concern when, in September 1985, the British government entered into a wide-ranging arms deal with the Jordanian government. It is fair to assume that elements of this, as with the Saudi Arabian Al Yamamah order, were really intended for Iraq. Scott concludes that 'the possibility that military exports to Jordan might be diverted to Iraq represented a continuing threat to the integrity of the government's policy on restricting defence related exports to Iraq' (E2.62). This seems like an unduly restrained conclusion in view of the evidence available. For example, through a series of parliamentary questions, Jim Cousins MP managed to unearth the fact that in the 1980s, under the general category 'arms and ammunition for military purposes', exports to Jordan were valued at £581.5m—over 30 times the figure (just £18.5m) for the 1970s. Notwithstanding the Jordanian defence package, it would appear that the UK armed Iraq through Jordan.

Not that Jordan was the only neighbouring state to act as a conduit or transhipment point. In considering other diversionary routes (although he does not consider all of those alleged to have been used), Scott reveals British government knowledge of the use of Kuwait and

Saudi Arabia, as well as Austria and Portugal as conduits, although the cases against certain other alleged conduits, such as the United Arab Emirates and Cyprus remain, to his mind, not proven. Again, the inquiry's conclusions are based on points drawn from British government documents and the opinions offered by the Ministry of Defence and Foreign Office, and so whether they represent definitive statements is open to question. As with Jordan, where Scott is able to confirm the likelihood that a state performed a conduit function, the detail available to him falls short of enabling him to estimate the volume of equipment involved.

Evidence of Saudi Arabia's conduit role had first appeared in 1981 and was an open secret within defence circles by the mid-1980s. Sir Stephen Egerton, a former UK Ambassador to Saudi Arabia, told the inquiry of reports of the use of 'a small military port of Jedda called Al Quadima [which] was occasionally used for transhipment of heavy equipment in transit to Iraq' and that, 'Al Quadima was in a restricted military zone, very difficult to get to. You were warned off the road if you got anywhere near and you were not allowed to follow anything coming out of it.' To take one example of diversion involving the Saudis cited by Scott—a former employee of Allivane International Ltd told the inquiry how a 1987 order for 15,000 rounds of 155 mm ammunition, with an end-user certificate signed by a senior officer in the Saudi Ministry of Defence, was ultimately shipped on by the Saudis to Iraq. Scott agreed that there was 'a fair probability' that this had indeed been the case. Wider interests—not least of which were the huge arms deals negotiated by the British government with Jordan and Saudi Arabia— combined to prevent the British government making any formal complaint about such diversions.

In the cases where Scott is unable to confirm allegations that diversion took place, does this mean that it did not occur, or merely that as a consequence of the inquiry's investigative limitations it has been unable to determine whether it occurred? Some cases suggest the latter. Take the example of the Skyguard air defence system manufactured by BMARC in Grantham. It was never officially exported to Iraq but was exported to known conduits such as Jordan, Saudi Arabia and Kuwait. Despite this, the Skyguard system was said by industry sources to have been in operation in Baghdad during the Iran–Iraq War. Furthermore, the former chairman of BMARC, Gerald James, has consistently claimed that Iraqis were trained in its use in the UK. The provision of training fell outside Scott's terms of reference, and he limits himself to saying that the documents supplied to the inquiry contained no indication that the Skyguard system had been exported to Iraq. However, if it had been passed on via a contiguous state, the export documentation for those states would require examination and would need to be followed up by determining quantity held against quantity exported.

A related issue, Project Lisi, involved the same company and similar allegations that diversionary routes were used to get otherwise prohibited arms to Iran and Iraq. In this case, the intention was to export naval guns to Iran via Singapore—within the defence industry a well-known transhipment point. After a cursory overview, Scott concluded that Lisi fell outside his remit and so did not need to be investigated further, leaving him with 'no conclusions to express' (D7.79). However, it was an issue taken up in 1995 by the Commons Trade and Industry Select Committee at the urging of then President of the Board of Trade, Michael Heseltine, after an internal DTI inquiry concluded that the guns 'could well' have been bound for Iran. In 1996 the committee concluded that it was indeed 'likely' that diversion had occurred.[3]

While the inquiry focused on Iraq, there were other cases where Scott accepted that he might need to consider the sale of arms and related equipment to Iran, given that the war between Iran and Iraq had led to the government's guidelines which applied to both belligerents in a supposedly impartial manner. One such instance involved the alleged activities of a European propellant cartel. Following the outbreak of war, both Iran and Iraq developed an almost insatiable appetite for explosives and ammunition. In the mid-1980s, Swedish Customs investigators exposed the so-called Bofors affair, revealing the extent to which Iran in particular was meeting this demand with the assistance of a network of major European explosives manufacturers, allegedly involving companies in Austria, Belgium, Britain, Finland, France, Italy, Netherlands, Norway, Spain, Sweden, Switzerland and West Germany, and organised around the European Association for the Study of Safety Problems in the Production and Use of Propellant Powders (EASSP)—formed in 1975 as a forum for discussing safety issues across the industry. Certain of these companies, prominent among which was the Swedish company Bofors, began to use the organisation as a forum for allocating orders from Iran and Iraq and devising means of getting these orders through to their prohibited destinations without attracting undue attention. They did so through the tried and tested methods of false end-user certificates, conduits and misdescriptions of consignments of explosive as being for industrial rather than military use.

Documents uncovered during the Swedish Customs investigation into Bofors in the mid-1980s had suggested that UK companies may have had some involvement with the cartel. They contained references to both Royal Ordnance—then still government-owned—and ICI–Nobel. For example, in a travel report dated June 1984, Mats Lundberg of Bofors spoke of the ICI management's concern at the involvement of this ICI subsidiary in the activities of the cartel: '[Sir John] Harvey-Jones [then chairman of ICI] forbids continued participation in our meetings and therefore Frank cannot participate, but wants individual contacts with the members. Someone will contact Frank before each meeting.'[4] In a number of cartel travel reports, Royal Ordnance is named as a competitor to the cartel, but at a cartel meeting in October

1984 'Guy' (Guy Chevallier) of French manufacturer SNPE informs the meeting that 'Truman' of Royal Ordnance had promised 'market cooperation' with the cartel.

It is another arms trade issue where the limitations of the inquiry's investigative reach combined with the limitations inherent in the terms of reference to prevent Scott looking into the matter in any great detail. The absence of an investigative arm meant that the inquiry had to rely on the Ministry of Defence and HM Customs and Excise for information. Despite the Swedish Customs investigation into the cartel, subsequent reports and court cases, the Ministry of Defence told Scott that it, 'had no knowledge or suspicion of a propellant cartel or a weapons cartel to which British companies belonged.' Notwithstanding the careful wording, the suggestion that the Ministry of Defence was unaware of the activities of the cartel is somewhat surprising. Scott's comments are inconclusive: 'The existence of international weapons/ propellants cartels, and the alleged involvement in them of UK companies are, per se, matters which fall outside my terms of reference ... It is also an issue in relation to which it would have been very difficult for me to obtain sufficiently cogent evidence to reach a concluded view without extensive investigation. Extensive investigation, even if the Inquiry were granted the necessary powers to conduct it, would have caused unnecessary delay to the publication of this Report. I have not, therefore, attempted to do so' (D7.14). This investigative limitation is also apparent when the inquiry deals with allegations that Royal Ordnance ammunition reached Iraq via conduits, and where Scott merely concludes: 'As to whether actual diversion took place after export, I am not in a position to investigate this fully, nor do I consider it necessary for me to do so' (D7.5).

The Scott report devotes much space — over 150 pages — to considering the labyrinthine saga of the Supergun, which had already been the subject of a limited investigation by the Trade and Industry Select Committee.[5] Here, Scott sought to answer questions relating to what the government knew about the Supergun project and when. There had been suggestions that the government knew of the project from its inception in June 1988. In a written submission, Chris Cowley had told the inquiry that Gerald Bull, the Supergun designer, had sought the approval of the British, US and Israeli governments before beginning work in Iraq. Having been gaoled for exporting military technology to South Africa, and then undertaken military work with CoCom-proscribed China (with the acknowledged approval of the US government), Bull was well aware that certain clearances were required before becoming involved with a sensitive destination like Iraq.[6] Scott rejects this account. He 'examined relevant files held by British Government departments and intelligence agencies and ... found no evidence that Dr Bull ever contacted the intelligence services.' (F2.5). However, he does not refer to and hence does not seek to explain the contents of a letter Bull sent in October 1989, a copy of which was sent to the inquiry, which referred to contact between Bull and the Foreign Office around the time Bull was looking to buy a plant in Northern Ireland through which he could get access to carbon fibre technology. In it, Bull wrote that 'the Foreign Office decided to run a press campaign through "leaks" ... The utter nonsense they spread was beyond belief ... I addressed a blunt memorandum to the Foreign Office on the whole matter. Through publicity, they were making me a target of terrorist groups ... After the memo was delivered, the whole matter was dropped from the press. Also we were assured that the action was taken by "a few irresponsible juniors and did not reflect the Foreign Office views of myself, our companies, the past etc".'

A second early source of information on the Supergun had been the then Conservative MP for Bromsgrove, Sir Hal Miller, who, from the seizure of the Supergun onwards, was consistent in his claim to have approached the DTI, Ministry of Defence and a 'third agency' as long ago as June 1988. This was at the request of the Halesown-based company Walter Somers, which had grown suspicious of an order for petro-chemical piping, to be manufactured to an unusually high specification, which it had been asked to produce by Bull's company, the Space Research Corporation. In reality, it was being asked to construct the barrels for the prototype Supergun. Scott rejects Miller's account which suggested existing knowledge of the project in intelligence circles in June 1988, explaining that memory fades over time and that he was not satisfied that Miller's account of his contacts was correct (F2.37). From this point, information on the Supergun flowed into the governmental machinery from a range of businessmen — Chris Gumbley and Gerald James of Astra, Paul Grecian of Ordtec, and later Paul Henderson of Matrix Churchill.

Yet, having dismissed the accounts of early governmental knowledge of the Supergun, Scott is left to explain an MI6 briefing note dated 6 October 1989 suggesting that knowledge of Walter Somers' involvement in the embryonic Supergun project went back to June 1988 — the month in which the contracts were signed. If the accounts of Chris Cowley regarding Bull and of Sir Hal Miller are discounted — as they seem to be in the report — where did this come from? Sigint via GCHQ? Scott does not know, saying; 'it would not be proper for me to reach a conclusion as to the source ... which is not accepted by either of the two people directly involved ... [it] must, therefore, remain an open unanswered question' (F3.55).

Ultimately, the report's coverage of the Supergun affair is inconclusive. Would this have been the case if Scott had sought documents from outside Whitehall? For example, could the documents seized by Belgian officials from Space Research Corporation's Brussels offices after the murder of Bull have helped? Again, while able to apply a near-forensic analysis to Whitehall documents, the absence of an investigative arm that looks beyond Whitehall in any meaningful way has limited Scott's capacity to answer all outstanding questions. The trail of documents he was given allows him to trace government knowledge back to 6 October 1989, but then it stops. In the event, he wraps up the long Supergun section without bringing much precision to bear on the question he had set himself, observing that 'there is clear evidence that, some time before October 1989, government officials had had information which raised the suspicion that Walter Somers' tubes were probably intended for use as artillery gun-barrels. There is no evidence that at that point officials suspected that they were for use in the kind of project which was eventually uncovered; but the evidence indicates suspicion that an Iraqi long-range artillery project with unusual features was in contemplation' (F4.80). As he further notes, 'also left unanswered is the question who it was among the British government officials who, prior to 6 October 1989, had formed the astute opinion that the Walter Somers tubes were probably intended for use as artillery gun-barrels' (F3.55).

One of the key themes to emerge from the whole 'arms-to-Iraq' episode is need to reconsider what we mean by arms and whether narrow definitions are really appropriate in an environment where a growing number of states are seeking to import the means to establish an indigenous arms production capacity. It would follow from this that there is a need for tighter control of dual-use technologies if the trade in arms is to be effectively controlled and proliferation concerns genuinely addressed. However, in his recommendations Scott has questioned whether dual-use technologies should be subject to export controls at all and 'whether, or to what extent, it should be permissible for export licensing decisions to be taken for foreign policy reasons' (K2.17). He goes on to produce a list of purposes for which export controls may be imposed which, although it includes complying with treaty obligations and the protection of UK armed forces, does not explicitly take account of long-standing proliferation concerns. The focus of these concerns may have shifted in the post-Cold War world, but they remain well-founded. Notwithstanding this, Scott concludes: 'I would doubt whether the maintenance of a technology gap between the United Kingdom and the Western countries on the one hand and Eastern bloc or third world countries on the other hand can still be regarded as a legitimate purpose of export controls' (K2.20).

While Scott makes a number of comments about the export licensing system, there is little consideration of wider systemic issues. For example, there is the question of end-use certification. Scott heard and received much evidence during the inquiry suggesting that the system was far from watertight, but it hardly features in the report. During the inquiry, Lt. Col. Glazebrook, one of the leading advocates of restraint within the Ministry of Defence, had explained that: 'End user certificates are not terribly reliable assurances that the person concerned ... will not pass the arms on to a third party. There have been a number of proven instances where false end user certificates have been produced ... and, consequently, it is really a question of what are you gaining by going to the trouble of asking for an end use certificate? My personal view is the only use is that after supply is taken, buyers if you find that it has been diverted to somebody else, then you can use it as a justification for refusing any further supplies ...' Neither did it really matter who had supposedly signed the certificates—that is, who was guaranteeing that they would not be passed on to a third party, because 'You had a signature block and it gave the name and it gave the appointment to the person there, but I had no means of checking whether it was a genuine signature or not.' Alan Clark told the inquiry that he 'would never attach any significance to assurances from customers such as these, or indeed practically anyone. They are not worth the paper they are written on', and that false end user information almost had the status of a commercial practice in the Middle East.

A good example of this process that came before Glazebrook was the application by Ordtec in early 1989 to ship an assembly line for the production of artillery fuses (a contract worth £500,000) to Aqaba on behalf of Gerald Bull's Space Research Corporation, with the consignee listed as 'Chief of Staff GHQ Jordan Armed Forces' and certified as intended 'for the sole use of the Jordan Armed Forces'. Again, he was rightly suspicious. As he explained to the inquiry: 'You need one fuse for each artillery shell. Shells are exceedingly expensive and therefore the numbers that you use in peace time for training are very limited. When you buy shells in the outset, you buy them complete with fuses normally, and therefore for a small country like Jordan to set up a special production line and train the staff to produce fuses for the sort of quantities that they would be likely to use on training did not make financial sense.' To put this further into perspective, this assembly line was designed to produce around 300,000 fuses a year (i.e. enough for 300,000 artillery shells), a volume more associated with the needs of a state at war than with Jordan. Nevertheless, this order, and a subsequent Ordtec application for booster pellets, again for SRC, were approved in the regulatory machinery. In the event, Ordtec went into liquidation before it could complete delivery of the assembly line (which was intended to be passed on from Aqaba to Baghdad) and so Iraq was never able to produce fuses with it.

Elsewhere in the report, a more detailed consideration of the relationship between government and arms trade, and of the mechanics of the arms trade with regard to Iraq and Iran, is hampered by the absence of any consideration of US foreign policy towards Iraq and Iran or the relationship between US and UK foreign policy in this area. The presence of the US and the implications of its position—the clear UK tilt towards Iraq in its war with Iran mirrored the US tilt—hang over a number of Foreign Office memoranda cited in the report, but are not considered much beyond this, thereby neglecting the wider policy framework within which the scandal occurred. For example, at one point in the report Scott notes that 'opposition from Washington to [UK] defence-related exports to Iran had no counterpart for exports to Iraq' (D1.15). But this is hardly the full story, as in practice the US played a pivotal role in facilitating the arming of Iraq, one that seems to have included encouraging other Western governments to do likewise, but one which Scott has neglected to address.

Furthermore, there was no attempt by Scott to extend the inquiry into the financing of the arms trade with Iraq—to interview and take evidence from businessmen, bankers, accountants, insurance company executives and others alleged to have been involved in it. Given that no arms deal can go ahead without the financing first being approved, this was a significant omission. There was no real attempt to 'follow the money' as, for example, Representative Henry Gonzalez had in the US through the House Committee on Banking, Finance and Urban Affairs investigation into Banca Nazionale del Lavoro and the US government's Commodity Credit Corporation programme for Iraq. This also appears to have been a route utilised by the UK intelligence services when monitoring the international arms trade. For example, in *The Unlikely Spy*, Matrix Churchill's Paul Henderson recalled that his first MI5 controller would question him about the financing of exports of militarily-useful equipment to the Eastern bloc countries he visited on business.

With regard to the arms trade, then, does the Scott Report represent a missed opportunity? A brief comparison with the reports of the contemporaneous Cameron Commission's investigation into illegal South African arms exports is instructive. The Cameron Commission was established in September 1994 after it was revealed that a consignment of South African arms allegedly intended for Lebanon had instead been bound for prohibited Yemen. It published its first report in June 1995.[7] This dealt directly with the Lebanon deception and was openly critical of a situation comparable to that existing in the UK, where arms marketing, sales and control functions are essentially exercised by the same department and where the institutional emphasis is on sale rather than restraint. Its broader terms of reference invited it to comment on the implications of its findings for South Africa's policy on arms sales, and it produced a second report in November 1995 which did just this—making extensive, clearly-articulated recommendations on future arms trade policy and decision-making procedures which would prevent the shortcomings of the past recurring.[8] Scott's observations on the administration of British arms sales fall well short of the proposals made by Cameron, although doubtless these would, in any event, prove unacceptable to the British government and defence industry.

Overall then, although the arms trade was at the heart of events that led to the establishment of the inquiry, and although it hovers over much of the report, it is often treated as little more than the context within which an inquiry into how we are really governed has been undertaken. Nevertheless, the very fact of the Scott inquiry has turned the spotlight on the role played by the British government in the international arms trade during the 1980s, fuelling the debates on transparency, accountability and oversight as well as on the question of the ethics of supplying arms to authoritarian or warring states generally. What the report exposes above all with regard to the arms trade is the absence of any real determination to prevent arms and arms-making technology from reaching Iraq. The continual arguing over end-use of dual-use goods, necessitating the application of the most beneficent gloss to Iraqi intentions, the redirecting of cautionary notes within the administrative system and so on, are not themselves the reasons why this equipment was allowed to go to Iraq—they are just symptoms of the wider, real reason: the profound absence of any political will to police these exports in a responsible manner, erring on the side of caution. This was itself a product of the combination of post-imperial, geopolitical and trade considerations which determined the course of UK and Western policy towards Iraq in the 1980s and dictated that rather than prevent arms reaching Iraq, it was the policy of the US, UK and other western governments to allow arms to reach Iraq so as to ensure it was not defeated in its war with Iran. The inquiry's focus at the administrative level meant that it did not really examine these wider foreign policy issues. As Jim Cousins MP, a member of the Trade and Industry Select Committee at the time of the Supergun investigation and one of the handful of MPs who have shown real persistence in the question of 'arms-to-Iraq', noted during the BMARC debate in June 1995: 'The issue of Iran and Iraq is not some marginal matter . . . It is one of the great secrets of the 1980s, and it will, sadly, take far more . . . than a select committee inquiry to get to the bottom of these very murky affairs.' Ultimately, it would appear that getting to the bottom of it was also beyond the Scott inquiry.

---

1 E.g. see the cases of Astra and BMARC documentation outlined in the report at B3.4–8, and in Appendix A, Part C.

2 See, e.g., C. Gearty, 'Our Flexible Friends', *London Review of Books*, 18 April 1996: 'Neither chemical nor lethal weapons as such were exported'.

3 Trade and Industry Committee: *Export Licensing and BMARC*, Third Report, Session 1995–96, HC 87-I and 87-II.

4 The Swedish Peace and Arbitration Society (SPAS): *International Connections of the Bofors Affair*, December 1987.

5 For an overview of this, see M. Phythian, 'Britain and the Supergun', *Crime, Law and Social Change*, 1993.

6 For the saga of the Supergun and the various claims as to what the British government knew and when, see M. Phythian, *Arming Iraq*, (Northeastern University Press, 1996).

7 *Commission of Inquiry into Alleged Arms Transactions Between Armscor and One Eli Wazan and Other Related Matters, First Report*, 15 June 1995. It is worth noting that while they both dealt with aspects of the same international arms trade, the two inquiries seemed to have differing perspectives on it. Justice Cameron began his report with a characterisation of the arms trade more in keeping with that offered by participants like Chris Cowley than that contained in the Scott Report. Cameron said

his inquiry; 'revealed a story rarely exposed to public view. It exposed a world of freewheeling and idiosyncratic characters; of intrigue, deception and subterfuge; of lucrative and often extravagant commissions and of high living; of deliberately disguised conversations; of communications shrouded in complex documentation and cryptic notes; of deals structured to conceal their true nature; a world with its own rules and code of conduct, in which intimidation, threats and actual peril are ever present; a world, also, of unpredictable allegiances and loyalties: the world, in short, of arms dealers'.

8 *Commission of Inquiry into Alleged Arms Transactions Between Armscor and One Eli Wazan and Other Related Matters, Second Report: Comment and Proposals on Conventional Arms Trade Policy and Decision-Making in South Africa*, 20 November 1995.

Public Interest Immunity

BY IAN LEIGH*

THIS CHAPTER examines the events surrounding the Matrix Churchill trial and the Scott report's findings and recommendations on Public Interest Immunity (PII) from the viewpoint of constitutional doctrine. Scott's findings are considered within a framework of constitutional values for the light they shed on the practical working of this area of potential conflict between the executive and the judiciary.[1] The discussion here focuses on the relevance of the rule of law and the separation of powers, each of which regulates relations between these two branches of the state. The question of the respective roles of judges, ministers and civil servants in relation to PII is also considered from the perspective of ministerial responsibility. Against this background, the report's recommendations on PII are criticised for their lack of a principled approach and their failure to contribute to accountable government.

Public Interest Immunity in context

The doctrine of Public Interest Immunity is no stranger to political and constitutional controversy; for example, in recent years PII certificates have been used in cases arising from the death of Blair Peach, the dismissal of Alison Halford, and shootings which led to the establishment of the Stalker inquiry. The contentious nature of PII is unsurprising, since, properly understood, it involves the suppression of relevant evidence in the public interest. The principles and procedure applicable to it have been developed almost exclusively by the judiciary and can be viewed from two distinct perspectives. Seen as part of the law of evidence, they are one of a number of situations in which evidence or documents are said to be privileged, that is bearing a confidential or sensitive quality which the law recognises by a prohibition on evidence of this kind being given in the public interest. In this guise what is now called Public Interest Immunity was formerly known as Crown Privilege. The terminology distinguished it from other forms of privilege applying to private relationships, such as the confidentiality of communications between a solicitor and his or her client. Viewed from a constitutional perspective, PII was one of the last vestiges of a collection of special immunities and privileges in law formerly enjoyed by the Crown. The change of name of the doctrine in the United Kingdom (the old terminology persists in some other jurisdictions, notably Canada) was

* Reader in Public Law, University of Newcastle upon Tyne.

meant to signify a broadening in law both of the types of interest protected and of who would be permitted to invoke the claim in the courts.

It is advisable at the outset to deal with some popular misconceptions which may have arisen as a result of the Matrix Churchill trial. First, PII is not only available where the Crown is a party to the proceedings; it may be invoked by the Crown in civil proceedings between private individuals and, in appropriate cases, can be used by other litigants also, whether private individuals or other public bodies. Where it is employed, the effect is not always to the benefit of the party claiming it. Since the evidence in question cannot then be given for any purpose, this disables the prosecution (or the Crown in a civil case) just as much as the other party—it is as though the evidence did not exist. The change in terminology from 'privilege' to 'immunity' was meant to underline this point but both terms are equally imprecise in subsuming under the one heading the interests of both litigants and third parties who hold relevant evidence, or who wish to raise the claim of immunity. The failure to distinguish more clearly between the position of these two groups caused extensive legal confusion in the Matrix Churchill case (where the Crown appeared in both capacities) over the question of whether PII could be waived and, if so, by whom.

A second misconception is the description of a PII certificate as a 'gagging order'. This terminology (adopted by the media in reporting of the Matrix Churchill trial) confuses PII with controls on the publication of evidence heard in the courtroom. There are a number of situations in which evidence may be given but the reporting of it is restricted (e.g. proceedings involving children or sexual offences), or where a trial is held with the press and public wholly or partially excluded (e.g. under the Official Secrets Act 1911). In these instances it is the public character of the administration of justice which is affected but not the evidence or the adversarial conduct of the proceedings. PII is quite different in its effect, since it places a limit on how one of the parties to the proceedings may present their case by prohibiting certain evidence from being given at all. This can result in a substantial injustice if the remainder of the evidence is misleading because incomplete or if, as a result, one party is simply unable to prove a vital ingredient of their case: the latter is particularly likely to happen in a civil action brought against the government where access to vital documents is denied.

PII claims can be categorised into two different types. The first, 'contents claims' proceed on the basis that the evidence or document in question is itself sensitive and should not be given in the public interest. The second, 'class claims' involve an assertion that the document or evidence belongs to a category which has traditionally not been permitted in evidence in the public interest. In the case of a class claim it is not necessarily asserted that there is anything which would be harmful to the public interest in the proceedings in question. The categories have been arrived at through previous judicial decisions and are subject to amendment through the normal development of the common law.

Whether the Matrix Churchill trial is treated as a novel and dangerous extension of previous practice into criminal cases turns on the distinction between criminal proceedings and criminal trials. There is a stream of legal authority exempting what has been known as 'informer privilege' in criminal cases and, as the doctrine of PII has been reconfigured by the judges, this separate line of authority has become co-mingled with it. What was novel in the Matrix Churchill trial was the making of a PII claim (otherwise than in relation to an informer) in the trial proper of a criminal defendant.

A final feature concerns the procedure for making a PII claim. In the 1942 decision of *Duncan v Cammel Laird*[2] the House of Lords laid down the principle that the courts would accept as conclusive a PII certificate signed by a minister of the Crown. The outcome was perhaps understandable in the wartime context of a civil action in which the plans of the ill-fated submarine *Thetis* were sought. However, the decision was strongly criticised and it was finally reversed by another House of Lords' decision in 1967, *Conway v Rimmer*. To this rediscovered power to overrule PII certificates was added a judicial power to inspect the evidence before deciding whether to uphold a certificate, formalised in what was known as the two-stage test. At the first stage the party seeking to challenge the certificate had to show how the evidence or documents were relevant to their case; if satisfied, the judge would inspect them. The second stage involved a judicial balancing of the public interest for and against disclosure. Judicial inspection was, therefore, by no means automatic and a certificate could be upheld without the judge seeing the documents or evidence. At the second stage the certificate could be upheld, partially upheld, or quashed; in the last two instances documents might be ordered to be released with redactions (that is, sensitive passages blanked out). The two-stage test, developed in the context of civil proceedings, fitted criminal procedure less happily because of inconsistency with the rules on advance disclosure of prosecution material to the defence and an apparent reversal of the burden of proof in the requirement that defendants establish the relevance of the material to their defence at the first stage.

PII in the Matrix Churchill trial

Public interest immunity certificates signed by four government ministers (Kenneth Clarke, Tristan Garel-Jones, Michael Heseltine and Malcolm Rifkind) were used in the trial of three businessmen from the engineering company Matrix Churchill for export control offences in November 1992. It was alleged that the intended use of machine tools in the manufacture of munitions in Iraq had been dishonestly concealed in the export licence applications in question. The defence had two strands, both of which required extensive access to government information (and, hence, the over-ruling of the PII certificates) in order to succeed. First, it was claimed that the company had been encouraged to conceal any military use and to emphasise the civilian applications of the machine tools at a meeting with Alan Clark (then a junior minister at the Department of Trade and Industry) in 1988. Secondly, that since one of the defendants (Paul Henderson) had regularly passed information to the intelligence agencies, the government had known of the true intended use of the machine tools, and no deception had taken place. To establish these defences, access was sought to a wide range of documents covering interdepartmental discussions and advice to ministers on licensing applications of machine tools to Iraq and documents from the intelligence agencies. The PII certificates covered documents in four categories: information from a confidential informer, documents passing between ministers and officials about the formation of government policy, documents relating to the work of intelligence and security services, and communications between the government and other states. The trial judge initially rejected the PII claims relating to the communications between ministers and officials about policy but upheld the certificates relating to intelligence documents. This second ruling was modified at a later point in the trial to allow for the release of redacted documents which then were extensively used in the cross-examination of officials. However, the case was abandoned following the answers in cross-examination from Alan Clark, which lent considerable support to the first strand of the defence, i.e. that he had encouraged the making of misleading export licence applications.

It was the collapse of the trial and the controversy surrounding the use of the PII certificates which led directly to the establishment of the Scott inquiry. So far as PII was concerned, the main points to be determined were whether (and, if so, how) it applied to criminal cases, and whether the certificates used at the trial were correctly signed, involving consideration of whether ministers were under a duty to sign and the accuracy of legal advice given by the Attorney General, Sir Nicholas Lyell.

The precise application of PII to criminal cases was somewhat unclear at the time of the Matrix Churchill trial. Some judicial comments suggested that the principles and procedure were the same as in civil litigation and government lawyers had obtained counsel's opinion to this effect, but the issue had never directly arisen in a clear case. Scott subsequently took a different view to the government in his report, arguing that it did apply in criminal cases, but in a different way to civil cases which made due allowance for the special need to protect a criminal defendant at risk of conviction and imprisonment. He regarded the first stage of the two-stage test as in effect otiose or at least subsumed within the disclosure procedure in a criminal case, with an automatic duty upon a trial judge to inspect documents covered by a PII certificate. As regards as the second stage, he strongly opposed the view that there should be a balancing of interests in a criminal case, because he regarded as unacceptable the possibility that evidence relevant to the defence might be suppressed in the public interest. Instead, the trial judge should consider whether, if the evidence was material and prima facie disclosable, it would be of possible assistance to the defence. If so the document would be disclosed. Only if it did not appear to assist the defence should the judge uphold the public interest behind the PII claim (K6.18). This view of the law was vigorously contested by the Attorney General, even after publication of the report.

Although Scott concluded that the claims of PII made at the trial in 1992 of the Matrix Churchill defendants were unjustified and unsound in law, he did not hold the individual ministers who had signed those certificates responsible. He concluded that they were entitled to rely on the (in his view, erroneous) legal advice they received and on the fact that the trial judge would inspect the document before upholding the claim. The certificates which he criticised were all class claims, and he argued that they were made in circumstances wider than the previous precedents endorse. For example, the class of documents concerning the formulation of government policy (the so-called Category B in the Matrix Churchill trial) had in effect been extended by the Treasury Solicitor to include documents passing between junior civil servants, rather than the 'high level' policy discussions originally envisaged between ministers and senior civil servants or among senior officials themselves. Scott's proposed antidote was to prevent the future use of class claims in criminal cases (although, and perhaps inconsistently, they would be retained in civil cases). The public interest in merely protecting a class of information could never in his view justify withholding from defendants information which was material to their defence. This would leave the government still able to rely on contents claims where appropriate. (In this he was influenced by evidence from the former legal advisor to the Security and Intelligence Services that their interest could be properly protected in criminal trials by contents claims alone.)

Scott also found ministers to have to been misadvised on whether they were obliged to make PII claims. Michael Heseltine had signed his PII certificate with considerable reluctance and only after the Attorney General advised him that he had a duty to do so, despite the apparent relevance of the documents to the defence, because of the class nature of the claim and the absence of a clear case for disclosure. His certificate stated, however, that he was merely asserting that the documents fell within the requisite classes and that he had been advised that it was for the trial judge to balance the public interest. Heseltine had also been assured that his concerns would be raised with the judge, but this was overlooked as it transpired: an oversight for which the Attorney General was strongly criticised by Scott. Scott also roundly rejected Sir Nicholas Lyell's repeated argument that ministers were obliged to make such claims. In fairness, however, it should be noted that the law, at least at the time of Matrix Churchill, did contain statements which could be used to support either opinion. Scott interpreted statements in earlier cases so that the minister's duty has not been fundamentally altered by the post-1967 capacity of the judge to inspect the documents and overrule a certificate signed by the minister. In his view the minister was still obliged to weigh the competing public interest and had no automatic duty to make a PII claim simply because a document falls into a particular class. This view received a powerful endorsement after the Matrix Churchill trial in the 1994 House of Lords' decision of *R v Chief Constable of the West Midlands, ex p. Wiley*.[3] Lord Woolf (with the agreement of the other Lords of Appeal) argued that, although the final word lay with the trial judge, the minister was not simply a 'rubber stamp' (or, in Jonathan Aitken's phrase, a 'postman'). However, in 1992 the law was not nearly so clear and substantial confusion had been caused by earlier comments of the Master of the Rolls, Sir Thomas Bingham, in the 1992 case of *Makanjuola v Commissioner of Police*,[4] where he had spoken of a duty to make such claims, subject only to a 'clear case exception' if it was obvious that the trial judge would overrule the claim. It was this passage which Sir Nicholas Lyell had relied on extensively when advising Michael Heseltine that he was required to sign notwithstanding his own misgivings.

PII and the rule of law

The Diceyan version of the rule of law expresses the need not only for the legality of governmental actions, but also a constitutional requirement that the judiciary should be free to judge such legality. It is at this level that rules of evidence in legal proceedings, such as PII, become crucially important. Also important is Dicey's insistence that government powers should not be arbitrary, and that there should be equality of treatment under the law for the government and the citizen.

   In the classic account given by Sir William Wade, PII is seen as a limited exception from the rule of law, which was abused by the government in the years following the seminal case of *Duncan v Cammel Laird*. According to this version of events, the judiciary gradually came to their collective senses and reined in the doctrine until in the 1967 landmark case of *Conway v Rimmer*[5] control was reasserted through the ability to overrule ministerial claims of PII. 'Thus did the House of Lords bring back a dangerous executive power into legal custody. Some of the earlier decisions, and the official concessions in administrative practice, will remain of importance. But the legal foundation of excessive 'class claims' has been destroyed.'[6] Generations of law students have learned of PII through this account in successive editions of Wade and, significantly, the Scott report cites with approval a passage from an earlier edition (G18.95). There are echoes of Wade in Scott's own criticisms of government lawyers for misinterpreting and abusing PII principles. However, the truth was both more complicated, and less conclusive than Wade's account would suggest. So far as equality of treatment is concerned, the Crown Proceedings Act 1947 removed a number of the special advantages formerly enjoyed by the Crown but, in relation to the disclosure of documents in litigation (the process known as 'discovery') it was seriously incomplete. It stated merely that the Crown was liable to an order for discovery, but provided that this was 'without prejudice' to any rule of law authorising or requiring the withholding of any document on the ground that the disclosure would be injurious to the public interest. The choice of language deliberately relied on the advantageous position of the Crown enjoyed under the Thetis case, namely that certificates signed by ministers were regarded as conclusive. Indeed, Lord Simon, who had delivered it as Lord Chancellor, wrote in his capacity as minister in charge of the 1947 bill that this should be the government's stance.[7]

Several causes can be advanced for the adoption of a less deferential judicial attitude. First, the growing judicial trend towards recognising that PII was not merely a doctrine at the behest of government, but one which private litigants could also invoke, drew attention to the special position of ministers. There were also both personal and institutional reasons for a less trustful attitude towards the political heads of departments of state. We may assume that the growing scepticism about the integrity of politicians in the post-Profumo era, affected not only public and press but, in time, the judiciary too. Belief in the reality of ministerial accountability to Parliament (which had been seen as the concomitant of the policy of judicial acquiescence) also began to be undermined. The enormous growth in judicial review of administrative action, often regarded as a legal revolution, has taken place over the same period. Indeed, some judges have recently argued that in periods where a dominant executive has little to fear on the floor of the House of Commons, then the judiciary should exert greater control in the interests of legality and individual liberty.

However, doubt has been cast on Wade's characterisation of the judiciary as reformed heroes. A recent article has argued persuasively that the judges encouraged the abuse of class claims of PII by the government through endorsing over-wide claims after *Conway v Rimmer*.[8]

Another commentator has also claimed that the way PII has been applied may undermine the rule of law, especially in cases in which the legality of actions by public bodies are challenged in administrative law, claiming there is 'an embarrassing conflict of values which besets the field of public law. ... Since effective judicial review of the legality of governmental decisions demands a rigorous scrutiny of the real grounds for such decisions, it is doubtful whether the aims of administrative law and the present treatment of claims of public interest immunity are compatible'.[9] He proposes that the public interest in the administration of justice weighed by the judge should look beyond the interests of the litigants and take account of the need to ensure the legality of governmental actions in administrative law cases, suggesting that the weight of the public interest should vary according to the seriousness of the allegations of misconduct and how high in government the action was taken.

Scott approached the issue in a criminal law context from a different direction—the fundamental public importance of a fair trial. In keeping with the Diceyan tradition which sees the courts as protectors of fundamental rights, he argued that the common law rules requiring advance disclosure of prosecution evidence provide the necessary safeguards. These principles, developed in the 'miscarriage of justice' cases of the early 1990s, require disclosure of material evidence to the defence. For Scott this test generally takes the place of PII in criminal trials: if evidence is not material, there is no duty to disclose it and no need for a PII certificate; if it is material, the defendant's right to it should prevail despite any opposing public interests favouring non-disclosure. A lawyer less enamoured of the common law tradition would instinctively have looked elsewhere for a solution, either to legislation or to some form of human rights protection for the right to a fair trial. Scott rejected legislative reform of PII without explanation. This is puzzling, not least because, as he was well aware, statutory reform of the disclosure rules was imminent in the shape of the Criminal Procedure and Investigations Bill. Since this Bill deals with the very principles of prosecution disclosure to which he attached such weight, much could have been said for integrating and codifying the PII principles in the same statute.

The report's failure to analyse the consistency of the common law with Article 6 of the European Convention of Human Rights[10] is another unfortunate omission. The Convention is not, of course, presently part of the domestic law of the UK, but judges may consider it when developing common law principles like those applicable to PII and disclosure of documents. Its value is as an external international standard in an area where domestic constitutional arrangements can too readily be accepted as axiomatic for reasons of familiarity and from blissful ignorance of the alternatives. A further advantage is that the Convention distinguishes more clearly than the common law between the interests of the litigants, the public and the press in open justice. Although under the present approach of the Strasbourg Court and Commission questions about the admissibility of evidence are left largely to national courts to determine, the consistency of PII with the Convention is, nevertheless, of interest, not least because of the continuing debate over domestic incorporation. Article 6 provides that: 'In the determination of his civil rights and obligations or of any charge against him, everyone is entitled to a fair and public hearing within a reasonable time by an independent and impartial tribunal established by law'. It then lists situations in which the press and public may be excluded, including interests of public order or national security in a democratic society, or the protection of the private lives of the parties, or 'to the extent strictly necessary' where publicity would prejudice the interests of justice. (Note that these reasons do not justify exclusion of the defendant, merely the public.) Among the additional rights conferred on the defendant in criminal proceedings are the right 'to examine or have examined witnesses against him and obtain the attendance and examination of witnesses on his behalf under the same conditions as witnesses against him.' This notion of a fair hearing has been established under the Strasbourg jurisprudence to require 'equality of arms'.

At first sight PII might be said to violate these principles by limiting the evidence which a criminal defendant may call in his or her defence, or the extent to which evidence called may be cross-examined. However, on closer examination the court is required (if the traditional approach is followed) to balance the public interest in a fair trial against the public interest protected by the certificate. Nevertheless, this way of putting the issue suggests that there are some circumstances in which the public interest in non-disclosure might displace the defendant's rights, whereas Article 6(3) of the ECHR requires access to witnesses and to examination and cross-examination on equal terms. The real problem is the 'equality of arms' principle. If PII hampers the prosecution as much as the defence, then Article 6 is satisfied. Scott, however, correctly recognised that in the cases he considered PII worked to the prosecution's advantage: it led evidence theoretically subject to PII (e.g. from intelligence officers) when it was convenient to do so and fell back on the protection as a tactical stratagem to limit the defendant's rights.

However, in every case the court is able to over-rule the claim and this may prove fatal to an Article 6 claim since the Convention organs will be reluctant to interfere with the trial judge's discretion. This was the outcome in *Edwards v UK*,[11] where a criminal defendant raised arguments under Article 6 concerning prosecution evidence which was not revealed at his original trial, which he claimed helped his defence, including the report of an official inquiry in respect of which a public interest immunity certificate had been signed. The Court of Human Rights held that his opportunity to raise these points when his case was heard by the Court of Appeal was sufficient to satisfy Article 6. However, this decision should not perhaps be treated as foreclosing such challenges altogether, since the Court engaged in no detailed analysis of Article 6(3)(d) nor of the 'equality of arms' point.

Although the adversarial quality of criminal procedure is inherent in Article 6, it is unlikely that the parts of PII procedure which exclude the defendant and his or her lawyers would be found to violate the requirement of a fair and public hearing since judicial inspection of documents takes place in the absence of *all* parties and lawyers—the state is given no special privileges in that respect. However, matters could be different if the prosecution were able to address arguments to the judge in the absence of the defendant. A procedure of this kind is permitted exceptionally under the common law (*R v Davis*)[12] and retained in statutory form in the Criminal Procedure and Investigations Act 1996. Scott endorses these controversial procedures without critical comment. The prosecution are permitted in exceptional circumstances to argue ex parte (in the absence of the defence) that material should not be disclosed, and, quite exceptionally, this may occur without the defence ever being informed. The procedure is intended to meet prosecution concerns about identifying informers and other categories of sensitive evidence. Arguably it is in breach of Article 6, although the issue has yet to be tested under the Convention.

The separation of powers

The position with regard to the separation of powers is also complex. It is the specific task of the courts to adjudicate on legal and factual matters, whereas the executive administers policy within the terms of the law. Since the late 1950s the judges have on a number of occasions refused to allow the jurisdiction of the courts to be ousted where issues concerning the legality of decisions by public bodies are concerned.

PII is a problematic area, however, because it is at the juncture of the areas of competence of two branches of the state. Looked at from the perspective of judging, a rule requiring the suppression of evidence in the public interest can be seen as interfering with the judicial specialism in the task of fact-finding and adjudication. Although traditionally the courts have been reluctant to overrule government claims about potential damage to the public interest, they also recognise the danger that a too ready acquiescence can invite political abuse. From the government's perspective, on the other hand, it is responsible to Parliament and the electorate for upholding the public interest; and the judiciary has no expertise in assessing the damage to the public interest through disclosure of documents.

Recent historical research, based on access to official files shows that concerns over whether ministers or judges were to have the final say on a claim of privilege, and debates over who should sign a certificate making such a claim were continuous in government from the 1920s on.[13] Consideration was given to statutory reform of the law in 1927 and again in 1947.

The implications of this can be pursued both at the level of principle — whether the judges or ministers should determine the categories of public interest protected by PII—and in relation to the operation of the doctrine in any piece of litigation (where the balancing role falls finally to the court). The clearest attempt to formalise the different roles is, perhaps, Lord Wilberforce's in the case of *Burmah Oil v Bank of England*: 'It is necessary to draw a reasonably clear line between the responsibility of ministers on the one hand, and those of the court on the other. Each has a proper contribution to make towards solution of where the problem lies. ... It is for the minister to define the public interest and the grounds on which he considers that production would affect it. Similarly, the court, responsible for the administration of justice, should, before it decides that the minister's view must give way, have something positive or identifiable to put into the scales.'

So far as the division of responsibility at the level of principle is concerned, plainly the classes of immune evidence are the product of the result of earlier judicial decisions and they can be adjusted accordingly by the judges in later cases. However, such decisions ought not to be merely a domestic matter for the courts. What is perceived to be prejudicial to the public interest at any given time is also partly a product of the prevailing climate of opinion conditioned by legislative and government policy. It would be nonsensical if PII did not adjust to movements in these, for then the courts would be cast in the role of continuing to prevent access to information in litigation which the government has freedom to release at will in other contexts. Although the United Kingdom still lacks legally enforceable Freedom of Information at central government level, there are indications of changing policies in the direction of openness. This ought to produce corresponding changes in the practice of the courts. Developments have occurred in recent years which presage a new approach to intelligence and national security:[14] legislation in 1989, 1994 and 1996 dealing with the Security Service, the Secret Intelligence Service and GCHQ; the creation of the Intelligence and Security Committee; the publication of the names of the agency heads, their budgets and of brochures describing the work of MI5 and the Joint Intelligence Committee. It would be surprising if this did not also affect the way in which the courts approach claims of national security, including PII cases.

There are also interesting issues about the separation of personnel, as distinct from functions discussed above. The leading speech in *Duncan v Cammel Laird* was delivered by the then Lord Chancellor, Lord Simon. This may be one instance where the textbook point about the Lord Chancellor's ministerial and judicial roles amounting to the corporeal refutation of the separation of powers doctrine has some substance. Similarly, Jacob has pointed out that the waxing and waning of PII has to be understood against the changing composition of the judiciary during recent decades. The dilution of the numbers of judges with direct experience of administration, either through political life or having acted as Treasury Counsel, upset a delicate balance between the rules governing the liability of the Crown and the specialised knowledge of those who administered them. Judges with less experience of governmental matters would be less inclined to see the need for secrecy. The argument may also work in reverse: judges with experience of unjustifiable claims to governmental secrecy may be hostile to apparently inappropriate claims. It was Scott himself who was confronted in the *Spycatcher* litigation (*A-G v Guardian Newspapers Ltd (No. 2)*),[15] with issues about the need for government secrecy and excessive claims made for it, which we may presume contributed to the sceptical approach so evident in his questioning of witnesses and in the report itself.

It is the Attorney General's position as a Law Officer, however, which raises the most serious questions of conflicts of interest. Perhaps anxious to avoid the perennial debate about creation of a non-political Minister of Justice, Scott left the issues unexplored when discussing PII. By convention a distinction has been drawn between the politically independent role the Attorney General plays in criminal cases and his role in civil cases as representing the government of the day. The difficulty is that the extension of PII into criminal cases bridges this divide. Scott recognised the potential conflict between the duties of the prosecution and the public interest advanced by a government department in a PII claim, and, consequently, recommended that in future departments should be represented separately in criminal cases. However, he provided no guidance for the Attorney General in advising ministers on future PII claims. A strong endorsement of constitutional independence and a development of the implications when advising on PII in criminal cases would have been appropriate as a counter-weight to the manifest dangers of political abuse of PII. Clear advice on this would also have been beneficial in view of the confusion revealed in evidence given to the inquiry about what the Attorney General's role was when consulted by ministers about PII claims and about the need for the Law Officers to see the documents for which immunity was claimed. By implication, Scott endorsed the view that departmental ministers must exercise personal judgement rather than relying on the Attorney General's advice, but he failed to elucidate what the latter's role should be.

Scott could be said to be following a separation of powers model to the extent that he sees PII as a system of checks and balances operating in the individual case, with both the minister and the judge having a role to play. This model sees ministers and judges as acting as successive safeguards in considering the public interest in a PII claim. According to Scott, ministers had been failing to play this role because of a misunderstanding of the law: the rule giving the judge the final say on disclosure had been misinterpreted by government lawyers as exonerating (or even forbidding) ministers from considering personally whether the public interest favoured disclosure. However, their respective parts are formulated through a complex (and controversial) exposition of legal doctrine and not, as one might have expected, on the basis of a principled consideration of the constitutional strengths, experience or knowledge of ministers and judges.

Ministerial responsibility: who is to sign?

Scott endorses the common law approach that signature of PII certificate should receive the personal attention of a minister. It was Lord Simon who stated in *Duncan v Cammel Laird* that the minister should sign as the political head of the department. In the same passage he allows that the permanent civil service head of a department may act where it is 'not convenient or practical for the political head to do so'. However, the concession is only as a matter of convenience, and if the court is not satisfied it may require the minister's personal attendance. This approach has much to commend it provided that those involved give the task the attention it requires. If it works well, the minister will give genuine consideration to whether it is necessary in the public interest to make such a claim: and the judge will be able to weigh this assertion in the context of the proceedings. Conversely, if it works badly the minister's scrutiny will be cursory and the judge will be overly reliant on his assertion of potential damage to the public interest. The evidence to the Scott inquiry clearly showed that the quality of ministerial scrutiny of PII claims before signature is variable and, understandably, dependent on whether the minister has encountered such documents before, the amount of time allowed for reading the brief and signing the certificate, and the pressure of other work. Whereas, Michael Heseltine signed only after taking detailed advice from the Attorney General, Kenneth Baker signed certificates as Home Secretary without calling for details of the documents involved. The idea that a minister who perhaps receives several dozen departmental submissions in his or her red box nightly will have much time to devote to detailed consideration of papers accompanying a draft PII certificate is optimistic. For this reason the alternative of a civil servant being permitted to sign such a certificate deserves consideration. This possibility was canvassed in the evidence of the Attorney General to the Scott inquiry but is not discussed in the report.

Judged against normal constitutional standards the surprising thing is that the practice requires ministers personally to sign the certificates. In statutory powers conferred on Secretaries of State, the courts do not require the minister's personal attention to be given. Instead, under the Carltona doctrine the actions of civil servants within the department are imputed to the minister (*Carltona Ltd v Commissioners of Works*).[16] Such decisions are treated in law as the minister's. This fiction parallels the parliamentary fiction of ministerial responsibility for the same acts. In each case it is a recognition that a busy politician in charge of a large department of state cannot hope to deal with anything but a small proportion of policy-oriented items of business. It is of course possible for a statute to require the personal attention of a minister for a particular matter: such examples are rare but do occur in the realm of protection of individual rights, e.g. warrants for telephone tapping. PII could be categorised as having this effect and, therefore, worthy of ministerial attention. However, the requirement of personal signature imposed through the common law under PII is very much against the constitutional norm and it is questionable whether there is a case for an exception to the Carltona principle here. The answer is intimately bound up with the question of whether there is a duty to make a claim.

If there is a justification for the involvement of the political head of a department, it can only be because there is a genuine discretion to be exercised; if making a claim is automatic once it is decided that documents fall into the relevant class, then it hardly requires the involvement of a minister.

Jacob argues that the debate about the need for a minister to sign a PII certificate should be understood against the background in the early 20th century of the emerging the doctrine of individual ministerial responsibility and the growth of a professional, unified civil service following the 19th century reforms. By 1942, both features of the constitution were so firmly established that the House of Lords could introduce the requirement that the PII certificate should be signed by the minister as the political head of the department. In so doing, the judges were aware that ministers would have available to them professional advice, and that they would be accountable for their actions to Parliament. This background assumption of parliamentary accountability is expressly mentioned in Lord Simon's speech in *Duncan v Cammel Laird*. Later, the courts would adhere to the rule strictly, holding that a claim made by a Permanent Secretary without consulting the Secretary of State was improperly made (*Re Grosvenor Hotel*).[17] Nevertheless, exceptions appear to have grown up in practice beyond those envisaged in 1942. Thus, when access was sought to the papers of a previous government (which, by convention, ministers do not see), certificates signed by successive Permanent Secretaries at the Department of Trade and by the Cabinet Secretary were accepted by the court (*Air Canada v Secretary of State for Trade (No. 2)*).[18] Similarly, officials have signed certificates during general election campaigns.

If one reason underlying the judicial requirement of ministerial signatures was a belief in accountability through the political process, the entire Matrix Churchill episode should surely give grounds for scepticism. Developments in the last thirty or so years undermining the doctrine of ministerial responsibility are well known. Especially relevant are the refinement (although abandonment might be a more accurate term) of the circumstances in which a minister will accept responsibility for the failings of officials; the direct answerability of civil servants to Parliament through select committees and as Accounting Officers, and to the Parliamentary Commissioner for Administration; the related loss of civil service anonymity; and, most recently, the move of most of the civil service into Executive Agencies. In the face of these developments, judicial insistence on ministerial signature of PII certificates looks increasingly anachronistic—a requirement which only makes sense within a constitutional understanding of accountability long since discounted for any practical purpose in the parliamentary arena.

Scott was plainly aware of these arguments and, indeed, elsewhere in the report he referred to the effect of the enormous growth in the business of government has had on the doctrine of ministerial accountability (especially K8.15). However, he failed to consider their implications for PII, despite the Attorney General's suggestion that ministerial signature of PII certificates should be replaced by those of Permanent Secretaries. Instead, Lord Simon's statement that the minister should sign as the political head of the department is quoted without analysis or reference to the changed circumstances since 1942. One is left wondering whether an exception to the Carltona doctrine is necessary on some unarticulated principled basis, such as the political nature of the decision, or whether its retention is a sign of the courts clinging doggedly to their own dignity and to the rule of law. It is at least doubtful whether an insistence on ministerial signature adds appreciably to accountability or the seriousness with which claims of PII are treated by government departments. Approaching the issue from first principles, an argument for civil servants' signatures might be that the view of the public interest in non-disclosure should be one which transcends the perspective of a temporary holder of political office, or even of any one government. A long-term perspective might be supplied either by the Permanent Secretary of a department or the Cabinet Secretary for wider classes. Nor can it be claimed that civil servants are inexperienced in making assessments of the public interest in this way. The Attorney General has stated that after the decision of the House of Lords in *Wiley*, systems have already been established for civil servants to advise ministers on the public interests favouring voluntary disclosure in prospective PII cases. The main objection to such a practice is likely to be lack of an accountable figurehead; but, as we have seen, the force of any such criticism depends on a rose-tinted version of constitutional orthodoxy.

Conclusion

In keeping with his own judicial background, Scott's approach shows a distinct preference for pragmatic, common law solutions to the problems of PII and disclosure of documents in criminal trials. This is at the expense of any wider consideration of constitutional principle or of the possibility of legislation. The report made no attempt to work out a principled basis for the allocation of functions between the judiciary, ministers and civil servants according to their expertise or the reality of their constitutional position. We are left at the end of the day with no cogent reasons why ministers are the most appropriate people to sign PII certificates, rather than civil servants, or what the role of the Attorney General should be as against that of other departmental ministers. Deeper reflection on the paradoxical claims of the rule of law, or more conscious consideration of the constitutional theory of the separation of powers or ministerial responsibility, might well have led on to consideration of the need for further reform. A significant opportunity to strike a blow for limited and accountable government, and to protect individual rights, has been missed.

The government's response even to Scott's limited recommendations on PII was grudging. At first, the Attorney General maintained that his view of the law was right all along. Finally, in the Commons debate on the Scott report a concession was announced, designed apparently (and successfully) to procure the last minute support of the wavering Conservative member for Torbay, Rupert Allason. The government secured its majority—by one vote. The concession? A reference of the whole issue to an interdepartmental working party of civil servants.

1   For legal analysis see I. Leigh and L. Lustgarten, 'Five Volumes in Search of Accountability: The Scott Report', *Modern Law Review*, September 1996; I. Leigh 'Reforming Public Interest Immunity', in M. Allen (ed.), *Web Journal of Current Legal Issues 1995 Yearbook*, (Blackstone Press, 1995).
2   [1942] AC 624.
3   [1995] 1 AC 274.
4   [1992] 3 All ER 617.
5   [1968] AC 910.
6   H.W.R. Wade and C.F. Forsyth, *Administrative Law*, (7th edn., Clarendon Press, 1994), p. 851.
7   J.M. Jacob, 'From Privileged Crown to Interested Public', *Public Law*, 1993, 121, 133–4.
8   A. Zuckerman, 'Public Interest Immunity—A Matter of Prime Judicial Responsibility', *Modern Law Review*, 1994, 703.
9   T.R.S. Allan, 'Abuse of Power and Public Interest Immunity: Justice, Rights and Truth', *Law Quarterly Review*, 1985, 200.
10 See D. Harris, M. O'Boyle and C. Warbrick, *Law of the European Convention on Human Rights*, (Butterworths, 1995), ch. 6.
11 (1992) 15 EHRR 417.
12 [1993] 1 WLR 613.
13 Jacob, op. cit.
14 L. Lustgarten and I. Leigh, *In From the Cold: National Security and Parliamentary Democracy*, (Clarendon Press, 1994).
15 [1990] 1 AC 109.
16 [1943] 2 All ER 560.
17 [1963] 3 All ER 426.
18 [1983] 2 AC 394.

Ministerial Accountability

BY VERNON BOGDANOR*

Scott's understanding of ministerial accountability

THE TERMS of reference of the Scott inquiry made no explicit reference to ministerial accountability. Scott was required to examine the facts relating to the export of defence equipment and dual-use goods to Iraq and decisions on export licence applications. But he was also asked to report 'on whether the relevant departments, agencies, and responsible ministers operated in accordance with the policies of Her Majesty's Government' (John Major, House of Commons, written answer 16 November 1992). In the event, he interpreted his terms of reference very widely. His 1,800 page report contains a massive amount of material on the relationship between ministers and civil servants and between ministers and Parliament, the product of an examination of around 130,000 documents. Indeed, Peter Shore has declared in the Commons that the report contains 'more description of the particular problem of the minutiae of policy-making and the administration of policy once it has been made than I have seen anywhere in my political life' (HC 313, 1995–96). Much of this material bears on that fundamental constitutional concept, ministerial accountability. Giles Radice, Chairman of the House of Commons Public Service Committee, which examined the Scott report for its own report on 'Ministerial Accountability and Responsibility', told Scott, 'In your terms of reference, you were not in fact asked ... to look at the issue of parliamentary accountability or ministerial accountability, and yet in a sense this is one of the key threads that runs through your whole report'; and David Butler has argued, in an unpublished lecture, that the Scott report 'represents the most exhaustive study ever produced of one aspect of that key Westminster doctrine, the individual responsibility of ministers'.

Scott summed up his conclusions on ministerial accountability at the very end of his report, K8.1–16. He further elaborated on his conclusions in oral evidence to the Commons Public Service Committee inquiry on 8 May 1996, and in his May 1996 Blackstone Lecture on 'Ministerial Accountability'.[1] The traditional understanding of ministerial accountability has been well summed up in the Treasury and Civil Service Committee's conclusion in 1994 that 'ministerial preparedness to resign

* Professor of Government and Fellow of Brasenose College, University of Oxford.

when ministerial responsibility for failure has been established lies at the very heart of an effective system of parliamentary accountability' (HC 27, 1993–94). Scott, however, contests this view. For he believes that the essence of ministerial accountability lies not in the threat of resignation but in the obligation to inform Parliament.

Before beginning his inquiry, Scott declared in his Blackstone Lecture, he 'would have associated ministerial accountability with a need for a minister to resign if serious errors had been committed in the department. This would, I suspect, be the understanding held by most people of the doctrine of ministerial accountability. But concentration on that existing aspect of ministerial accountability has, to my mind, distracted attention from more important although less dramatic aspects of this constitutional principle'. 'I do not', Scott told the Public Service Committee, 'regard the debate—and I do not want to underestimate it—between accountability, responsibility, blame, as being the key and most important feature of ministerial accountability; I regard the provision of information as being the key to the doctrine. I think willingness on the part of ministers to inform Parliament and through Parliament the public, or perhaps sometimes the public directly, of the matters in respect of which they are accountable is critical. It is accountability, so far as ministers are concerned, on two levels. It is accountability in respect of policy, and ministers must of course answer for the policy of their departments, but it is more than that, it is also accountability for what the departments of which they are in charge have been doing or not doing. So far as that is concerned, it is accountability not in regard to policy but in regard to facts, what has happened, what has been done, what has been done in government, which is after all government on behalf of the public.'

Thus in his report, Scott declared that 'The obligation of ministers to give information about the activities of their departments and to give information and explanations for the actions and omissions of their civil servants lies at the heart of ministerial accountability' (K8.2). It follows, then, that if information is withheld from Parliament or the public or misleading answers are given to Parliament or the public, then the obligation of accountability has not been discharged. 'If, and to the extent that, the account given by a minister to Parliament, whether in answering parliamentary questions, or in a debate, or to a select committee, withholds information on the matter under review, it is not a full account and the obligation to account for what has happened, or for what is being done, has, prima facie, not been discharged. Without the provision of full information it is not possible for Parliament, or for that matter the public, to hold the executive fully to account. It follows, in my opinion, that the withholding of information by an accountable minister should never be based on reasons of convenience or for avoidance of political embarrassment and should always require special and strong justification' (D4.58). Sir Robin Butler, the Cabinet Secretary and Head of the Home Civil Service, endorsed this proposition in his oral evidence to the Scott inquiry.

In the concluding section of his report, 'Ministerial Accountability', Scott listed seven examples which have come to light as a result of his inquiry 'of an apparent failure by ministers to discharge that obligation' (K8.1). Perhaps the most important of these was the deliberate failure, in answers to parliamentary questions in April and May 1985, to disclose the existence of the Howe guidelines, which had been agreed in December 1984; and the failure of government statements, in 1989 and 1990, both in answers to parliamentary questions and in letters to the public, 'to disclose either the terms of the adjustment to the guidelines that had followed the cease fire or the decision to adopt a more liberal policy on defence sales to Iraq' (K8.1). These answers and letters were, Scott believed, misleading, although he accepted that ministers did not consciously intend to mislead.

Misleading Parliament

There are, then, in Scott's view two facets to the provision of information to Parliament and public. The first is that misleading information should not be given. The second is that information should not be unreasonably withheld. The first of these is more straightforward than the second. Paragraph 1 of the Civil Service Code declares that 'Ministers must not knowingly mislead Parliament and the public and should correct any inadvertent errors at the earliest opportunity. They must be as open as possible with Parliament and the public withholding information only when disclosure would not be in the public interest'. This paragraph is intended to clarify the section of *Questions of Procedure for Ministers*, which defines the obligation of individual ministerial accountability, and which will be amended accordingly in due course. It is the adverb 'knowingly' which enabled the minister most at risk from the findings of the Scott inquiry, William Waldegrave, Minister of State at the Foreign Office between July 1988 and November 1990, to evade censure by the House of Commons. Indeed, the number of occasions on which he gave misleading answers to Parliament and the public has given rise to the witticism that there are three different ways of breaching the principle of ministerial accountability. These are, in ascending order of seriousness, the grave, the very grave and the Waldegrave! More seriously, some critics have suggested that the addition of 'knowingly' was itself an attempt by the government to evade the application of ministerial accountability and to save Waldegrave.

Scott rejected this view. 'The qualification of "mislead" by the addition of the adverb "knowingly" does not, to my mind, make any material difference to the substance of the obligation resting on ministers not to mislead Parliament or the public' (K8.5). The key issue was whether the minister intended to mislead. 'Before the word was there', he told the Public Service Committee, 'I think the word was implicit. I do not think it would have been regarded as a breach of the previous formulation for a minister, inadvertently and unconsciously, to give misleading information. I think there was a concomitant obligation when he discovered it to put it right'. 'I am a judge', Scott said, 'and I have heard witnesses in many, many different cases, and it is very often that a judge finds that the evidence given by a witness is not true, but it is another question whether the judge finds the witness has intended to give false evidence. The witness has intended to give the evidence he has given, nobody is saying it was an inadvertent statement, but that is not to say the witness has deliberately told an untruth. There is no ambiguity, if one thinks about it, between a finding that a statement made by an individual is not accurate and a finding that the individual has not intended to deceive.'

The situation appears to be that William Waldegrave was well aware of the facts which persuaded most impartial observers, including Scott himself, that the guidelines on arms sales had been altered. But Waldegrave did not believe that the alterations amounted to a change of policy. They were, rather, in Scott's words, 'a justifiable use of the flexibility believed to be inherent in the guidelines' (D3.124). Therefore, in his view, Waldegrave had no 'duplicitous intention'. Part of the difficulty is, of course, that what amounts to a change in policy is, to some extent at least, a matter of judgment.

But there is a further point. Waldegrave had been arguing strenuously with other ministries, and in particular the Department of Trade and Industry, against relaxation of the guidelines. He struggled hard to avoid conceding any change in policy, approval for which would have had to be obtained from his Secretary of State, Sir Geoffrey Howe. It must have been psychologically difficult for Waldegrave to admit that he had lost that particular battle, and psychologically necessary perhaps for him to insist to Parliament and the public that the guidelines had been reinterpreted rather than altered. Ministers, Scott told the Public Service Committee, 'just talked themselves into a position that objectively could not be justified but they did not appreciate it at the time.'

Whether or not one accepts this defence of Waldegrave, it is clear that the formula 'knowingly mislead' is too narrowly drawn. It does not provide for a situation in which a minister has been negligent or incompetent, in which he failed to apprise himself of things that he ought to have known. In 1982, following the Argentinian invasion of the Falklands, Lord Carrington resigned, together with two other Foreign Office ministers. On different occasions, Lord Carrington has given different reasons for his action. The Franks Committee in fact exonerated the Foreign Office ministers, declaring that no blame could be attached to any individual minister. Yet, in a letter written to *The Times* (22 February 1996), intended to defend William Waldegrave,

Lord Carrington declared that 'The assessment made by the Foreign Office of the likelihood of an Argentinian invasion of the Falklands was wrong and I, as Foreign Secretary, properly took responsibility and resigned.' He was suggesting that it was his responsibility to have tested the assessments of his officials as to the likelihood of an invasion and to have taken precautionary measures to prevent it. He resigned because he had failed to apprise himself of information of which he ought to have apprised himself.

The same accusation was made against Waldegrave. In the House of Lords debate on the Scott report (26 February 1996), Lord Callaghan declared that he was either deceitful or incompetent. If he was 'not a knave, what was he, a simpleton?'; Lord Hailsham replied, 'Neither. He is a Fellow of All Souls College, Oxford', to which Callaghan's riposte was 'Perhaps then he was a clever silly. That is it.'

As well as not knowingly misleading Parliament, ministers are also required to 'be as open as possible with Parliament and the public, withholding information only when disclosure would not be in the public interest'. The test of what is in the public interest is to 'be decided in accordance with established Parliamentary convention, the law, and any relevant Government Code of Practice'. There is no requirement, understandably, for an answer to be complete, a requirement which it would be almost impossible to meet. Ministers are under a duty to tell the truth, but they are under no duty to tell the whole truth. Ministers very rarely tell deliberate untruths, and then only in highly exceptional circumstances where perhaps it can be justified, such as in answering questions on interest or exchange rate changes, or on contacts with bodies such as the IRA. There are hardly any cases of ministers telling a direct lie, and when they do, as with John Profumo in 1963, resignation is the normal consequence.

In answering questions, ministers are under an obligation, then, to answer accurately. But they are under no obligation to volunteer information unnecessarily. The onus is in a sense on MPs to frame their questions in a manner appropriate to elicit the required information. Thus, an answer to a parliamentary question satisfies the principle of ministerial accountability, as understood by Scott, even if it is misleading, so long as it is not intentionally misleading, and even if it is incomplete, so long as it would not lead a reasonable listener to a false conclusion. In its evidence to the Public Service Committee, the Association of First Division Civil Servants said: 'There may, as one cynical civil servant put it recently, be three drafts in future placed before all ministers: the complete answer in accordance with *Questions of Procedure for Ministers*; the answer which deliberately withholds information, but does not knowingly mislead; and the answer which designedly leads Parliament to believe one policy is in place where the overwhelming evidence is to the contrary, but does so unintentionally.'

Scott's interpretation of the principle of ministerial accountability allows it to be satisfied too easily. The hurdle is too low. A minister can say 'I have satisfied the principle because I have answered the question, even if my answer is incomplete and misleading, because it is not intentionally misleading.' Only when a minister has told a deliberate lie, as with Profumo, will he or she have fallen foul of the doctrine. As Graham Mather told the Public Service Committee, 'Ministerial responsibility for departmental acts has been defined away almost to nothing.' The consequence is that, when there have been serious mistakes in public policy, no accountability can be enforced. Ministers will escape, to use the by now well-worn joke, Scott-free. But, if ministers are not responsible when things have gone wrong, should civil servants be held responsible?

Ministers and civil servants

Under our system, civil servants, except in the role of Accounting Officer, have no direct responsibility to Parliament. They are responsible to their minister. It is part of the principle of ministerial accountability that, when there have been mistakes as a result of civil service failures, the minister must demonstrate to Parliament that action has been taken to correct these mistakes and to prevent any recurrence. There may need to be disciplinary proceedings taken against particular civil servants as provided for by the Civil Service Management Code, but such proceedings will not be initiated by the minister. Nor is it for Parliament to impose a penalty upon a civil servant since, constitutionally, officials are the servants of the Crown, i.e. of ministers, and not of Parliament.

The Scott report gave a number of instances of negligence or error on the part of officials. It accused both officials and ministers of failing to keep the Prime Minister informed of the line on defence sales to Iran and Iraq agreed upon by junior ministers (D3.102). It accused DTI officials of 'unacceptable negligence' for doing nothing for a year to ensure the return of goods exported to Iraq under temporary licence (D6.70). It found that an official slanted his advice so as to accord with the known views of his minister, Alan Clark (D6.148). It criticised an Assistant Under-Secretary at the Foreign Office for not detecting a misleading submission by a junior official which was placed before a minister (D6.159). It underlined the failure of officials to bring certain intelligence information to the attention of William Waldegrave (D6.169). It accused officials of failing to bring information on the destined use of machine tools to the attention of Alan Clark (F3.88). It criticised officials for not bringing to the attention of the Secretary of State at the DTI (Nicholas Ridley) the involvement of Sir Hal Miller in the Supergun case (F4.37).

So far as is known, however, no disciplinary proceedings have been taken against any of the officials criticised in the Scott report. The reason is clear. It would appear hypocritical for a government, whose ministers escaped censure by the skin of their teeth — by one vote indeed in the censure debate in March 1996 — to allow such action against those who were carrying out their policies.

Ministers criticised in the Scott report, such as William Waldegrave and Sir Nicholas Lyell, were, however, able to defend themselves publicly and robustly. The government indeed declared that it rejected Scott's criticism of these ministers and, by using its parliamentary majority, was able to ensure that ministers escaped censure. Civil servants, by contrast, are in a far less enviable position. They can not make any public statements rejecting them. They may have to suffer the loss of their reputations in silence. That, indeed, was what happened after the Crichel Down inquiry conducted in 1954. All but one of the criticised officials had their careers blighted.

Scott's interpretation of the doctrine of ministerial accountability thus diminishes real constitutional responsibility almost to vanishing point. Ministers are able to discharge the duty of accountability by statements which turn out to have been incomplete and misleading, but not knowingly so, while officials are accountable only to ministers and so can not give Parliament their own version of what has occurred, even where the ministerial version is in fact misleading. The result in practice is that it is difficult to pin responsibility for fault upon anyone. 'Is it not the difficulty for this committee', John Gunnell asked Sir Robin Butler when he appeared before the Public Service Committee, 'that, in a sense, we are dealing with a lot of issues in which things have gone wrong, and in the end it would seem that ministers are not to blame, because they did not knowingly mislead Parliament, civil servants are not to blame, because they were the servants of the ministers, and therefore, we are left in a sort of area where nobody is really to blame for anything that happened, and does not that rather confuse the position of accountability?' The mistakes investigated by the Scott inquiry turn out in the end to be 'Nobody's Fault'. Scott has thus raised, unintentionally perhaps, a constitutional problem which relates not only to the export of defence equipment and dual-use goods to Iraq, but one which is endemic in our system of parliamentary government.

Making ministerial accountability effective

In the adjournment debate on Crichel Down, the Home Secretary, Sir David Maxwell-Fyfe, gave the classic interpretation of the doctrine of ministerial accountability. He distinguished four different categories to indicate the degree of accountability of ministers for the actions of civil servants. They are:

(1) Where there is an explicit order by a minister, in which case the minister must protect the civil servant who has carried out his order.

(2) When the civil servant acts properly in accordance with the policy

laid down by the minister, in which case, the minister must protect and defend him.

(3) Where an official makes a mistake or causes some delay, but not on an important issue of policy and not where a claim to individual rights is seriously involved, in which case the minister acknowledges the mistake and accepts responsibility although he is not personally involved, and states that he will take corrective action in the department; he would not, in those circumstances, expose the official to public criticism.

(4) Where action has been taken by a civil servant of which the minister disapproves and has no prior knowledge, and the conduct of the official is reprehensible, in which case there is no obligation on the part of the minister to endorse what he believes to be wrong or to defend what are clearly shown to be errors of his officers; but, of course, he remains constitutionally responsible to Parliament for the fact that something has gone wrong, and he alone can tell Parliament what has occurred.

If Parliament is to be able to determine in which category a particular case belongs, it must be able to discover the details of what has occurred. A minister, after all, has an interest in implying that what might seem to be an instance of category 1 or 2, in which case he or she might be held to blame, is in reality an instance of category 3 or 4, so that in reality it is officials are to blame. A minister has an interest in offloading responsibility on to his or her officials who can not, constitutionally, speak out in public.

The Maxwell-Fyfe categories were laid down to show that ministers were not vicariously responsible for the actions of their officials in cases where they were not personally involved or had not been informed, though in fact this was no new doctrine. The categories, however, left open the opposite danger, that civil servants would be held vicariously responsible for the failings of their ministers. The principle of ministerial responsibility, after all, is in two parts: the first provides that ministers take the credit for what goes right, the second that ministers take the blame for what goes wrong. Ministers, quite naturally, are disposed to accept only the former. Yet a system in which ministers take the credit when things go right but blame civil servants when things go wrong is a recipe for the progressive demoralisation of the civil service.

The fundamental problem is that the principle of ministerial accountability imposes obligations upon ministers which are owed to Parliament, but under modern conditions of party government Parliament finds it difficult to ensure that these are actually fulfilled. *Questions of Procedure for Ministers* and other codes regulating ministerial behaviour lay down admirable principles to which ministers ought to adhere. Scott declared, and Sir Robin Butler agreed, 'that the withholding of information by an accountable minister should never be based on reasons of convenience or the avoidance of political embarrassment and should always require special and strong justification' (D4.58). Under our adversarial political system, this is likely to remain no more than a pious aspiration. The crucial problem is that Parliament lacks mechanisms which can be brought into play when ministers seek to evade the rules of accountability. In theory, Parliament can seek the resignation of the minister concerned, but, under modern conditions of party discipline, that will hardly ever be successful.

It is one of the weaknesses of the Scott report that it proposes no mechanisms by which Parliament can ensure accountability. The proposals which it makes for change put the onus entirely on ministers to act according to the rules. But if ministers were always prepared to act according to the rules, then it might not have been necessary to establish inquiries such as Scott at all. Scott, after all, believes that constitutionally improper things occurred over exports to Iraq as the following exchange from the Public Service Committee hearings between Anthony Wright and Scott shows:

Wright: 'Did something constitutionally improper happen ?'
Scott: 'Yes, I think it did and I said so.'
Wright: 'Did ministers behave in ways that ministers ought constitutionally not have behaved?'
Scott: 'I have said so, yes.'
Wright: 'Was Parliament denied information that Parliament constitutionally ought to have been provided with?'
Scott:. 'I think so, yes.'

Yet, no penalties were exacted for such constitutionally improper behaviour and Scott suggested no mechanisms through which a repetition could be prevented. In his evidence to the Public Service Committee, however, and in his Blackstone Lecture, he does propose reforms which would enable Parliament more easily to ferret out who was responsible when something goes wrong.

Reforming the system

Four reforms are proposed. The first is a Freedom of Information Act. The second is a revision of the Osmotherly Rules so that civil servants could, when something has gone wrong, give evidence to parliamentary committees on matters of fact (as distinct from policy) in their own names, as opposed to being required to be the minister's mouthpiece. The third is the institution of an official whose responsibility it would be to monitor answers to parliamentary questions to ensure that they were not misleading. The fourth is to make the convention of ministerial accountability justiciable. Scott's proposals (see HC 313) will be discussed in turn.

It is a corollary of the Maxwell-Fyfe categories that Parliament should have the right to obtain information on past decisions, including the advice which civil servants gave to ministers, so that it can ferret out who in reality was to blame. As Scott put it in his report: 'If ministers are to be excused blame and personal criticism on the basis of the absence of personal knowledge or involvement, the corollary ought to be an acceptance of the obligation to be forthcoming with information about the incident in question. Otherwise Parliament (and the public) will not be in a position to judge whether the absence of personal knowledge and involvement is fairly claimed or to judge on whom responsibility for what has occurred ought to be placed' (K8.16). Under our present constitutional arrangements, however, it is ministers themselves—or the Prime Minister—who decide what they are responsible for. Ministers are the judge and jury in their own case, and with a disposition to find themselves innocent. Scott thus favours a Freedom of Information Act as a corollary of ministerial accountability.

A second way in which it might be possible to ferret out who was to blame would be to allow civil servants to give evidence to select committees on their own behalf when something has gone wrong. The minister's obligation, Scott believes, assuming that he has not got any personal knowledge, was to facilitate the giving of information held by civil servants in his department about the incident in question. That would require a revision of the constitutional position of civil servants, as embodied in the Osmotherly Rules.

Scott proposes a distinction between questions of policy, for the government and questions on factual matters, the application of policy. 'I do not see why civil servants should not, as part of the manner in which ministers render their accounts to Parliament, give information about what they have done in the discharge of their duties, not in the formation of policy, but in the application of policy or in doing governmental acts in the course of their duty.' Civil servants were of course able to give evidence on their own account to the Scott inquiry itself because the Prime Minister had instructed them to cooperate with it as fully as possible. It did not seem that damage was done to the processes of constitutional government by this procedure. On the contrary, it enabled Scott to ferret out, in perhaps rather excruciating detail, what had happened. Why should not select committees have the same powers?

There is at present no effective means of testing a minister's insistence that an answer to a parliamentary question was reasonable or that a refusal to answer was justified in the public interest. Where a minister refuses to provide information, MPs can not complain about it as a matter of privilege. They can, admittedly, complain about the provision of information which they believe to be misleading. But this is an arduous process. A complaint must overcome four hurdles: acceptance by the Speaker, a Commons debate, consideration by the Committee on Standards and Privileges, and a second debate—if it is to succeed. There are no recent examples of this method being used with success.

The reports of the Nolan Committee on Standards in Public Life have accustomed us to the idea that it is no longer sufficient to rely upon tacit understandings to secure constitutionally correct behaviour. Codes of conduct need to be monitored by a person of independent standing, as with the new Parliamentary Commissioner for Standards, Sir Gordon Downey, whose task it is to monitor MPs. Scott told the Public Service Committee that where ministers used the 'public interest' exception to their obligation to provide information, then 'It would be possible to have some figure rather like the Comptroller and Auditor General, who would be regarded not as a servant of government but as a servant of the House, who would have clearance to look at any underlying departmental papers he might call for and who would report at, say, yearly, half-yearly intervals, on the way in which the public interest exception underlying a refusal to provide information in response to a question had been used and whether it was satisfactory.' In response to questioning, he accepted that the Ombudsman could fulfil this function. MPs would be able to approach the official when they believed that answers to parliamentary questions had been inadequate. In order to make his/her judgment, he/she would have access to government documents, for often the problem is not so much that MPs do not receive adequate answers as that they do not know what questions to ask because they have not seen the relevant documents. Although he/she would not be able to compel a minister to answer a PQ or make an answer more complete, he/she would report regularly to a select committee (perhaps the Committee on Standards and Privileges) and a hostile report might be very damaging to the minister's reputation.

There are, however, problems with this proposal. The Ombudsman's main role is to investigate maladministration, but a statement made by a minister in Parliament cannot be regarded as an administrative action. The Ombudsman's task is to look at the administrative relationship between government and the public not at ministerial accountability to Parliament, a very different function. In a submission to the Public Service Committee, Sir William Reid, the Ombudsman, put forward further objections. He feared, first, that the idea might catch on like wildfire — MPs (and peers?) might be inclined to ask the Commissioner to investigate almost any type of answer, whether out of a genuine seeking after the truth, or by way of general opposition to the government of the day, or for other less cogent reasons. MPs would use the new machinery to make purely party points and the Ombudsman would be drawn into political battles. The remedy, however, would surely lie in the Ombudsman's own hands. It would not be difficult for him to dismiss contumacious or frivolous requests from MPs, just as, no doubt, he does vexatious complaints from members of the public. MPs would then soon stop wasting their time and there would probably be few serious complaints, and so a hostile report by the Commissioner would come to be feared by ministers.

The Ombudsman also feared that it would be too onerous to add to his existing responsibilities a further, novel and contentious extension. Therefore a separate Parliamentary Commissioner for Accountability should be established or the post brigaded with that of the Parliamentary Commissioner for Standards, which is held on a part-time basis. Sir Gordon Downey, however, is involved in ensuring that MPs live up to their obligations in relation to their interests, while the role of the Parliamentary Commissioner for Accountability would be to enforce the obligations of ministers on behalf of backbench MPs. Moreover, in Sir William Reid's words, 'the creation of yet another post to be designated a Parliamentary Commissioner for X is likely to make greater the incipient confusion in parts of the press about who is the Parliamentary Ombudsman', and this would make it more difficult for the Ombudsman to fulfil his task as citizen's protector. Nevertheless, there remains a strong case for an independent person, whether the Ombudsman, the Parliamentary Commissioner for Standards, or an entirely new officer, to monitor the extent to which ministers fulfil their constitutional obligations.

The fundamental issue perhaps, is whether the function of a Parliamentary Commissioner for Accountability would be so political as to compromise his or her position. Roger Freeman, the Chancellor of the Duchy of Lancaster, believed that this would be the case, and that such a figure would diminish the responsibility and probably the effectiveness of the Commons and its select committees. Tony Newton, the Leader of the House, doubted whether it could put in commission to anybody else its duty to hold ministers to account. They may be right, but it is fair to say that exactly the same qualms were expressed before the Ombudsman was established in 1967. Further, the proposal to establish a Commissioner to assist MPs pin down ministerial responsibility accords with recent institutional changes designed to codify constitutional understandings rather than establish a codified constitution.

Scott's final proposal, if none of the above alternatives commands acceptance, is the most radical and perhaps the most unrealistic of the four. It is that the obligation on ministers to provide information to Parliament be put into statutory form. He declared in his Blackstone Lecture, 'it would not be Parliament and its machinery that would have the final responsibility of enforcing the obligations, it would be the courts. The constitutional obligation, at present non-justiciable, would have become justiciable. Whether that would be a desirable state of affairs would be open to debate. But it must be recognised that if the obligations of accountability are not accepted by ministers, both in principle and practice, as binding, and are not, where necessary enforced by Parliament, the remedy can only lie in reducing at least that part of our unwritten constitution into statutory form.' Such arguments may come to be heard more frequently if reforms are not instituted to make ministerial accountability a reality rather than a fiction.

Conclusion

It is perhaps in showing how inadequate our conventional notions of ministerial accountability are in actually pinning down responsibility, whether on ministers or civil servants, that the central value of Scott's over-long and convoluted report lies. It has already been all but forgotten. Few can remember the precise issues involved, just as few can call to mind the issues involved in Crichel Down or Westland affairs. Yet the significance of these episodes is that they cast a shaft of light on hitherto unexamined constitutional assumptions relating to accountability. They show perhaps that the emperor has no clothes.

Paradoxically, however, the highlighting of the issue of the individual accountability of ministers in the Scott report distracts attention from a much more serious governmental failing which Scott was not asked to investigate. The fact remains that the events described in the report and, in particular, the government's continued willingness to sell military goods to a ruthless dictatorship constitute a failure of collective government policy on a massive scale. The government was tilting its policy towards Iraq and supplying it with materials right up to the moment when Iraq invaded Kuwait. Indeed, a ministerial meeting on 19 July 1990, chaired by the Foreign Secretary, proposed a major shift in the guidelines only six weeks before the invasion. Ministers assumed that Iraq was so exhausted by her eight year war with Iran that it would settle down to using technology for peaceful purposes. They quite failed to understand the aggressive dynamism of Saddam Hussein's Iraq. That was a serious policy failure. Yet, as with other cases, such as the poll tax or 'Black September' when Britain was forced out of the ERM, no ministers were held accountable for the disaster.

Thus the deepest lesson of the Scott report is the need for some reference point over and above the government of the day, some neutral authority, so that the constitution is no longer what the government says it is. The deepest lesson of the Scott Report is that we have no constitution and that it is time we had one.

---

1   Reprinted, *Public Law*, 1996, 410–26.

Parliament and the Executive

BY PHILIP GIDDINGS*

'THE MAIN objectives of governments are the implementation of their policies and the discomfiture of opposition; they do not submit with enthusiasm to the restraints of accountability . . . governments are little disposed to volunteer information that may expose them to criticism . . . The enforcement of accountability depends largely on the ability of Parliament to prise information from governments which are inclined to be defensively secretive where they are most vulnerable to challenge.'[1] Those prescient words were written seven years ago but they could well have served as the theme for the Scott report's assessment of the accountability relationship between the executive and the House of Commons in Britain. The quotation expresses well the political and partisan context within which the business of parliamentary government is carried out in the United Kingdom. That context provides the key to understanding and evaluating what the report has revealed about howministerial accountability to Parliament operated in relation to the export of defence-related equipment to Iraq.

Thirty years ago Anthony Birch drew a useful distinction between two contrasting views ('languages' according to Birch) of the British constitution—the liberal view and the Whitehall view.[2] The former is rooted in the canons of liberal democratic theory and sees the sole source of legitimacy for government as the sovereign electorate, represented in the House of Commons, which is the focus of governmental power and responsibility: a system of parliamentary government. While holders of the liberal view consider the Whitehall view reactionary and anachronistic, the latter draws on the monarchical origins of English government and emphasises the way in which the central governing role of the Crown—now largely vested in the Queen's ministers—has been accommodated to, rather than supplanted by, emerging democratic pressures and processes. Holders of the Whitehall view consider the liberal view simplistic, naive, perhaps even subversive. For them Her Majesty's Government rules through Parliament.

In reality, it is a case of 'both . . . and', not 'either . . . or'. To understand the complex and dynamic processes of government in the late twentieth century, account has to be taken of the significant presence of both liberal and Whitehall views within our political and administrative culture. Whilst this dual character of our culture is

* Lecturer in Politics, University of Reading.

evident in the Scott report, Scott himself and some who have commented on the report have failed to appreciate that duality. Many assume, mistakenly, what they perhaps wish were the case, that the British constitutional system is based entirely on liberal democratic presuppositions—Birch's 'liberal view'. In consequence, when Scott and others taking that liberal view encounter features of the system which reveal the continuance of the other constitutional perspective—e.g. in attitudes to the disclosure of information—they respond with surprise, if not censure, at practices which have been, and still are, integral to the Whitehall view. If a primary task of government is to manage the Commons, rather than be ruled by it, then the disclosure or withholding of information will be part of the strategy of management which Whitehall—in both its political and administrative forms—will employ.

Legislation

Scott's liberal assumptions were illustrated in his report's account of the legislative history of the control of the export of defence and defence-related equipment: 'The government's statutory powers under the 1939 Act are based on wartime emergency legislation lacking the provisions for Parliamentary supervision and control that would be expected and are requisite in a modern parliamentary democracy.' He went on to complain that 'the lack of any indication in the empowering legislation of the purposes for which export controls can legitimately be used has led, in my opinion, to a dangerous confusion between the law on export controls and government policy on export controls.' He supported that opinion with references to the principles of both democracy and the rule of law (K2.1).

Although government's 'unfettered power' and the use of its powers to achieve its policy objectives attracted Scott's censure, they reflect Whitehall's perception of the desirability, some might say the necessity, of government having (and therefore taking) the power to act in an unrestricted way in pursuit of its policy in the national interest, in this case linked to some extent with defence of the realm. This point emerged when consideration was being given to amending the legislation (C1.41–110). Ministers and officials were reluctant to 'concede' [sic] parliamentary supervision of the exercise of the executive's powers. In discussions with the opposition front bench about the 1990 bill, the brief to ministers advised that they should be willing to consider an additional clause providing for a negative resolution procedure—but only if the point were raised and pressed by the opposition (C1.94–95). The opposition did not press (there is a conflict of evidence about why, which is not of concern here), so the measure making permanent the sweeping powers derived from the 1939 Act went through with only a brief debate—and with no provision for parliamentary supervision of the exercise of the powers.

Scott's criticism (C1.108–10) of the failure to take the opportunity to provide for parliamentary supervision is a powerful statement of the liberal view: 'The democratic checks and balances of the United Kingdom's unwritten constitution require, if they are to be effective, that power conferred on government to make subordinate legislation should, as a general rule, be subject to parliamentary approbation or control. . . . The imposition of new prohibitions on citizens, the creation of offences, the prescription of penalties, are, under a democratic constitution, matters essentially for parliamentary legislation rather than executive dictate. If and to the extent that these matters are to be delegated to the executive then . . . proper parliamentary supervision should be maintained. The wider the ambit of the powers, the more necessary is the maintenance of parliamentary scrutiny and control. The neglect of these principles is to give substance to the charge . . . that the constitution has become an elected dictatorship' (C1.108). Scott was scathing about the continued use of the emergency powers granted in the 1939 Act long after the wartime emergency had ceased: 'Nothing can, in my opinion, excuse the continued reliance by government on the emergency powers after the emergency had long since passed other than, if it be an excuse, the pursuit of the Grail of administrative convenience' (C1.109). Ministers and Parliament had failed, over 45 years, to take action to remedy a continuing abuse of power—and this despite a succession of opportunities (1958, 1964, 1969, 1980, see C1.33)—a clear failure of parliamentary control.

Nor has Scott changed these views since his report was published. In his evidence to the Commons Public Service Committee (8 May 1996, HC 313, 1995–96) he confirmed his description of the continued use by successive governments of wartime emergency powers of export control as 'a cynical evasion by government of its constitutional duties'. Not to provide for any form of parliamentary supervision of the exercise of subordinate powers might be explicable in wartime, he said, 'but it is outrageous in peacetime'.

Mechanisms of accountability

Much attention is given in the Scott report to the adequacy of ministerial and official responses to parliamentary questions and letters from MPs. Public debate has focused on the vexed issue of when a change in guidelines is a change of policy and what is meant by 'intentionally misleading' and similar phrases. These semantic debates are akin to the various attempts to make a conceptual distinction between responsibility and accountability: people will want to define such terms in ways that enable them to be used as they want to use them. We are not likely to make much progress in debate simply by swapping definitions. What is more interesting to the observer about the Scott material on parliamentary questions and ministerial correspondence is what it shows about the approach of ministers and officials to the task of responding to MPs' inquiries.

For Members of Parliament these forms of accountability have, in practice, a variety of objectives. For some—very few—the purpose is simply to secure information and explanation. But for most it goes further. Some hope that by seeking information and explanation they can exert pressure for change in a decision taken or likely to be taken. For some the purpose is to attribute blame (or, less often, praise) for what has or has not been done. It may even be that some hope the exposure of blame will secure a propitiatory outcome, such as an apology, a dismissal or a resignation. In each case the common assumption is that the possibility of such outcomes will influence the decision-makers who are being held to account, so that they will act in a way which is responsive to the wishes of those who are holding them to account. Sanctions such as dismissal or enforced resignation are perceived to increase the likelihood of such responsiveness. Even when accountability produces only wider availability of information and explanation, responsiveness may be increased through what has been called the 'mobilisation of shame'. Ministers and the officials advising them, however, are not unaware of the hopes/intentions of MPs' questions and letters. They are particularly aware of the implications of these outcomes for the reputation of ministers and their parties. As has been pointed out, the means which are used to secure accountability are also used to wage party warfare: the process of scrutiny is mixed with that of discrediting the government.[3]

In preparing and approving answers ministers and officials will be, and as Scott showed evidently were, as much concerned with the political dimension of the responses given as with discharging what some see—on the basis of the guidelines set out in *Questions of Procedure for Ministers*—as their constitutional duty to keep public and Parliament fully informed. Indeed, for some officials it is a matter of professional pride that replies should be so tightly drafted as to reveal as little as possible beyond that which it is to ministerial advantage to reveal. There is no point in giving free ammunition to one's critics. As Christopher Dunabin of the First Division Association put it in evidence to the Public Service Committee (20 March 1996): 'There is a commonly accepted culture that the function of the answer to a parliamentary question is to give no more information than the minister thinks will be helpful to him or her, the minister, in the process of political debate in the House. Individual officials are aware of that assumption and in preparing a draft answer will act accordingly.' Nor is this a particularly modern view. H.E. Dale wrote over fifty years ago: 'It might be said, cynically, but with some measure of truth, that the perfect reply to an embarrassing question in the House of Commons is one that is brief, appears to answer the question completely, if challenged can be proved to be accurate in every word, gives no opening for awkward "supplementaries", and discloses really nothing.'[4] And in their classic study of parliamentary questions in 1962 Chester and Bowring specifically endorsed that interpretation when discussing the approach of ministers and officials to the drafting of answers to parliament questions.[5]

The significance of such a defensive culture was powerfully underlined to the Scott inquiry by the former Permanent Secretary at the Ministry of Defence, Sir Michael Quinlan. In a submission (D4.61) entitled *Answers in Parliament* he compared the parliamentary activity of seeking and giving information to a game, describing it as a competitive activity conducted, within rules, largely for a purpose different from that of its apparent object. He commented that 'the fact that the competition can work to the detriment of balanced public understanding rests less with individuals than with the dynamics (especially the high-profile immediacy of questions) of the Westminster system itself'. Other considerations might legitimately motivate ministers to be wary about what they disclose—such as the sensitivities of foreign governments, international negotiations, the need to maintain individual and commercial confidences. Such considerations were not unique to Whitehall, but the most pervasive pressure, and the one distinctive to government, was the unflaggingly adversarial political context. That generates a culture of secretiveness which has been a long-standing feature of British central government.   ·

In addition to that general context, it has been a widely accepted practice that governments decline to answer questions about the details of arm sales, supply of arms and export licences. As Scott noted (D1.28), this practice was well-enough established to be incorporated in the bible of parliamentary procedure, *Erskine May*, and successive administrations have used it to bolster refusals of information sought by MPs. He cited as an example the answer to a question from David Howell in June 1984 which showed how the block could be used as a way of declining any information about, for example, arms sales, not just information for which there is a widely accepted reason for maintaining confidentiality.

There were three other instances where Scott explicitly criticised the unsatisfactory way in which departments had responded to parliamentary questions or letters from MP. One was the application of the Howe guidelines to export credit policy: Scott argued (D2.111–12) that the inclusion of a defence allocation in the protocols signed with Iraq between 1983 and 1987 was inconsistent with the government's professed policy of even-handedness between Iran and Iraq while they were at war and that this allocation should have been revealed. An oblique reference to it was eventually made in a memorandum to the Trade and Industry Select Committee in 1991; but the opportunities to inform Parliament offered by questions (about the protocols from Allan Rogers MP in June 1990 and in December 1986 from Michael Latham MP about a ministerial visit to Iraq) were not taken. Scott considered this failure was not consistent with the obligation (derived from *Questions of Procedure for Ministers*) 'to give Parliament . . . and the public as full information as possible about the policies, decisions and actions of the government'.

Secondly, there were letters from MPs and questions in 1989 and 1990 querying the government's policy on sales of arms and defence-related equipment to Iraq. Scott criticised the replies as inaccurate (D4.24) and found that answers to questions in both Houses had failed—deliberately—to inform Parliament of the current policy. In a much quoted passage, he concluded that, 'the overriding and determinative reason was a fear of strong public opposition to the loosening of restrictions on the supply of defence equipment to Iraq and a consequential fear that the pressure of the opposition might be detrimental to British trading interests' (D4.42). Again drawing on *Questions of Procedure for Ministers*, Scott commented: 'The importance, if ministerial accountability is to be effective, of full and adequate information is, in my opinion, self-evident. If, and to the extent that, the account given by a minister to Parliament, whether in answering PQs, or in a debate, or to a select committee, withholds information on the matter under review, it is not a full account, and the obligation to account for what has happened, or for what is being done, has, prima facie, not been discharged. Without the provision of full information it is not possible for Parliament, or for that matter the public, to hold the executive fully to account. It follows, in my opinion, that the withholding of information by an accountable minister should never be based on reasons of convenience or for avoidance of political embarrassment and should always require special and strong justification.'

Thirdly, there were answers to PQs about Supergun. Scott took as typical those asked by Richard Caborn MP in December 1990 and again concluded (F4) that the government's responses had been inadequate: 'There can have been no ground for not giving Mr Caborn an answer to his question. The failure to respond adequately to the question constituted, in my opinion, a further example of failure to discharge the obligation of accountability.' To complete the picture, he also criticised the government's attitude when the Trade and Industry Select Committee attempted to take evidence from two retired Ministry of Defence officials, when it argued that as officials give evidence to select committees on behalf of ministers (according to the so-called Osmotherly Rules), retired officials could not perform this function. Scott's view was: 'A minister's duty to account to Parliament for what his department has done ought, in my opinion, to be recognised as extending (in the absence of any special limiting factors) to an obligation to assist an investigating select committee to obtain the best first hand evidence available on the matters being investigated. The refusal to facilitate the giving of evidence by Mr Harding and Mr Primrose may be regarded as a failure to comply fully with the obligations of accountability owed to Parliament.' In his subsequent evidence to the

Public Service Committee (3 April 1996) Sir Michael Quinlan insisted, contrary to Scott, that he and his colleagues had simply intended 'that we should find some other way, which was consistent with the convention, of getting them the information'.

Reflecting on the parliamentary handling of the Howe guidelines, Scott set out his fundamental criticism of the government's approach: 'The obligation of ministers to be forthcoming with information in answer to PQs about their departments' activities lies, in my opinion, at the heart of the important constitutional principle of ministerial accountability. The public interest in a full discharge by ministers of this obligation should be a constant heavy weight in the balance (between the public interest in favour of full disclosure against the public interests which might be adversely affected by full disclosure). Throughout the period that the inquiry has had to examine, there is to be found, in my opinion, a consistent undervaluing by government of the public interest that full information should be made available to Parliament. In circumstances where disclosure might be politically or administratively inconvenient, the balance struck by the government comes down, time and time again, against full disclosure' (D1.165).

To sum up on accountability, Scott found that the parliamentary mechanisms — ministerial statements, PQs, MPs' letters, select committee investigation — had not adequately fulfilled the requirements of the principle of ministerial accountability. The basis for his conclusion was that government had withheld information or disclosed it partially or in a misleading way. In response to ministerial criticisms of those findings he offered the curious doctrine that if ministers were sincere in their attempts to withhold information then that sincerity might excuse the constitutional impropriety of misleading Parliament.

Scott was able to make his findings because of the exceptional access the inquiry team were given to departmental papers, officials and ministers — a unique insight into the complex ways in which the administrative process of British central government actually works (or in some instances does not work). Indeed, the extent of that access is probably the explanation of one of the major failings of the report: its lack of clarity. So much detail was given, and judgements were so often qualified or balanced, that, as the parliamentary debates on the report so clearly demonstrated, its overall message was deeply ambiguous. In evidence to the Public Service Committee (3 April 1996) Scott robustly rejected — 'that is complete nonsense' — the view that his report did not have any conclusions.

Scott's reasoning also throws light on the semantic debate about accountability. He accepts, particularly when dealing with Sir Nicholas Lyell's role in briefing prosecuting counsel in the *Matrix Churchill* trial (G13.123–5) a distinction between a minister's constitutional accountability for all that is done or not done in his department but in which he was not himself directly involved, and his personal responsibility for that in which he has been or should have been involved. He elaborated on this in reply to questions from the Public Service Committee, where he distinguished between accountability on two levels, that with regard to policy and that with regard to what he called facts — 'what has happened, what has been done'. So far as the latter is concerned (Q394): 'Ministers cannot be expected to have firsthand knowledge of everything their departments are doing; it simply is not practicable. I for my part . . . do not feel inclined to attach blame to a minister who in the absence of any personal involvement in or any personal knowledge of the matter in question has presided over a department where something has gone wrong. I think blame in the ordinary sense should follow one or other, or a combination, of personal involvement and personal knowledge of the matter.'

That view reflects, and corresponds very closely with, the attempt to redefine (or, as some would say, restate) the doctrine of ministerial responsibility made by Sir Robin Butler in evidence to Scott and endorsed by his predecessor as Cabinet Secretary, Lord Armstrong of Ilminster, in his evidence to the Public Service Committee (3 April 1996). Lord Armstrong said that while a minister was accountable for all that happens in his department, there were aspects for which he could not be held personally responsible, either because they were actions taken in contradiction to the guidance or objectives he had laid down, or for other reasons (upon which he did not elaborate). He did not consider that such cases would necessarily be a resigning matter, but a minister was not exempted from a measure of responsibility — he would be required, for example, to take action to ensure that whatever had gone wrong did not happen again. Such distancing of the minister from responsibility (as opposed to accountability) for actions or inactions in which he was not directly involved raises in acute form the question with which the committee was wrestling: who in such cases is responsible?

Parliamentary reaction to the report

The handling of the Scott report is itself an illustration of how the mechanisms of parliamentary accountability operate. First, the way in which it was published and distributed provoked considerable criticism. Although it was his original intention that his report should be available to everyone simultaneously, Scott accepted that the government should have some advance copies because ministers would be required to make a response as soon as it was published. In consequence, a very limited facility — three hours in secure conditions — was also granted to the opposition, but in circumstances which were close to farce. The government produced a highly selective 'information pack' which concentrated upon the findings which were favourable to ministers but which was widely considered to be a distortion. Scott himself described the immediate aftermath of publication — 'the sound bite episode' — as trivial and not a matter of importance (Public Service Committee, 3 April 1996).

In the immediate aftermath of publication, attention focused on the fate of the two ministers perceived to be at greatest risk from criticism in the report—William Waldegrave, Chief Secretary to the Treasury but Minister of State at the Foreign Office at the time of revision of the Howe guidelines, and Sir Nicholas Lyell, the Attorney General. Scott found that Waldegrave had knowingly, but without duplicitous intent, misled Parliament by giving answers to PQs and MPs' letters which were. in his opinion, incomplete and inaccurate. Scott also found that Sir Nicholas Lyell bore major responsibility for the inadequacy of the instructions to prosecuting counsel in the Matrix Churchill trial and was personally at fault in that respect. With such critical findings from an independent senior judge, it was inevitable that there would be substantial opposition and media pressure for the two ministers to resign.

In the event, neither resigned, nor was either moved to another ministerial office. So the ultimate sanction against ministers was not brought to bear. In the Commons debate on the Scott report (26 February 1996)—on an adjournment motion—the government had a majority of just one. In that debate, as in its equivalent in the Lords (26 February 1996), its supporters were forced to attempt a detailed defence of the conduct of the two ministers—and others—in response to opposition criticism, even though the Conservative line was that Scott had cleared the government of the two major charges which had been made against it, namely that it had armed Iraq and that there had been a conspiracy to allow the Matrix Churchill defendants to go to prison rather than reveal government involvement.

The government has accepted that the Scott report revealed deficiencies which ought to be corrected. The President of the Board of Trade, Ian Lang, made a series of announcements when opening the Commons debate on 26 February. He announced that action had been taken to improve the distribution of intelligence material. He undertook to publish a consultation paper on export controls and licensing procedures. The government has accepted in principle the need for greater supervision by the Attorney General of HM Customs prosecutions in relation to export control matters. It also accepted that the long-standing practice according to which ministers decline to answer parliamentary questions on the sale of arms or defence related equipment should be re-examined. And, most important here, it encouraged the Commons Public Service Committee to expand its inquiry into the accountability of executive agencies into a wider inquiry encompassing ministerial accountability and responsibility. Therefore, although the Scott report itself may have disappeared from the media headlines, its findings remained the subject of parliamentary debate as government and opposition, frontbenchers and backbenchers, seek remedies for the deficiencies it identified.

Assessment of the Scott report

Scott's central conclusion—summarised in response to questions from Tony Wright during the Public Service Committee's hearings (3 April 1996)—was that ministers had behaved in ways that were constitutionally improper by denying Parliament information with which it should constitutionally have been provided. The mechanisms for ministerial accountability had not worked satisfactorily and they had not done so because ministers and officials withheld information from Parliament and public, or presented information in ways which were calculated to mislead. On this central judgement one has to ask, was Scott correct? The question here is not whether information was withheld or answers given that were calculated to mislead, but whether such responses fell short of the requirements of the doctrine of ministerial accountability. The case for saying 'no' rests on two grounds: past practice and political context.

The first ground states that there was nothing new here: such action or inaction is what ministers and officials have always done (see *Erskine May*) in their efforts to make the best case possible for government policy and practice. This argument is rather more subtle than seeking to excuse a sin by claiming everyone is at it anyway and always has been. It derives its force from the point that British constitutional conventions are based on practice, not principle—i.e. the convention is what the practice has been. That is not (necessarily) a justification of the desirability of the practice: it remains open whether the practice should be changed (and thus the convention with it). But it is a contradiction in terms in the British context to criticise a long-established practice as contrary to constitutional norms—for which reason, of course, some argue that those norms should be codified in a written constitution.

The second ground for rejecting Scott's central judgement is that his analysis seriously undervalued the political (partisan) context within which the convention of ministerial accountability operates. He was not unaware of that context—his attention was specifically drawn to it in evidence, particularly from officials seeking to explain the way in which letters and answers were drafted. Indeed, his central judgement (D1.165) argued that government has consistently, and wrongly, opted for political and administrative convenience rather than full disclosure. So the question is whether, in reaching this view, he gave sufficient weight to the partisan political context within which Parliament conducts its affairs and to the fact that lives were at stake. With the export of defence-related material to Iraq that also included the diplomatic and commercial considerations to which Lord Howe drew his attention but which he explicitly rejected as a justification for providing Parliament with incomplete or misleading information (D4.60).

Scott's case rested squarely on the perceived need for accurate information to enable Parliament to hold the executive to account. He cited in support of that view not only the 1994 Treasury and Civil Service Committee Report on Ministerial Accountability but also evidence given to it by the Cabinet Secretary, Sir Robin Butler, as well by two academics, Keith Dowding and John Stewart (K8.2). Without the provision of full information, Scott concluded (K8.3), it is not possible for Parliament . . . to assess what consequences, in the form of attributions of responsibility or blame, ought to follow. Against this, it was strongly argued in the House of Lords Debate (26 February 1996) — by Lords Howe, Rippon and Lord Armstrong of Ilminster, amongst others — that Scott would have benefited from the assistance of assessors who could have weighed the political and administrative considerations which are necessary to any rounded judgement about the 'attribution of responsibility or blame'. For here is where the tension between 'the securing of accountability' and 'party warfare', between 'scrutinising' and 'discrediting' government [to use Turpin's categories] is at its most acute. The difference between Scott and his critics lies in the allowance to be made for the latter, political dimension.

For Scott, accurate information is the key to effective accountability — and the current arrangements fail to secure it. He relied heavily — probably too heavily, given its status as merely guidance to ministers — on paragraph 27 of *Questions of Procedure for Ministers* which referred to 'the duty to give Parliament, including its select committees, and the public as full information as possible about the policies, decisions and actions of the Government, and not to deceive or mislead Parliament and the public'. He noted (K8.4) that this document was being revised in the light of the Nolan Committee's work. The government had already announced one clarification — that information should be withheld only when disclosure would not be in the public interest, 'which should be decided in accordance with established Parliamentary convention, the law and any relevant Code of Practice'. Scott did not consider this provision sufficient and called for a comprehensive review by Parliament and government of the practice whereunder information on exports of arms and defence-related goods need not be given by ministers. In his view (K8.13), the limitations that the public interest requires to be placed on the obligations of accountability owed by ministers need urgently to be rethought.

For many, it is but a short step from that position to advocacy of 'freedom of information' legislation. Supposing, for the sake of argument, that that step is not taken, what alternative way is there of improving accountability arrangements to meet the criticisms made by Scott? Would, for example, the appropriate redrafting of *Questions of Procedure for Ministers* and a much more restrictive list of 'blocked' categories in *Erskine May* do the trick, perhaps supplemented by some relaxing of the Osmotherly Rules and a more vigorous inquisitorial style by select committees? Prophecy is a risky business, especially in politics, but the effectiveness of such an incrementalist package would seem to depend on two issues—knowledge and culture.

Knowledge is crucial in two respects. First, the vexed issue of intention: rules and conventions of the *Questions of Procedure for Ministers* and *Erskine May* kind depend to a large extent upon the willingness of ministers and officials to play the game in the proper spirit—not to cheat, if you like. Here, the ministerial defence to Scott— we did not knowingly mislead—can be valid, if proved, unless ignorance is itself culpable. It remains necessary to correct what was misleading as soon as its misleading nature is known.

Second, how will Parliament know it has been misled, knowingly or otherwise? Assuming that investigations of the scale of the Scott inquiry are likely to be exceptional, are the normal processes of scrutiny likely to uncover deficiencies in ministerial answers? One suspects a positive answer to that question can be given only by relying on unauthorised disclosures—i.e. leaks.

That takes us to culture. Our present system works as it is does because of two very powerful mutual interests. The common interest of ministers and their officials in preserving the reputation of their depart-ment, and the common interest of ministers and their backbench supporters in protecting the government from criticism by its political opponents.

The former, allied to a powerful Whitehall professional ethic and the old Official Secrets Act, used to be a strong defence against unauthorised disclosure. The present government has substantially changed the secrecy laws and discloses a good deal more information, including information about its inner workings (e.g. *Questions of Procedure for Ministers* and details of Cabinet Committees) than was previously the practice, although it has not gone as far as advocates of a Freedom of Information Act would like. It has also introduced a Code of Ethics as part of its programme of civil service reform. Whether those changes will yield an increase in disclosure sufficient to achieve the desired enhancement in accountability remains open to doubt.

The second common interest goes to the heart of the partisan political context of our parliamentary system: government backbenchers are in the business of defending ministers—not assisting their political oppo-nents to criticise, and still less to discredit them. Unless the partisan dimension can be taken out of the scrutiny process (which in practice will mean excluding its application to individual ministers), its effective-ness will always be limited by this inhibition—at least when the government of the day has a cohesive overall majority.

Conclusions

Before we draw too many conclusions on the basis of the Scott report, we ought to enter a caveat: how typical is the material of the general run of government business? Peter Shore, in his evidence to the

Commons Public Service Committee (24 April 1996) drew a strong distinction between 'internal' and 'external' issues highlighting—as Lord Howe has—the commercial, diplomatic and security dimensions to trade policy with Iraq and Iran and the fact that on several occasions the lives of British subjects were at risk. This is not the case with most government business, nor with most parliamentary questions or select committee inquiries. It is true, however, that the political interest and convenience of the government is a constant factor.

We can see, first, from the Scott report that the system of ministerial accountability operates in a highly political context, in which government seeks to manage Parliament as part of the process of gaining and using electoral support for its policies and their implementation. Second, we see that in such a context full disclosure of information has not been, and will not be, perceived as an unqualified benefit. In setting its desirability against other requirements of the public interest, the political and administrative interests of the government will always be an important factor. Thirdly, to the extent that this factor is seen as an undesirable limitation upon the effectiveness of accountability arrangements, it is open to question whether incremental changes to Whitehall's and Westminster's procedures will make a significant difference, unless there are parallel changes in the administrative and political cultures in which they would operate.

1   C. Turpin, 'Ministerial Responsibility: Myth or Reality?' in J. Jowell and D. Oliver, *The Changing Constitution*, (Clarendon Press, 1989).
2   A.H. Birch, *Representative and Responsible Government,* (Allen & Unwin, 1964).
3   C. Turpin, op. cit.
4   H.E. Dale, *The Higher Civil Service of Great Britain,* (Oxford University Press, 1941), pp. 104–5.
5   D.N. Chester and N. Bowring, *Questions in Parliament*, (Clarendon Press, 1962), pp. 238–9.

The Attorney General

BY DIANA WOODHOUSE*

THE ATTORNEY GENERAL'S actions in relation to Matrix Churchill, together with Scott's report, have drawn public attention to his constitutional position. This chapter examines the responsibilities of the Attorney General, in particular the situations where he is required to act in the 'public interest' and the perhaps inevitable suspicion that at times this becomes confused with the government's interest. It also considers the difficulty of holding him accountable through the convention of ministerial responsibility and suggests that on occasion it has been to the government's advantage for the Attorney General, rather than any of his colleagues, to be the responsible minister. Finally, it examines Scott's conclusions regarding the actions of the Attorney General and assesses the extent to which he accounted to Parliament for them.

Constitutional position

In constitutional terms the position of the Attorney General is at best awkward and at times barely sustainable. He is required to serve two masters, the government and the law, and thus to combine the role of a politician with that of a lawyer. As a result, he is sometimes expected to exhibit partisanship and to pursue the government's interest and at other times to be independent, impartial, upholding the public interest.

The Attorney General is an elected Member of Parliament and, as such, has constituency responsibilities and takes the party whip. He is also a government minister and, although no longer a member of the Cabinet, is bound by the convention of collective responsibility and required to support government policies. He and the other Law Officers (the Solicitor General and the two Scottish Law Officers) give confidential legal advice to the government and represent it in civil actions.

However, the Attorney General also has a range of responsibilities where he acts as 'guardian of the public interest' (HC Debs, 12 November 1984). In the criminal field he can instigate proceedings and his consent is required for certain prosecutions under the Official Secrets Act, the Prevention of Terrorism Act and the Public Order Act. In addition, he is constitutionally responsible for the actions of the Director of Public Prosecutions to whom he can give instructions, and he has statutory responsibilities in relation to the Crown Prosecution Service

* Principal Lecturer in Law, Oxford Brookes University.

© Oxford University Press

and the Serious Fraud Office. Whilst he is not responsible for individual prosecution decisions, he can insist on a prosecution being brought or stop one from proceeding further. He also provides guidelines which relate to the bringing of prosecutions, such as those concerning the disclosure of documents to the defence: particularly relevant in the Matrix Churchill trial. In the civil jurisdiction, he can apply to the courts for an injunction to stop the publication of a book or article on the grounds that the information it discloses is not in the public interest. He can also bring proceedings against public bodies who are failing to fulfil their legal obligations.

At times the Attorney General is required to represent the government interest and at times the public interest. These are not always the same, as indicated in *Questions of Procedure for Ministers*, which states: 'In criminal proceedings the Law Officers act wholly independently of the government. In civil proceedings a distinction is to be drawn between proceedings in which the Law Officers are involved in a representative capacity on behalf of the Government, and action undertaken by them on behalf of the general community to enforce the law as an end in itself.' The requirement that the Attorney General acts 'wholly independently of the government' and separates the government from the public interest raises questions about his relationship with ministerial colleagues. In a classic statement of the position, Sir Hartley Shawcross said in 1951 that it was his duty in deciding whether or not to authorise a prosecution, 'to acquaint himself with all the relevant facts, including . . . the effect which the prosecution . . . would have upon public morale and order, and with any other considerations affecting public policy'. To this end he may 'consult with any of his colleagues in the government', but their assistance 'is confined to informing him of particular considerations which might affect his own decision, and does not consist, and must not consist, in telling him what that decision ought to be'. 'If political considerations which affect government in the abstract arise, it is the Attorney General, applying his judicial mind, who has to be the sole judge of those considerations (HC Debs, 29 January 1951).

The Attorney General is thus expected to take into account all relevant factors, including, if appropriate, information given by government ministers, but must not consider government or party embarrassment, for this is irrelevant, nor must he allow political pressure. Of course, the line between listening to colleagues and being influenced by them is a thin one, a fact recognised by Scott in his report on Matrix Churchill. 'The proposition that decisions whether or not to prosecute for criminal offences should be reached by a prosecuting authority without regard to political considerations is an important tenet of our unwritten constitution.' However, 'political considerations are not capable of exact definition and ministers may have a legitimate contribution to make to decisions as the allocation of finite resources, whether of manpower or of money, to the investigation and prosecution of particular classes of case' (C3.8). The resourcing issue may be particularly relevant in cases which involve long and complex investigations and trials, e.g. fraud cases, which also have a poor record of success. However, resourcing may also be a political decision, related to wider government policies and party sectional interests. The Attorney General therefore has to be astute in his consideration of ministerial contributions and underlying motivations in order to satisfy Scott's final contention that 'consideration of party political advantage or disadvantage should never play a part in decisions as to whether or not to prosecute'.

Given the inexactitude of 'political considerations' it is perhaps not surprising that there have been occasions when a decision about a prosecution or the seeking of an injunction has been alleged to show political influence. The most dramatic demonstration of the potential difficulties in the Attorney General's position occurred in 1924. The Labour Attorney General, Sir Patrick Hastings, considered an article in the communist *Daily Worker* to be an incitement to mutiny and instructed the Director of Public Prosecutions to prosecute the editor, John Campbell. After angry protests from government backbenchers, and conversations with ministerial colleagues, including the Prime Minister, the Attorney General announced that the prosecution was to be withdrawn. The timing of the announcement was unfortunate for it was made immediately after a Cabinet meeting at which the Attorney General was present and the prosecution was discussed. This resulted in the accusation that the Cabinet had not merely endorsed his decision but had instructed him. The opposition seized the opportunity to bring a censure motion against the minority government and it was defeated and resigned from office.

In more recent times a number of decisions of the Attorney General have been questioned with regard to their independence or the seeming confusion of public and government interest. In 1975 doubts were raised over the decision to seek an injunction to prevent publication of the *Crossman Diaries*.[1] The basis for the injunction was that publication would damage the public interest by undermining Cabinet confidentiality and thus the convention of ministerial responsibility. However, there were accusations that by preserving a culture of secrecy the Attorney General was in fact acting in the government's interest, and that the public was better served by openness. This drew from Sam Silkin the assurance that in seeking the injunction he had neither been influenced by his Cabinet colleagues nor by the Cabinet Secretary. In the event, the court accepted the need for confidentiality but refused to grant an injunction, considering that the Diaries concerned events not recent enough to be harmful.

In 1979 Sir Michael Havers was faced with the politically contentious decision whether to prosecute companies which had broken the embargo on shipping oil to Rhodesia (now Zimbabwe) by routing it through South Africa. He decided that prosecution was inadvisable because of problems of jurisdiction and evidence. However, there was also the possibility of the government being politically embarrassed by a defence of implied approval which might reveal its compliance (shades of Matrix Churchill). Thus whether the Attorney General was acting in the government or the public interest was brought into question.

Similar questions arose in 1984 when he decided to prosecute Clive Ponting, a senior civil servant in the Ministry of Defence who had leaked a document to a Labour MP. He claimed the document showed that the Secretary of State for Defence had misled the House of Commons over the sinking of the Argentine cruiser, *General Belgrano*, during the early stages of the Falklands Campaign when peace negotiations were still in progress. Michael Heseltine had told the House that the cruiser was steaming towards the British fleet and was thus a danger, while the document indicated that it was moving in the opposite direction. Prosecuted under section 2 of the Official Secrets Act 1911, Ponting claimed that he had acted in the public interest, a defence then available and was acquitted by the jury despite the summing-up of the trial judge who equated 'the public interest' with 'the government interest'. This confusion by a judge of the two interests heightened concern that in practice it was not possible to keep consideration of them separate and that the Attorney General's decision had in fact been politically motivated. Such accusations were vigorously denied by the Prime Minister and Sir Michael Havers. Mrs Thatcher wrote to Neil Kinnock, the leader of the Labour Party, stating unequivocally that the Law Officers had not consulted with other ministers, while the Attorney General told the House, 'I decided that the case fell within my published guidelines and that there should be a prosecution. Neither I nor the Solicitor General nor any of my officials sought the view or consulted with any other minister, nor was the view of any other minister conveyed to us before the decision was taken' (HC Debs, 12 February 1985). This was subsequently supplemented by a firm denial that Mrs Thatcher had directed him in any decision he had made about a criminal prosecution. The statements suggested a situation whereby the Attorney General and his staff isolated themselves from ministerial contact. This would seem to be more than was required, indeed might be seen as detrimental to the decision-making process which requires all factors relevant to the public interest to be considered. As Sam Silkin, with the authority of having been Attorney General, commented: 'In a case such as the Ponting case it is hard to believe that there are no aspects of the public interest upon which consultation with colleagues could have assisted the Law Officers in reaching their eventual and independent decision.'[2]

Similar comments would seem relevant to the Zircon affair. Zircon, code-name for a defence project, was the subject of a programme made for the BBC in 1986 by an investigative journalist, Duncan Campbell, and revealed how the government had kept its existence and associated expenditure secret from Parliament. Shortly before the programme was due to be screened, the government persuaded the Director General of the BBC to withdraw it, while the Attorney General sought an injunction to prevent Campbell from revealing the information contained in the programme elsewhere on grounds of national security. The Attorney General instructed the Director of Public Prosecutions to investigate possible breaches of the Official Secrets Act. This resulted in a middle of the night search of the BBC Glasgow office and Campbell's home with seizure of a large amount of material, much of it irrelevant to the investigation. The heavy-handed nature of these incidents raised concerns about who had authorised them and whether the decision with regard to possible prosecution was politically motivated. In a Commons debate the Home Secretary insisted that the Attorney General 'does not consult his colleagues—indeed he debars himself from consulting colleagues on any matter relating to a prosecution' (HC Debs, 3 February 1987). As with Ponting, this would seem either to be an overstatement of the previously accepted position or an indication that the conventions relating to the taking of public interest decisions have changed in which case the Attorney General may on occasions be deprived of relevant information .

Political embarrassment was also suspected by some as the motivating force behind the *Spycatcher* saga which included a civil action in Australia against an ex-MI5 agent, Peter Wright, and an application for injunctions in Britain to prevent the publication of the book and its serialisation by the newspapers. The ground here was that it was in the public interest that a member of the security services should owe a lifelong duty of confidentiality, for only thus could its operations be assured and national security protected. The Attorney General's argument seemed somewhat less plausible when he sought to keep the injunctions in place even after *Spycatcher* had been published in America and pirate copies of the book became available in Britain: if publication was damaging, the damage had already been done. This point was recognised by the Law Lords who refused the Attorney General's requests for injunctions.[3] The action in Australia was also lost and the book revealed little to damage the operations of MI5. However, it did make revelations that might be seen as politically embarrassing to the government, including allegations that MI5 had been engaged in burglary and the bugging of political parties and trade unions and that the service had been involved in a plot to destabilise the Labour government of Harold Wilson.

It would seem that where politically contentious decisions are concerned, the Attorney General is unlikely to escape criticism whatever declaration he makes. If he admits that he has consulted with his colleagues, then he is accused of succumbing to political pressure and taking the possible political consequences for the government into account. If he insists that there has been no consultation, then his decision may be impugned for failing to consider all relevant factors. The truth is that in serving two masters, the government and the law, a conflict of interest will always be suspected and the opposition will seek to make political capital out of any high-profile decision. He is, after all, a politician and thus fair game on the floor of the House and in the media. As Sir Michael Havers commented when Attorney General: 'One is sometimes put in an impossible position' (HC Debs, 12 January 1987).

Spycatcher and Zircon raised an important question as to whether the Attorney General decides for himself that confidentiality or national security will be undermined by the release of particular information or whether he is advised by his ministerial colleagues on this. If the latter, it comes dangerously close to taking instructions unless he requires a detailed exposition rather than just the minister's word. Even then, it would seem that the independent decision-making of the Attorney General is confined to weighing the public interest in publication against the public interest in repressing allegedly sensitive information and is not concerned with determining whether national security is in fact threatened.

This role of facilitator rather than decision-maker seems confirmed by Matrix Churchill where, with regard to Public Interest Immunity certificates, the Attorney General, Sir Nicholas Lyell, acknowledged that he had not read any of the material covered. He had accepted the word of civil servants and ministers that the documents were of a class for which protection should be claimed. Thus his advice to ministers to sign the certificates was purely technical. In a similar way, the decision to seek an injunction may at times be a technical one based in part on the chances of success, rather than one of substance.

Ministerial responsibility

In all cases concerning the public interest the Attorney General is accountable solely to Parliament through the convention of ministerial responsibility. There is no accountability to the courts by way of judicial review. The absolute nature of his discretion was clearly stated in the *Gouriet* case in 1978. Mr Gouriet wanted the Attorney General to seek an injunction against the Post Office Workers Union to prevent its members boycotting mail from South Africa claiming this was against the public interest. Lord Wilberforce held that the decision of the Attorney General was 'unassailable' and could only be challenged in Parliament, to whom, as a minister, he was accountable.[4] This was reaffirmed in 1994. An application for judicial review was made by the Taylor sisters who had been convicted but were subsequently released after the Court of Appeal held that newspaper coverage had made a fair trial impossible. The sisters wanted the Attorney General to initiate proceedings for contempt of court against the papers concerned but he declined to do so. The High Court again stressed the absolute nature of the Attorney General's discretion, repeating that his responsibility for decisions taken in the public interest was political and thus to Parliament alone.

Parliament, or more accurately the House of Commons, therefore has the responsibility for holding the Attorney General accountable for his decisions. This, however, is a task for which it is hardly suited, given the lack of expertise of MPs and the nature of Commons proceedings. Moreover, there are other limitations on its ability to hold the Attorney General accountable. He cannot be questioned on any case that is under consideration, pending or in process (sub judice), and he is unlikely to be drawn on the details of how or why he made a particular decision. Instead, he will retreat behind the cloak of quasi-judicialdom and assert that in his opinion (all that really matters), given all the facts, it was the correct decision at the time. In making this assertion, he knows that he can rely on the government majority in the House to support him

There therefore seems to have developed a predictable format for the questioning of the Attorney General on a politically contentious decision. The opposition asks whether he was influenced by ministerial colleagues and to what extent he took account of the political consequences. He affirms the independent nature of the decision. Government backbenchers seek to confirm the difficulty of his job whilst congratulating him on doing it so well. Finally, if the situation requires, the Home Secretary and/or the Prime Minister will also assert the independence of the Attorney General. Seldom is the legal correctness of a decision challenged in the House of Commons. The breadth of the Attorney General's discretion when acting in the public interest makes such challenges unsustainable. In any case, the arguments utilised have to be technical rather than political and are therefore of little interest to most MPs. Moreover, they change the nature of the debate and are easily rebutted by technical answers. Thus where decisions taken in the public interest are concerned, accountability is frequently inadequate.

Legal advice to the government

The Attorney General is accountable to the Prime Minister for the quality and correctness of the advice he gives to the government and can, like any other minister, be dismissed, or be required to resign, if he fails to perform adequately. The advice he gives is confidential. Indeed, according to *Questions of Procedure for Ministers*, even the fact that advice has been sought from him or the other Law Officers cannot be revealed without their permission. The consequence of breaching this convention became apparent in 1986 during the Westland affair when extracts from a letter written by the Solicitor General to Michael Heseltine, then Secretary of State for Defence, were leaked to the press.

The Solicitor General insisted upon an inquiry to determine the source of the leak. This was undertaken by the Cabinet Secretary who found officials at the Department of Trade and Industry to be culpable and the responsible minister, Leon Brittan, was forced to resign.

The requirement that legal advice remains confidential, unless the permission of the Law Officers is given, guards against the possibility of subsequent legal action either by the government or against it, while at the same time protecting the professional interest of the lawyer. However, it may also frustrate the accountability process, for although the law officers are, in the first instance, accountable to the government as 'client', if ministers justify their actions on the basis of legal advice received, then accountability for that advice would seem to pass to Parliament and the details of it should be disclosed.

Such disclosure was successfully resisted in the Maastricht debate in 1993 on the European Communities (Amendment) Bill, where the advice of the Attorney General was used to extricate the government from a difficult position. The opposition tabled an amendment to remove Britain's opt-out from the social chapter, contained in a protocol to the Treaty. The Foreign Office minister, Tristan Garel-Jones, declared that this would prevent the ratification of the Maastricht Treaty. The hope, it seems, was that such a serious consequence would deter rebel government backbenchers from voting for the amendment as a protest against European integration. However, it soon became apparent that this strategy would not work. Less than a month later the Foreign Secretary, Douglas Hurd, told the House that the amendment would not affect the ratification of the Treaty. He explained that the previous view had been based on wrong legal advice by Foreign Office lawyers. The correct version was that which had now been given by the Attorney General, Sir Nicholas Lyell. The change in the government's stated position meant there would be no gain in backbench Eurosceptics voting for the amendment.

The episode posed questions about who gives legal advice to ministers and about the nature of that advice. *Questions of Procedure for Ministers* states that consultation with the Law Officers 'will normally be appropriate' when 'the legal consequences of action by the government might have important repercussions in the foreign, Community or domestic field'. It would seem therefore, that the Attorney General should have been involved from the beginning, a point accepted by Mr Hurd. The complete reversal of the legal position brought the comment in the House from Sir Russell Johnson (Liberal) that 'where there is a political will there is a legal way', whilst Peter Riddell writing in *The Times* likened the government to a spiv businessman with a sharp lawyer. The way in which the Attorney General was used by the government undermined the credibility of his office. Moreover, Sir Nicholas Lyell refused to explain to the House the advice he had given the government, maintaining that such information would break with precedent. It would certainly have been unusual but then it was not usual for the advice of the Law Officers to be cited by ministers in debate. As far as the House of Commons was concerned, without the appropriate information it was unable to hold the Attorney General to account, despite the fact that his actions had enabled the government to change its position to suit the political circumstances.

The use of the Attorney General to depoliticise a matter of public concern and to deflect responsibility from other ministers suggested that even if he does not act politically where the public interest is concerned, he may be used politically in his role as adviser to the government. There are advantages for the government in presenting him as the responsible minister because he can hide behind legal confidentiality and technicalities not available to his colleagues.

The role of the Attorney General in the Maastricht debate was controversial. However, it paled into insignificance when his full role in the Matrix Churchill case became apparent. Central to the controversy again was the revelation of legal advice which usually remains confidential. This time the Attorney General, Sir Nicholas Lyell, took the unprecedented step of outlining the advice he had given to ministers on the signing of Public Interest Immunity certificates in a letter to *The Times* (13 November 1992). Significantly, he stated that he had told ministers that they had no choice but to claim Public Interest Immunity if the documents concerned were of a class to which immunity attached. This seemed to be an attempt to transfer responsibility from the ministers concerned, namely Michael Heseltine, Kenneth Clarke, Tristan Garel-Jones and Malcolm Rifkind, and to depoliticise an issue over which there was considerable public concern. Whether the advice was right or not—and thus whether ministers should have signed the certificates—would thus become a matter of legal opinion rather than political debate, as became evident when Scott reported that the Attorney General's advice had been based on a 'fundamental misconception of the law'. Sir Nicholas Lyell rejected this, citing support from 'the great majority of senior members of the Bar—who understand these matters—as well as the higher judiciary' (HC Debs, 19 February 1996). He therefore traded legal opinion with legal opinion, avoiding political questions and the requirements of political accountability.

However, there were other matters relating to Matrix Churchill which were less easily categorised as a matter of legal opinion. Scott found the Attorney General was responsible for a failure to inform the trial judge that Michael Heseltine, then President of the Board of Trade, had strong reservations about claiming Public Interest Immunity. Heseltine was concerned that the interests of justice required that some material should be disclosed to the defence. Scott considered that the prosecution counsel, Mr Moses, had not been given adequate instructions with regard to these reservations and concluded that 'major responsibility' for this must in his opinion be borne by the Attorney

General. He noted that there had been an absence of the personal involvement by the Attorney General which Mr Heseltine's stance and its implications had made necessary (G13.123–5). Scott was also concerned that a letter from Mr Heseltine to the Attorney General on the issue had been left unread for between three and seven weeks and it was apparent from the report that the Attorney General had never himself read the documents about which Mr Heseltine had expressed concern, or indeed any of the documents which were covered by PII certificates.

Scott's conclusion that the Attorney General was personally at fault was disputed by Sir Nicholas, but Scott was not swayed. He accepted 'the genuineness of his belief that he was personally, as opposed to constitutionally, blameless for the inadequacy of the instructions sent to Mr Moses'. However, he continued, 'I do not accept that he was not personally at fault. The issues raised by Mr Heseltine's stand on the PII certificate did not fall into the category of mundane, routine, run of the mill issues that could properly be dealt with by officials in the Treasury Solicitor's Department without the Attorney General's supervision' (G13.125).

The distinction made by the Attorney General between personal and constitutional blame was an attempt to distance himself from culpability. He was implying that the convention of ministerial responsibility which makes a minister accountable for errors within his department does not necessarily imply personal fault. Thus the minister could be required to explain what had happened and take amendatory action, but the question of resignation did not arise. Sir Nicholas Lyell was adopting the position that matters relating to PII certificates were administrative matters and therefore not something in which he had been involved. As a consequence, if errors had been made, he was not to blame.

Scott showed no recognition of such a divide. Indeed, he reinforced the traditional position in which the Attorney General, like other ministers, is liable for errors within his department of which he knew, or should have known, regardless of whether or not they were operational. He considered that the Attorney General should have overseen matters relating to the certificates: the fact that he had not done so, and was therefore unaware of the inadequacy of the instructions given to Mr Moses, did not reduce his liability.

The Scott report brought the Attorney General's handling of Matrix Churchill firmly within the ambit of ministerial responsibility and thus a matter for which he was responsible to Parliament. Moreover, the criticisms made by Scott in this respect were concerned with the Attorney General's oversight of his department not with his competence as a lawyer. There were calls for his resignation from the opposition and some sections of the press. Even several Conservative backbenchers expressed reservations about his continuation in office. However, the

Attorney General refused to countenance resignation or even admit that he had mishandled Matrix Churchill in any way.

His response, when questioned in the House of Commons, was to continue to deflect political criticism with legal technicalities. When asked by Mr Hain (Labour) how he could remain in office 'after Scott's savage condemnation of his incompetence and the subsequent public collapse in confidence in his role' (HC Debs, 19 February 1996), he replied that his integrity was 'unquestioned'. He continued: 'The one instance in which the report says that I was personally at fault rests on Sir Richard Scott's different view of the law'. He insisted that the wording on the PII certificate signed by Michael Heseltine was such as to alert the trial judge to the minister's reservations and pointed to the fact that the judge had examined the documents and that the defence lawyers agreed that the trial had been fair. He therefore reworked Scott's criticism that he had been negligent in failing to involve himself personally in matters relating to the certificates into a 'different view of the law' and dismissed it on the basis of the end result.

The one allegation made in the report which did not lend itself to this treatment was that concerning the letter from Michael Heseltine. Scott stated that it had been unread for a period of between three and seven weeks. The Attorney General maintained that Scott had been wrong in making this charge, asserting that the letter was not unread. Moreover, he maintained that he had not been given the chance to refute the allegation before publication of the report, thus implying that it had been unfairly made. He insisted that with regard to Matrix Churchill he had acted 'carefully and properly throughout'.

The Attorney General had no intention of relinquishing office. In his opinion he had done nothing wrong and he was not prepared to accept the verdict of others who considered him to be culpable. The stance taken by Sir Nicholas Lyell contrasts with that of Lord Carrington who, after the invasion of the Falklands in 1982, tendered his resignation despite his belief that neither he nor his staff had been at fault. For his part, the Attorney General rejected suggestions that public confidence in his office had been lost, and with the support of the Prime Minister, who was determined to ride out the Matrix Churchill affair without a sacrificial resignation, remained a Law Officer to the Crown. Thus the findings of an inquiry, commissioned by the government, that the Attorney General was personally at fault proved to be of little consequence.

Matrix Churchill and the position of the Attorney General

The survival of Sir Nicholas Lyell as Attorney General demonstrates the inadequacy of the mechanisms for public accountability. Whether or not he was personally at fault, the public perceived that he was and believed he should resign. His failure to do so reinforced negative perceptions about politicians and those who hold public office and also about Parliament's ability to hold ministers to account. Beyond that, the Matrix Churchill affair highlighted again the ambiguous role of the Attorney General, who is portrayed as a lawyer making independent and impartial decisions, but whose actions nevertheless have considerable political consequences and who, as a minister, relies on prime-ministerial patronage for his position. The high profile taken by the Attorney General in the Matrix Churchill case also brought to the fore once again concern over the separation of the public interest from the government interest. Public Interest Immunity certificates, as their name indicates, are meant to protect information which it is not in the public interest to disclose without good cause. In the Matrix Churchill case there was the suspicion that non-disclosure was in the government's interest. Such suspicion, whether justifiable or not, undermines public confidence in both political and legal systems.

This is one of the reasons why from time to time suggestions are made for a Ministry of Justice which would fulfil the public interest role of the Attorney General along with other responsibilities currently undertaken by the Lord Chancellor. This would leave the Attorney General free to act in the government's interest as its principle law officer and remove the problem of actual, or perceived, confusion over government and public interest. However, such a ministry is not under consideration. It therefore seems likely that the role of the Attorney General will remain controversial and that high-profile decisions will continue to attract criticism.

1   *Attorney General v Jonathan Cape Ltd* [1976] QB 752.
2   *The Times*, 29 September 1984.
3   *Attorney General v Guardian Newspapers* (No. 2) [1990] 1 AC 109.
4   *Gouriet v. National Union of Postal Workers* [1978] AC 435.

Intelligence and Government

BY ADAM TOMKINS*

THE SCOTT inquiry was probably the longest and most public investigation into Britain's national security constitution that we have ever seen. Yet in the immediate aftermath of the report's publication in February 1996 and in the literature which has so far been produced on the Scott story, very little has been said about national security and secret intelligence. On one level this is not surprising. There is no chapter of the Scott report headed 'intelligence' to which one can turn to find with ease what Scott has to say about the successes and failures of the intelligence services in the story he uncovered. Instead, one has to pick through the report's less fashionable passages such as the detailed lists of specific cases of the application of the Howe guidelines on exports to Iran and Iraq in chapter D2 (a mere 435 paragraphs) and again in chapter D6 (a further 485 paragraphs) piecing together obscure references about export licence 3G/53234/88 and a telegram sent by Mr O of the Secret Intelligence Service to Mr P of the Security Service in December 1988 (D6.73 and D6.78). This, perhaps, is the very stuff of the Scott addict's obsession.

But apart from its narcotic function, such activity also reveals a hitherto private world of government decision-making and secret intelligence. This is exactly the constitutional value of the report: despite its lack of political bite (no minister resigned; the government survived) the story remains one of not only high but unprecedented constitutional importance. Although public lawyers and political observers may long have suspected that all was not well in the murky world of intelligence and government, now we know. Never before has a public inquiry uncovered so much information so close to the heart of British central government on such a sensitive issue. While there are many aspects of the Scott story with an intelligence connection, the focus is on just one: the export licensing process. Companies such as Matrix Churchill were prosecuted for breaches of export licensing law—in the Matrix Churchill case three company directors were charged with deception offences relating to their export licences. The question which concerns us is what the intelligence community, ministers and officials knew, at the time the export licences were first applied for and then processed, about the true nature of Matrix Churchill's business with Iraq.[1]

* Lecturer in Law, King's College, London.

Secret intelligence, defence sales and the export licensing process

A thorough examination of the export licensing process and the role of secret intelligence in that process as it applied to Iran and Iraq during the entire period covered by the Scott report would take several hundred pages. To make matters more comprehensible we focus on the characters that became the protagonists of the drama: Matrix Churchill. It is important that the reasons for this are not misunderstood. The report concerns matters far broader and deeper than merely what happened to one Iraqi-owned Coventry-based company in the late 1980s and early 1990s. Their sad story of another 600 unemployed in the West Midlands does not need a multi-million pound public inquiry for it to be told. But the collapse of the Matrix Churchill trial in November 1992 was the immediate reason behind the establishment of the Scott inquiry; the case (*R v Henderson and others*) was the only one to be expressly mentioned in its terms of reference (see A2.2); and as it has become the one about which we know most, due to the focus on it in the Scott report itself, it is the one about which most can be said with certainty. Moreover, the fact that what happened to Matrix Churchill also happened elsewhere heightens rather than reduces its importance. As a close reading of the report will disclose, other branches of the Iraqi arms procurement network, other companies, other failed prosecutions, could quite easily have become the household names instead: BSA, Wickman Bennett and so on. Matrix Churchill is thus a story in itself, but it is also a representative story, revealing a malaise at the centre of British government.

A little needs to be said first about government decision-making in this field. Three government departments were directly involved in the control of export licensing: the Foreign Office, the Ministry of Defence and the Department of Trade and Industry. Of these, the DTI was the department which was responsible for most of the administrative work. The Export Licensing Unit, located within the DTI, granted licences in consultation with the other two departments. Many matters could of course be dealt with at official level, but when issues were referred to ministers, export licensing was generally a matter for second-tier, non-Cabinet ministers. During the period 1987–1990, the three Ministers of State were William Waldegrave at the Foreign Office, Lord Trefgarne, the Minister for Defence Procurement, and Alan Clark, the Minister for Trade (in July 1989 the last two swapped positions). The three departments and their ministers were assisted by a number of advisory groups and committees, most notably the Restricted Enforcement Unit, the Working Group on Iraqi Procurement and the Ministry of Defence Working Group.

This network of government decision-makers was supported by the intelligence community, constituted for our purposes by five separate organisations. First there are the three agencies colloquially known as MI5, MI6 and GCHQ. The Security Service (or MI5) is responsible for protecting national security, in particular, against 'threats from espionage, terrorism and sabotage'. Established in 1909, but not given statutory authority until the Security Service Act 1989, it has close links with the Home Office. The Secret Intelligence Service (MI6) is responsible for obtaining and providing 'information relating to the actions or intentions of persons outside the British Islands', tasks performed in the 'interests of national security' or the 'economic well-being of the UK' or 'in support of the prevention or detection of serious crime'. The Secret Intelligence Service, put on the statute book along with GCHQ by the Intelligence Services Act 1994, has close links with the Foreign Office. Government Communications Headquarters (GCHQ) is responsible for signals intelligence (SIGINT). Two other intelligence organisations played an important role in the Scott story: the Defence Intelligence Staff and the Joint Intelligence Committee. The former was formally established in a Ministry of Defence restructuring in 1964. It has no specific statutory authority but is thought to be responsible for providing and analysing intelligence on military matters and defence policy to the ministry. The Secret Intelligence Service also has a branch located there, 'whose existence is not normally acknowledged' (F2.36). What the relationship is between the two is unknown. Finally, the Joint Intelligence Committee, located in the Cabinet Office, is responsible for coordinating intelligence across government.

OCTOBER 1987–FEBRUARY 1988. So much for the background. Three sets of Matrix Churchill export licence applications fell to be examined. In August 1987 Matrix Churchill applied for licences to export machine tools to Hutteen in Iraq. The application stated that the nature of Hutteen's business was 'general engineering' and that the purpose of the goods was the 'manufacturing of general engineering products' (D2.279). As the Scott report comments, such a brief statement is the very 'antithesis of a "precise" purpose' which the application called for, yet this degree of imprecision was apparently routinely accepted by the DTI (*ibid*, see also D2.271). Perhaps if a more rigorous approach had been taken from the beginning, the Scott story could have been avoided altogether. With regard to the Matrix Churchill applications, there was some concern initially within the Ministry of Defence that the goods might be destined ultimately for the USSR, but after seeking further specifications, this fear was allayed and in October 1987 it was agreed that the machine tools could be exported to Iraq as they would not constitute a significant enhancement of Iraq's military capability (D2.272).[2]

An intelligence report on Hutteen was drawn up by the Secret Intelligence Service in late 1987, stating clearly that Iraq had been signing contracts with British-based companies 'for the purchase of general purpose heavy machinery and for the production of armaments in Iraq'. Five companies were named, including Matrix Churchill, BSA and Wickman Bennett. The report also stated that 'Iraq intends to use the machinery purchased to manufacture its own munitions' (D2.265–66). This was not the first intelligence on Hutteen. The Defence Intelligence Staff had known for some years that Hutteen was an armaments factory. The November report was, however, the first intelligence that was passed on to the export licensing departments of the Foreign Office, Ministry of Defence and DTI (D2.267). The source for this intelligence was Mark Gutteridge, a senior executive and exports manager at Matrix Churchill. Throughout the late 1980s he had been in regular contact with MI5 and from at least May 1987 he had been meeting an MI5 officer, known to him as Michael Ford and to the Scott report as Mr P. In May 1987 Mr P drew up a contact note in which he wrote that Iraq was 'buying up milling machines specifically tooled up for arms production'.[3] It also recorded the concern (which was to become important in early 1988) that this business should not be interfered with since 'it is of high value and will be taken up by the West Germans' if Matrix Churchill are forced to withdraw (D2.265).

By the date of this intelligence report the Matrix Churchill export licence applications of 1987 had already been approved. Could they now be revoked? According to the Scott report, it was generally agreed among relevant witnesses to the inquiry that if its contents had been known by the officials in the export licensing departments of the Foreign Office, Ministry of Defence and DTI at the time, the 'export licences would not have been granted' (D2.282). Despite this, the possibility of revoking the licences was not even discussed until January 1988, a delay of which the Scott report is very critical. Why did the government departments concerned not act on the intelligence more quickly?

As far as the Ministry of Defence is concerned, the report states that 'the failure of anyone there to take prompt action on the report as soon as it was received within the department was . . . a failure of system within the Defence Intelligence Staff rather than a failure on the part of any individual. There was, at the time, no clearly understood system within DIS under which intelligence with implications for export sales policy would be brought to the attention' of the relevant people. Scott describes the Ministry of Defence/DIS system as having been 'unsatisfactorily haphazard' but is happy that institutional reforms within the ministry had resolved this problem by the end of 1994 (D2.287) — though we are not told the nature of such reforms.

As regards the Foreign Office, Scott singles out an official in the Middle East Department, a Mr Patey, who is described as 'plainly unsatisfactory . . . his failure to react to [the intelligence report] until early January 1988 was, in my opinion, a failure for which no adequate explanation has been offered'. As regards the DTI, the official most directly concerned — Mr Tony Steadman, head of the Export Licensing

Unit—did not receive the security clearance necessary to permit him to see such intelligence until January 1988, some eight months after he had taken up that post (described by Scott as 'plainly unacceptable' (D2.293)). His superior, Mr Eric Beston, may have read the intelligence report, but if so not until January 1988. Scott describes the system as rather hit and miss (and this was a miss) but is less critical of the DTI than of the Ministry of Defence and Foreign Office, since the issue of probable munitions manufacture should have been primarily their concern (D2.292)—we are told that the DTI system was subsequently improved, but not how.

As it turned out, even by the middle of January 1988 only 13 of the 141 machine tools for which Matrix Churchill had received export licences had actually been shipped. It was therefore still not too late to revoke the licences, but they were allowed to stand. Why? The Export Licensing Unit contacted Matrix Churchill in January 1988 explaining that they were being reconsidered due to their suspected munitions use. Matrix Churchill were highly concerned about the significant loss of trade that this would entail, and a meeting was arranged for 20 January 1988 between the Minister for Trade, Alan Clark, and the Machine Tools Trade Association (MTTA) of which Matrix Churchill was a member. Paul Henderson, the managing director of Matrix Churchill was to attend the meeting. Tony Steadman and Eric Beston were the officials who briefed Alan Clark for this meeting.[4] Their briefing referred to the November 1987 intelligence report and stated that the MTTA companies should be advised to 'maintain a low profile . . . press or public attention would make it more difficult to permit fulfilment of the contracts' (D2.302). Significantly, it added that 'the providers of the intelligence are most anxious that their source [Gutteridge] should not inadvertently be put at risk . . . For this reason, they, like DTI and other officials, would favour allowing the present contracts to be completed and export licences refused only for any future suspect business' (D2.304).

Although it was only a DTI minister who was directly involved in the January 1988 meeting, ministers in the Ministry of Defence and Foreign Office also received submissions on this issue. The Ministry of Defence submission to Lord Trefgarne stated that 'the intelligence community recommends against revoking the licences as they fear for the safety of their source and they also believe that far more important information could cease to become available as a result' (D2.311). As Scott makes clear, this was misleading: the intelligence community did not fear for Gutteridge's life or limb: they merely felt that if his identity were to become known, his value as a source would be at an end (*ibid*, also D2.322)—a somewhat different concern.

By this time, the November 1987 report was not the only intelligence available. An anonymous employee of Matrix Churchill wrote to the Foreign Secretary, Sir Geoffrey Howe, in January 1988 stating that her employers were 'working on a £30 million order for CNC lathes to be used for munitions production in Iraq' (D2.318). This was copied to the Ministry of Defence and to the Secret Intelligence Service, yet although, in Scott's words, it 'should have been recognised as highly significant'(D2.320), no action was taken on it. The report views this episode with an understandable lack of sympathy. The report states that the Matrix Churchill export licence applications were 'attended by muddle and confusion' (D2.326) and that key officials demonstrated 'unacceptable carelessness' (D2.342).

Scott's concerns focus on the handling of applications and on the rather gung-ho pro-trade attitude of DTI officials rather than on matters of intelligence. Yet serious questions need to be raised in respect of the latter. Here was a story that could and should have been an intelligence success. The intelligence services had worked together to glean, analyse and distribute information which directly related to government policy on defence sales to Iraq, and moreover they had done so in time. The government, through the intelligence services, had ascertained that British-based companies such as Matrix Churchill were being used by the Iraqis as sources of arms procurement and manufacture. This was contrary to its clearly stated policy as articulated in the Howe guidelines and it was in a position to put a stop to the matter by denying export licences. Instead, the intelligence services put pressure on the government departments concerned not to revoke the licences. As Alan Clark described it in his evidence, this was 'an absurd paradox. Intelligence was telling you what [the exports] were being used for, but the machines had to be provided in order to protect the source telling you how they were being used. It was a total circularity'.[5]

OCTOBER 1988–FEBRUARY 1989. In October 1988 Matrix Churchill lodged a new export licence application with the DTI, known as ELA 53234. This was one of the applications in respect of which its directors were later charged and prosecuted by HM Customs. It involved twelve vertical spindle machining centres and two high speed lathes, to be exported to Nassr in Iraq (D6.73). As with Hutteen, the Defence Intelligence Staff had long suspected that Nassr had an arms production facility (D2.267). ELA 53234 related to the so-called ABA Project which was being orchestrated by Cardoen, a well known Chilean arms dealer. The application was as imprecise as the 1987 ones had been: Nassr's business was stated as 'mechanical engineering' and the purpose for which the goods were to be used as 'production of metal components' (D6.73). As Scott observes, considering the fact that by October 1988 it was known that Nassr was a munitions factory, the absence of any precision in the statement was glaring. No attempt was made by the DTI to obtain further details (D6.75).

The Ministry of Defence's working group on export licence applications, which advised the ministry (based on a military assessment of the goods in question) initially recommended that ELA 53234 should be refused, on the ground that it would constitute a significant enhancement. But the Ministry of Defence was not the only interested party. The security and secret intelligence services were also concerned about the way in which this new Matrix Churchill application would be handled. Mr O of the Secret Intelligence Service sent a telegram to Mr P of MI5 in December 1988, saying that 'the problem of source protection again raises its ugly head ... we are saying that the applications should be considered ... on the merits of export guidelines. There is of course a fine dividing line between lathes and tools for industrial use and those for military use' (D6.78). The reference here to source protection was ambiguous, but in Scott's view it was intended to mean that source protection was not a factor as far as SIS were concerned (D6.80). MI5 was not so sure. In his response to Mr O, Mr P wrote that 'it is important to maintain source protection. There seem to be so many uncertainties that granting this particular set of export licences will at least give time for [the intelligence agencies] to discover more about Iraqi intentions' (D6.81). The Defence Intelligence Staff took a completely different view, arguing that ELA 53234 offered Iraq a 'significant enhancement which is contrary to the current ministerial guidelines ... DIS will oppose most vigorously any shipment of machine tools to [Nassr]' (D6.84). Thus the three intelligence agencies most directly concerned each took quite different lines: MI6 (i.e. SIS) appeared neutral—its Iraqi concerns really lay elsewhere and were primarily focused on nuclear capacity (D6.82 and 87) and it was not so bothered about conventional exports such as those Matrix Churchill proposed. MI5 wanted to protect its source and was therefore prepared to allow the goods to be exported. The Defence Intelligence Staff, concerned with more broadly based matters, was interested in all Iraqi military enhancement and procurement, whether nuclear or not, and, interestingly, was the only agency to present its concerns in the light of government policy as articulated in the Howe guidelines.

Ministers from the Foreign Office, Ministry of Defence and DTI were to decide the fate of ELA 53234 in February 1989. Much of January was therefore taken up with the preparation of ministerial briefings. From the intelligence point of view, the most interesting of these is the Foreign Office's for William Waldegrave, which stated that 'we have reason to believe that the refusal of these export licences could force Matrix Churchill to close down. If this happened, we would lose our intelligence access to [Iraq's] procurement network' (D6.94). The official responsible for this submission (Mr Lillie) stated in his evidence that the submission had been cleared with the Secret Intelligence Service. SIS officers, however, argued that both the tone and the content of the submission was misleading: Mr C3 told the inquiry that he did not consider that 'it accurately reflects our knowledge at the time on Iraqi military procurement and production, nor of Matrix Churchill's part in it . . . I consider it to have been misleading to say that forcing Matrix Churchill to close down would lose our intelligence access . . . I consider too much weight was given, in the submission, to retaining Gutteridge' (D6.96). The Ministry of Defence submission incorporated the Foreign Office briefing. Astonishingly, it did not draw the minister's attention to the concerns which had been strongly expressed by the Defence Intelligence Staff apparently because its officials took the view that 'it was far more important to protect the intelligence source and more particularly the flow of information than it was to uphold the guidelines' (D6.103). In the view of the Scott report, the Ministry of Defence minister (Lord Trefgarne) was 'ill served' by his officials, who 'failed to put before [him] a balanced recommendation' (D6.103).

On the basis of these submissions, the ministers agreed to grant ELA 53234. One Ministry of Defence adviser, Lt. Col. Glazebrook, had described the machine tools that were to be sent to Nassr as being 'sufficient to equip a factory designed to produce 500,000 × 155 mm shells per annum'. In the event, not all of the goods had been exported by the time the licence expired. A renewal was applied for and approved in July 1990, but in August 1990 Iraq invaded Kuwait and the consequent UN embargo intervened before the remaining goods (the machining centres) could be exported (D6.106 and 246).

MARCH 1989–NOVEMBER 1989. The final set of Matrix Churchill export licence applications which need to be examined are those considered by the relevant departments in late 1989. There are three pairs of applications to be discussed here: ELAs 52039 and 0440 concerning the export of high speed lathes and machining centres for Nassr in relation to a scheme known as Project 1728 (D2.336 and D6.58); ELAs 22351 and 23006 concerning eleven high speed lathes and 24 machining centres for Nassr, involving the Chilean arms dealer Cardoen (D6.112); ELAs 27311 and 27315, concerning Nassr's so-called Central Tool Room Project (D6.115).

Again, as before, the Ministry of Defence working group recommended that these applications should be refused. So too, this time, did William Waldegrave at the Foreign Office (D6.123). In July 1989 Alan Clark and Lord Trefgarne swapped ministerial positions, the former became the Minister for Defence Procurement and the latter became the Minister for Trade. As Minister for Trade Clark had been much more supportive of British trade with Iraq than either Lord Trefgarne or William Waldegrave. He took this enthusiasm for trade with him to the Ministry of Defence, which had traditionally had slightly different concerns from those of the DTI and had accordingly been more cautious. Lord Trefgarne, on the other hand, began to change his position once he arrived at the DTI, taking to its line (in favour of trade) much more keenly than Mr Clark took to what had traditionally been the Ministry of Defence line. Thus a significant tilt towards favouring trade with Iraq developed and it became Mr Waldegrave who was to a greater extent left in the minority (D3.132–39).

In late 1989 both Mr Clark and Lord Trefgarne expressed their disagreement with Mr Waldegrave's view that the remaining Matrix Churchill applications should be refused. In this they were supported by submissions from their officials. The Scott report is very critical of these controversial submissions, primarily on the ground that they failed to take into account three pertinent intelligence reports of September 1989. The first two, from the Secret Intelligence Service, identified Project 1728 at Nassr as a 'large Iraqi missile project' (D5.25) and said that Iraq had negotiated with British-based companies for the export of 'specially manufactured components, machinery, production tools, production lines' for the production of missiles. Copies were sent to the Foreign Office and to the Defence Intelligence Staff, but not to other Ministry of Defence desks and not to the DTI. The third report, also from September 1989 and distributed in the same way concerned the Central Tool Room Plant at Nassr, identified as being for the design and manufacture of shells, cartridges and mortars, adding, however, that there were insufficient machines in the establishment to make large quantities of these armaments, apart from missiles 'where there might be sufficient resources for a production run' (D5.25).

Why did the relevant officials fail to draw this intelligence to the attention of their ministers? The submission to Alan Clark was prepared by Mr Barrett, the number two at the Defence Export Services Secretariat. The intelligence reports were not circulated to DESS, but Mr Barrett should nonetheless have known about them because he and the relevant SIS officers met regularly as members of the Working Group on Iraqi Procurement composed of government officials and intelligence officers 'set up in order to provide a venue in which to discuss Iraqi procurement ... The idea behind the meetings was to discuss all the latest snippets of information that SIS and other Whitehall departments had obtained on the Iraqi network' (C2.73). In evidence Mr Barrett accepted that he had failed to mention intelligence imparted at the Working Group meetings in his submission to Alan Clark. This was put down to a lapse in memory (D6.128). In the event of such memory failure, there was no fall-back in the system: the intelligence would simply be forgotten (had it been DESS practice to clear relevant ministerial submissions with the Defence Intelligence Staff then this error might have been corrected in time).

The submission to Lord Trefgarne prepared by Mr Steadman, head of the Export Licensing Unit at DTI and by his superior within the ministry, Mr Beston, said that 'there was no evidence that British made machine tools would be used other than for the purpose originally stated' (i.e. general metalworking or engineering). As Scott concluded, this was 'a positively misleading' statement (D6.133). He describes the DTI submissions to Lord Trefgarne as 'highly unsatisfactory', 'unbalanced' and 'seriously inaccurate' (D6.135 and 144). What was the cause of this state of affairs? The report puts it down to a fundamental lack of concern by the two officials about the possibility, even probability, that the machine tools would be used for munitions manufacture.

The effect of these inadequate submissions was compounded by a quite different problem concerning the Foreign Office brief to Mr Waldegrave, prepared by Mr Sherrington, who was new to his job at the Middle East Desk. No one referred the intelligence reports to him despite the fact that they had been circulated to the Desk. Although he was not cleared to see relevant intelligence until early in October 1989, his submission was not finished until 31 October. His submission stated that 'our friends (i.e. the Secret Intelligence Service) have . . . said that they believe that the lathes may not, at any rate initially, be used for the direct manufacture of munitions' (D6.150). As we have seen, and as Mr O, an SIS officer told the Scott inquiry, 'all the evidence' from SIS in fact showed something quite different (D6.151). How had this evident misunderstanding between the Foreign Office and SIS come about? While Mr Sherrington was at the Middle East Desk, he was frequently visited by Mr O, and quite naturally thought, therefore, that he should use him to obtain SIS clearance for his ministerial briefings which might concern SIS, but this was a misconception: there were in fact quite different channels for SIS approval. Mr O never considered that his conversations with Mr Sherrington were being taken by him as constituting formal SIS approval for his submission to Mr Waldegrave. Nobody realised that this mistake had been made (D6.149–54).

In Scott's view this mistake was an unfortunate accident for which no individual was to blame, although the report is critical of those involved for not detecting it more quickly and acting more rapidly to rectify it. When they did realise what had happened, the SIS officers involved (Mr O and Mr C3) made no written note to correct the erroneous representation in the submission to Mr Waldegrave. This failure is described as 'a serious error of judgment' (D6.154). Similarly, Mr Sherrington's line manager is criticised for having taken insufficient care in overseeing the submission (D6.157). Of David Gore-Booth, then head of the Middle East Desk and later British Ambassador to Saudi Arabia, Scott says 'I found it a matter of regret that the impatience with the inquiry evinced by Mr Gore-Booth throughout his oral evidence seemed to prevent him from facing up to the possibility that deficiencies in MED procedures or errors by MED personnel might have contributed to the lamentable fact that a misleading submission had been placed before Mr Waldegrave' (D6.259).

The unsurprising consequence of this depressing catalogue of forgetfulness, laziness, complacency and error was that on 1 November 1989 the three ministers concerned met and agreed to grant the Matrix Churchill export licence applications. In the view of the Scott report, they did so on an entirely false footing brought about by a 'failure to take into account the abundance of current and previous intelligence' (D6.169). Most of the blame for this is not attributed to ministers but to officials. Also criticised, however, is the distribution of the intelligence reports. Why, for example, were they sent to Defence Intelligence Staff but not to the Defence Export Services Secretariat? SIS claimed that this was largely because when DESS, as a Whitehall intelligence customer, explained (in September 1986) to SIS what would be relevant to them, they failed to mention that they had any connection with export licensing: their requirements appeared to be strategic intelligence on supplier countries rather than about recipients (D6.178). Scott nonetheless concluded that the poor distribution of intelligence within the Ministry of Defence was 'clearly an unacceptable state of affairs and indicate[d] shortcomings in the system operating within the Ministry of Defence' (D6.182) although adding that the DIS system of distribution has been reformed (we are not told what these reforms are).

There is one final episode of this story. An intelligence report of October 1989 noted that the Chilean arms firm, Cardoen, was under contract with various Iraqi organisations to build a large munitions factory. Two of the 1989 Matrix Churchill export licence applications were connected with Cardoen. It further stated that a 'UK firm' was to supply 24 machining centres for various types of fuses as well as 18 high speed lathes for this project. The firm was identified as Matrix Churchill at a meeting of officials on 8 December 1989. However, the ministers were not told that this development ended any plausible doubt about military use of the Matrix Churchill exports and that the basis on which they had granted the licences five weeks earlier had turned out to be unfounded; nor was consideration of the licences reopened, although in Scott's opinion it should have been (D6.188).

JULY 1990. One of the major controversies of the Scott story was whether government policy on export sales to Iran and Iraq secretly changed after the cease fire in the Iran–Iraq war in 1988.[6] By the summer of 1990, Nicholas Ridley, the Secretary of State at the DTI, had become anxious about the content and presentation of government policy in this area and expressed his concern in a letter to the Prime Minister, Margaret Thatcher, in June. Mrs Thatcher's response was to establish an ad hoc committee, chaired by the Foreign Secretary, Douglas Hurd, to examine the government's position with regard to defence sales to Iraq and to report back to her. This was to be a high-powered meeting and it brought about considerable preparatory paperwork. It was decided that the best way to proceed was for the committee to consider a paper, which was to be coordinated by the Cabinet Office with contributions by all the relevant government departments (Foreign Office, Ministry of Defence and DTI).

One part of this Iraq Note concerned the role that had been played in the export licensing process by secret intelligence and said that 'ministers have allowed the supply of some Matrix Churchill machine tools for ad hoc reasons of an intelligence nature' (D3.155). No draft of the Note was passed to the secret intelligence services, but after the final draft had been agreed, it was sent to SIS, where Mr T2, a senior officer took exception to the statement about intelligence reasons for allowing Matrix Churchill exports. He wrote in a letter to the Cabinet Office that 'our understanding of the situation is somewhat different. At an early stage of our coverage of Iraqi procurement activities in the UK, we did indeed express some reservations about a proposal to take action against Matrix Churchill ... on the grounds that it might compromise our operational interest in the matter. However, we later withdrew our reservations, and made it clear to those concerned in other departments that ... we had no objection to departments taking whatever actions they might think fit on any applications for export licences by Matrix Churchill. These discussions took place some 18 months to 2 years ago (i.e. mid-1988–early 1989)' (D3.155).

The Note was not amended in the light of these observations because by the time they had been received in the Cabinet Office Iraq had invaded Kuwait and rather different considerations had come into play. After August 1990 there was no suggestion that British policy on defence exports to Iraq should be further liberalised! The correspondence from the Secret Intelligence Service to the Cabinet Office is nonetheless interesting as it reinforces the sense that there was a considerable, substantive and long-lasting misunderstanding between SIS and government departments as to the position the former had adopted with regard to Matrix Churchill. This misunderstanding infected official submissions to ministers throughout 1989. It appears from the Iraq Note that it was to continue to infect government decision-making, even at the highest level, right up to the point of the Iraqi invasion of Kuwait.

To conclude on the export licensing process, it appears that although there was throughout the period under consideration an abundance of relevant intelligence, this was either (a) overridden for reasons of source protection, notwithstanding knowledge of intended military use, or (b) ignored, overlooked or forgotten (D8.10). This 'failure of the licensing departments to make effective use of available intelligence was compounded by the failure of ... SIS officers to draw attention to inaccurate statements about current intelligence' contained in ministerial submissions (D8.12). One final point concerns the role of the Joint Intelligence Committee. SIS's failure to amend misleading submissions was caused at least in part by the fact that they were primarily concerned with Iraqi acquisition or development of weapons of mass destruction rather than conventional weapons. The priority attached to nuclear-related intelligence was not one which SIS had invented for itself: it was merely following JIC instructions (D8.14). As regards export licensing, the JIC also bore further responsibilities for the failure of coordination which peppered this story. Despite the considerable volume of available intelligence, 'no one person was familiar with all the accumulated intelligence' (D8.11) until the Iraq Note was drawn up in July 1990. The evident lack of coordination or central monitoring of intelligence relating to British involvement in Iraqi arms procurement from 1987 onwards represents a major JIC failure.

Evaluation

We can now turn to a more general evaluation of the roles played in the government decision-making process by secret intelligence. Writing on matters of secret intelligence is always fraught with difficulty for the obvious reason that much of the material is secret. Even when former diplomats, civil servants and intelligence officers write in specialist journals, there is a persistent absence of detailed information and much of what is written has to be taken on trust. That said, the Scott report does offer glimpses into what is normally a closed off world—the view may still be clouded, but it is nonetheless a clearer picture than we are usually privileged to see. The question remains, what are we to make of the intelligence story that has been revealed? The purpose here is to identify the matters which, in the light of the Scott report, require further investigation. This is a task which academics can undertake only to a limited extent. All that can be done here is to point out the way forward.[7] Until 1995 there would perhaps have been little point in doing even this, but Britain is now blessed with at least some form of parliamentary oversight of the security and secret intelligence agencies. The Intelligence Services Act 1994 provided for the establishment of an Intelligence and Security Committee, composed of nine parliamentarians (drawn from either House) 'to examine the expenditure, administration and policy' of MI5, SIS and GCHQ. Operating within the so-called 'ring of secrecy', as all of its members have been formally notified under the Official Secrets Act, it meets (in Whitehall, not in Westminster) every week during parliamentary session. Currently chaired by Tom King MP, it has now published three reports: an introductory interim report, a special one on MI5's expanding roles in the field of organised crime and its first annual report.[8]

The committee has already made it plain that it will be concerned with some big questions. It is set to examine, among other things, overall government/intelligence structure, especially the government's assessment of intelligence. 'Our first major inquiry shall address how the agencies have adapted in general to the new situations post-Cold War and, in particular, how tasks and the priorities attached to them have altered, and whether the resources now provided are appropriate to those tasks and used in a cost effective way.' It also intends to examine 'the dissemination and uses made of the agencies' product by government customers, in particular the briefing of intelligence and security information and procedures to ministers and senior officials and the suitability of the present ministerial structures for dealing with these matters'. It is to be hoped that the lessons of the Scott report will be taken into account. So what should the committee be looking for?

There are three areas arising from the report that call for further evaluation. The first concerns the episode in January 1988 when pressure was put on government departments by MI5 and the Secret Intelligence Service not to revoke export licences (for reasons, apparently, of source protection). This raises questions about the proper constitutional relationship between ministers and intelligence agencies: who controls whom, who sets whose agenda, what happens when agendas are markedly different? The second area concerns the episodes in February 1989 and November 1989 when ministers granted export licences to Matrix Churchill despite the abundant intelligence directly connecting Matrix Churchill exports with arms production in Iraq. Questions are raised here about intelligence distribution (who gets to see what?) and about intelligence quality (what do those who get to see the intelligence actually think of it?). Why did officials who did see relevant information not pass it on to ministers? Thirdly, the overall lack of intelligence coordination (until July 1990) revealed throughout these episodes raises questions about the functioning of Britain's central intelligence machinery, namely the Joint Intelligence Committee.

MINISTERS AND INTELLIGENCE AGENCIES: THE CONSTITUTIONAL RELATIONSHIP. Quite what the proper constitutional relationship between ministers and intelligence agencies should be is unclear from both a formal, legal point of view and from a practical point of view.[9] Oddly, it seems that there can be both too much, and too little ministerial control. That there can be too much ministerial control is shown in the story broken by Cathy Massiter that MI5 were 'breaking their own rules' in their surveillance of CND in the early to mid 1980s. The role of the Ministry of Defence in using MI5 for partisan purposes has never been adequately debated.[10] That there can be too little ministerial control is illustrated in the series of events related by Peter Wright in *Spycatcher*.[11] If true, these revelations depict a security agency which had become an independent power centre, uncontrolled by ministers, and determining its own targets, priorities and mandate.

The formal legal position with regard to MI5 under the Security Service Act 1989 is that the Director General (appointed by the Secretary of State) is placed in 'control' of the operations of the Service. He or she has direct access to the Prime Minister, but the Act also provides that the Service is under the 'authority' of the Secretary of State.[12] There is a statutory duty to deliver an annual report to the Secretary of State and to the Prime Minister. This report remains secret. The same formulation was adopted in the Intelligence Services Act 1994 in respect of SIS and GCHQ.

Apart from this general framework, the legislation is almost completely silent on what relations should be between government departments and the security and secret intelligence services. The only other legislative references to ministers concern the issuing and duration of warrants. The MI5 publication, *The Security Service* (1996) states that 'the Home Secretary receives advice from the Director General on the threats to national security. He also discusses with the Director General matters of policy affecting the Service, for example, to do with resources, or legislation ... The Security Service is [however] not part of the Home Office. It is a separate entity, with a distinct statutory basis under which the Director General is personally responsible to the Secretary of State'. Thus the official sources are hardly precise and take no account of the kind of difficulties evidenced in the Scott report which Alan Clark described as 'absurd'.

According to Lustgarten and Leigh, there is some degree of formalised contact between Home Office officials and MI5. They 'talk in general terms about priorities and the operational landscape but no attempt is made to exercise day-to-day supervision, let alone control, over the Service'. There is an evident presumption of regularity. MI5 is not seen as a wild tiger needing to be caged, but as an organisation disposed to carry out its functions in a legal and honest way. Home Office officials also feel restricted by the need-to-know principle: 'our own natural curiosity might lead us further in than is necessary ... There is greater reluctance on our part to ask questions, than of the Service to answer them'. Thus they conclude, 'the relationship between the Home Office and the Security Service is a matter of trust. To an outsider it seems more akin to a religious faith than empirically based judgment'. The views of the Home Office with regard to the information that ought to be presented before ministers are also illuminating. In their view there cannot be an 'automatic duty to inform ministers of everything, given their numerous other responsibilities and the fact that many matters, seemingly vital at the time, later prove false or of exaggerated consequence. Only matters of intrinsic importance should be raised with ministers'. But what does this mean, in practice? According to Lustgarten and Leigh, what seemed to be the paramount element in this amorphous concept was the potential to embarrass the government.[13]

The connected question of relations between the Foreign Office and the Secret Intelligence Service is, as we have seen, alluded to in a number of places in the Scott report. One revealing instance concerned British relations with Jordan, normally looked upon as one of Britain's closest allies in the Middle East. During the late-1980s and early-1990s, however, there was considerable concern in the Foreign Office that it was acting as a conduit for arms sales to Iraq. The Foreign Office felt that it had to make strong representations but the matter had to be dealt with very carefully, as it was not perceived to be in Britain's interests in any way to offend that country. It appears that the Foreign Office decided that an appropriate way to proceed would be through intelligence channels and asked SIS to pass a message on to Jordan concerning its links with Iraq, apparently causing considerable anxiety within SIS which was highly reluctant to carry out this delicate policy matter. Though Iraq invaded Kuwait before the matter could be resolved, it is a rare insight into the political tensions that can arise between an intelligence agency and its parent department (E2.26).

Thus the first contribution that the Intelligence and Security Committee should make in the light of the Scott report is to investigate and to provide a thorough report on the proper constitutional relationship between government ministers and the intelligence services that manages to go beyond the mere snatches and glimpses that we have so far been allowed to see.

DISTRIBUTION, QUANTITY AND QUALITY OF INTELLIGENCE. In his evidence, William Waldegrave referred to a constant problem about the use of gathering information which is not actually used. With reference to the export licensing process, he said that those who took these decisions did not actually have the right information. While the information had 'gone into the government machinery, [it] did not come out in the right place'. Alan Clark echoed this view in his evidence to the inquiry. He complained that he had 'no personal knowledge' as a minister. He was 'a spectator'. He referred to the 'obsessional possessiveness' of the intelligence agencies. These views are apparently shared across government: according to Lord Howe, for example, one of the most difficult tasks in Whitehall is to ensure the prompt availability of intelligence 'everywhere it should have been available while at the same time ensuring that it was not available anywhere else'. It is like trying to 'design and operate a high-speed, multi-directional, leak-proof sieve'.

The problem of distribution is compounded by that of quantity. In his evidence, John Major explained that the Foreign Office alone receives in the region of 40,000 intelligence reports every year: 'They would be of varying grades. Some ... would be extremely valuable, others not so. Quite a strong filtering process is needed. It is clearly absurd that ministers should read 40,000 pieces of intelligence, but it would be filtered through the appropriate machinery and, where intelligence was thought to be relevant, validated and reliable—reliable being a key point—the officials would endeavour to put that before ministers.'

Once intelligence has been properly distributed, there remains the problem of the quality of what ministers get to see. Too frequently, it appears, they simply did not take what they saw seriously enough. David Mellor, former minister at the Home Office and at the Foreign Office, for example, stated in evidence that intelligence reports did not contain 'shattering information about who was doing what to whom

... they didn't tell you all you wanted to know about life'. Similarly, David Gore-Booth, former head of the Middle East Desk at the Foreign Office, stated that 'intelligence is a very imprecise art'. Lord Howe stated in his evidence to the inquiry that 'in my early days I was naive enough to get excited about intelligence reports. Many look at first sight to be important and interesting and significant, and then when we check them, they are not even straws in the wind. They are cornflakes in the wind.'[14]

David Gore-Booth argued that intelligence would have needed to have been 'incontrovertible' for it to have prevented exports to Iraq. This is problematic, as we know from him and from Howe that intelligence is a very imprecise art—so how could it ever be incontrovertible? Herein lies the second issue which calls for thorough review by the Intelligence and Security Committee: namely, how to make the cornflakes in the wind more effective.

CENTRAL INTELLIGENCE MACHINERY.   At the heart of the intelligence failures outlined in the Scott report lies the Joint Intelligence Committee and the British government's central intelligence machinery. The roles of this machinery have been enhanced in recent decades with the growing importance within the Cabinet Office of the Joint Intelligence Secretariat, the Intelligence Coordinator and the JIC. In 1993, as part of the government's policy towards (slightly) greater open government, the Cabinet Office published a short document entitled *Central Intelligence Machinery*, in which John Major wrote that 'it is a strength of the British system that Ministers do not receive conflicting or piecemeal intelligence assessments on situations of issues of concern. Through the JIC they are provided with assessments agreed between departments which provide an objective background to the discussion of policy'. Clearly, this system did not quite work in the Matrix Churchill case but what is the JIC supposed to do?

The JIC was established in 1936 as a joint services sub-committee reporting to the Chiefs of Staff of the armed services. During the second world war the Home Defence (Security) Executive was established to iron out duplication between the various intelligence agencies and to prevent overlap with regard to domestic surveillance. After the war this role was taken over by the JIC and the HD(S)E was abolished. In 1957 the JIC was brought within the Cabinet Office. In 1968 the post of Intelligence Coordinator was established, responsible for advising the Cabinet Secretary on the coordination of the intelligence machinery and its resources and programmes, and an assessments staff was created to prepare papers for JIC discussion.

The JIC is responsible, subject to ministerial approval, both for setting the UK's national intelligence requirements and for producing a weekly survey on intelligence, colloquially known as the Red Book. This contains assessments prepared by geographically-based groups made up of those in the relevant departments with special knowledge of the area for ministers and officials on situations of current concern.[15] Meeting weekly, it includes representatives of the Foreign Office, the Ministry of Defence, and the Treasury, as well as the heads of the three intelligence agencies (MI5, SIS and GCHQ), the Intelligence Coordinator and the Chief of Assessments Staff. Its Chairman is responsible for ensuring that its roles are adequately discharged and has a right of direct access to the Prime Minister. After the Falklands War, the chairmanship passed from the Foreign Office to the Cabinet Office but subsequently reverted. The published terms of reference for the JIC are as follows:

The Committee is charged with the following responsibilities: to give direction to, and to keep under review, the organisation and working of British intelligence activity as a whole at home and overseas in order to ensure efficiency, economy and prompt adaptation to changing requirements; to submit, at agreed intervals, for approval by ministers, statements of the requirements and priorities for intelligence gathering and other tasks to be conducted by the intelligence agencies; to coordinate, as necessary, interdepartmental plans for intelligence activity; to monitor and give early warning of the development of direct or indirect foreign threats to British interests, whether political, military or economic; on the basis of available information, to assess events and situations relating to external affairs, defence, terrorism, major international criminal activity, scientific, technical and economic matters . . .

The last major review of the JIC and the central intelligence machinery occurred in the aftermath of the Falklands War when a committee of Privy Counsellors under the chairmanship of Lord Franks was appointed to review the circumstances which led to the Argentinian invasion of the islands. Its terms of reference included the government's access to and assessment of relevant intelligence in the months immediately prior to the invasion. While the Franks report[16] was not critical of the 'reliability of the intelligence that was regularly received from a variety of sources', it was 'surprised that the events in the first three months of 1982 . . . did not prompt the Joint Intelligence Organisation to assess the situation afresh'. It continued, 'we remain doubtful about . . . aspects of the work of the Joint Intelligence Organisation . . . We do not seek to attach blame to the individuals involved [but there is a] need for a clearer understanding of the relative roles of the assessment staff, the Foreign Office and the Ministry of Defence, and for closer liaison between them.'

While in theory monitoring and assessment are matters for the JIC, in practice it appears that Defence Intelligence Staff has a considerable role to play as well. As Michael Herman (a civil servant for 35 years) has written, while its official remit focuses on defence intelligence, 'in practice DIS has always been landed with urgent non-defence analysis tasks, simply because there is no other body to take them on. The result smacks of analysis reacting to events instead of trying to anticipate them. If there was a British intelligence failure before the invasion of Kuwait it may have been because it was 'No one's job to study the parlous state of the Iraqi economy in detail and draw on the results in assessing Saddam Hussein's intentions'.[17] Herman is clearly critical of the methods of intelligence assessment employed by the JIC and DIS. Of the former, he says 'it incorporates the principle of the search for truth through the medium of the seminar', which leads to blandness, the establishment of a lowest common denominator of agreement and the search for the drafting solution which papers over the cracks and consequently softens meaning. This is all compounded by the fact that the JIC is composed of departmental interests and stitches departmental segments together rather than looking at subjects as a whole. While the Franks report felt that the JIC was 'too passive in operations to respond quickly and critically to a rapidly changing situation which demanded urgent attention', according to Herman this may have been because those concerned were too busy handling the Falklands crisis departmentally to make an adequate overall intelligence assessment.

The theme of overdepartmentalisation is echoed by Davies, who, in his recent examination of what he terms the 'producer/consumer interface', argues that the primarily departmental concerns of MI5 and the Secret Intelligence Service significantly weakens the position of the Joint Intelligence Committee.[18] In the case of SIS and GCHQ this is in large part because although their tasks are set by the JIC, their customers are individual departments, primarily the Foreign Office. Customers have requirements: indeed, SIS and GCHQ regularly receive detailed lists of these. As the 1995 report of the Intelligence and Security Committee put it, 'agencies meet regularly with customer departments to ensure that they are meeting their needs ... customers put forward proposals for new or amended requirements ... at any time'. This system predates and effectively bypasses the JIC. The idea that the intelligence agencies exist to provide intelligence for some common good thus appears to be a false assumption: in practice, they serve more diverse, and more private aims. The benefits of intelligence accrue to departments.

Whatever the true position, quite clearly the roles, composition and working practices of the JIC urgently need to be reviewed in the light of experience since the Falklands conflict and in the light of the failure, demonstrated in the Scott report, to coordinate intelligence on Iraqi arms procurement in the late 1980s.

Conclusion: towards standards in intelligence?

In the light of the Scott report three broad areas concerning intelligence and government decision-making require further investigation. The most appropriate body for this would be the Intelligence and Security Committee. One way would be to adopt the framework of 'standards in public life' as laid down by the Nolan Committee.[19] Its first report made a number of recommendations, based on seven principles of public life, which 'apply to all aspects of public life'. The Intelligence and Security Committee could, perhaps, apply these to the field of secret intelligence. They are selflessness, integrity, objectivity, accountability, openness, honesty and leadership. Two of these are especially pertinent here: accountability and openness. The Nolan Committee stated that by accountability it had in mind that 'holders of public office [should be] accountable for their decisions and actions to the public and must submit themselves to whatever scrutiny is appropriate to their office'. On openness, it stated that 'holders of public office should be as open as possible about all the decisions and actions that they take. They should give reasons for their decisions and restrict information only when the wider public interest clearly demands.' It recommended that all public bodies should draw up codes of conduct incorporating these principles of public life. If the Intelligence and Security Committee were to adopt these basic standards in the context of secret intelligence, then perhaps the intelligence failures identified in the Scott report might be avoided in the future.

1   The Supergun story and the Matrix Churchill prosecution (sections F and G of the report) also raise interesting questions concerning secret intelligence.

2   This is a reference to the Howe guidelines as they stood in 1987: guideline (iii) provided that 'we should not in future sanction new orders for any defence equipment which in our view would significantly enhance the capability of either side [i.e. Iran or Iraq] to prolong or exacerbate the conflict'.

3   See also D. Leigh, *Betrayed: The Real Story of the Matrix Churchill Trial*, (Bloomsbury, 1993), p. 102.

4   This was the meeting that was later relied on by the defendants in the Matrix Churchill trial and in respect of which Alan Clark was famously cross-examined as the trial collapsed around him (G17.29 for his evidence).

5   See R. Norton-Taylor, *Truth is a Difficult Concept: Inside the Scott Inquiry*, (4th Estate, 1995), p. 107.

6   See A. Tomkins, 'Government Information and Parliament: Misleading by Design or by Default?', *Public Law*, 1996, 472.

7   This echoes Scott's own approach. In his chapter of recommendations, he wrote 'I do not feel qualified to make recommendations as to how the systems in place in the respective agencies and departments might be improved. I propose, therefore, simply to identify the respects in which there evidently are, or were, problems' (K7.1). He identifies a number of matters already mentioned here: distribution (K7.2–4), over-reliance on memory (K7.5), the slowness of getting security clearance (K7.5), and misrepresentations of SIS views in submissions to ministers (K7.7).

8   Cm 2873 (1995), Cm 3065 (1995) and Cm 3198 (1996).

9   This problem is frequently compounded by the issue of whether the intelligence agencies (especially MI5 and SIS) prefer to cooperate, to interfere with or to ignore each other. Richard Thurlow argues that even when the security and secret intelligence services were first established in 1909 there were 'continuing tensions' and even 'rivalry between the Home and Foreign Offices', and that because of 'institutional rivalries there was little coordination or exchange of information between MI5 and SIS before 1940'. Between the two world wars, institutional rivalry, frictional hostility, ambition and pride delayed the emergence of a coordinated security service until 1931. Even then, overlapping areas of counter-espionage and counter-intelligence with SIS caused continuing organisational problems. *The Secret State: British Internal Security in the Twentieth Century*, (Blackwell, 1994), pp. 6 and 51.

10 L. Lustgarten and I. Leigh, *In From the Cold: National Security and Parliamentary Democracy*, (Clarendon Press, 1994), p. 364.

11 See K.D. Ewing and C.A. Gearty, *Freedom Under Thatcher: Civil Liberties in Modern Britain*, (Clarendon Press, 1990), pp. 152–3.

12 Security Service Act 1989, s.1(1). When the Home Affairs Select Committee invited Stella Rimmington

to appear before it, it was the Home Secretary who refused to allow her to do so and he appeared instead.

13 Lustgarten and Leigh, op. cit., pp. 427–8.

14 For preceding paragraphs see R. Norton-Taylor, *Truth is a Difficult Concept: Inside the Scott Inquiry*, (Fourth Estate, 1995), pp. 99–100, 106–7.

15 See M. Herman, 'Assessment Machinery: British and American Models', 10 *Intelligence and National Security* (Special Issue), 1995, pp. 13–33.

16 *Falkland Islands Review: Report of A Committee of Privy Counsellors* (Cmnd 8787, 1983). See W. Wallace, 'How frank was Franks?', 59 *International Affairs*, 1983, 453–8, and L. Freedman, 'Intelligence Operations in the Falklands', *Intelligence and National Security*, 1986, 309–35.

17 M. Herman, loc. cit.

18 See P. Davies, 'Organisational Politics and the Development of Britain's Intelligence Producer/Consumer Interface', *Intelligence and National Security*, 1995, 113–32.

19 See *First Report of the Committee on Standards in Public Life*, Cm 2850, 1995.

Ethics in Government

BY BARRY O'TOOLE*

IF ETHICS in government is about the application of moral standards in the course of official work, then the Scott report seems to have unveiled an enormous amount of unethical behaviour in British government over a number of years. The report appears to catalogue lying, deception, disingenuity, political self-interest, personal ambition and political and military support for repugnant foreign regimes. If it is read as such, then the report would seem to have revealed behaviour by ministers and officials which is contrary to many of the most important canons of conventional morality. However, appearances can be deceptive. Perhaps it is simply too glib to put such a gloss on the activities of ministers and officials in numerous departments over a considerable number of years and in relation to matters of public policy as complex as those concerning the sales of military equipment to warring regimes. Perhaps the above definition of ethics needs to refined so that it is not simply about the application of moral standards in the course of official work, but about the application of those standards in relation to the performance of duty.

Few would disagree that the highest duty of democratic government is to protect and promote the public interest. There would be more disagreement, however, about what the public interest is, and about how it is to be determined and by whom. Problems arise mainly from the complexity of government, the multiplicity of participants in government, and the enormous pressures brought to bear on government from hundreds, possibly thousands of sources, both from within and from outside. Problems arise, too, because not only is government complex in the ways outlined, it is not a machine: it is made up of individuals who have their own ideas about what is right and wrong, about their duty in relation to official work, and ultimately about what the public interest is. Moreover, these individuals, even at the exalted level of Secretary of State or Permanent Secretary, for example, are primarily concerned with their own relatively small aspect of public policy. Very rarely, if at all, will they be able to set themselves above the fray and take a dispassionate and disinterested view of the entire canvass of government activity. They suffer from tunnel vision, blinded to other aspects of public business by the necessity of concentrating on their own specialist activity.

* Senior Lecturer in Politics, University of Glasgow.

Given this complexity, and given the constraints on human understanding, it is perhaps more useful not just to try to think of the public interest as if it were something concrete and comprehensible, against which all actions can be judged, but also to think in terms of the public interest in different circumstances, for different departments, for different individuals and in relation to each decision. In other words, it could be argued that there is both an overall public interest, which it is the duty of government as a whole to protect and promote, and a public interest as perceived by individuals and smaller collectivities, such as government departments or agencies, which it is their duty to protect and promote. This academic convenience, however, does not answer the question, 'what is the public interest?' at whatever level; nor does it deal with the problem of how these various levels and views of the public interest can be made mutually compatible, even if there was a satisfactory definition.

Scott: *the public interest and defence equipment sales*

If nothing else, the Scott report reveals that, even if the term 'the public interest' can be set aside for the time being, different departments and different individuals had radically different views of the world in relation to the sale of arms and defence-related equipment to Iran and Iraq. The three departments primarily involved, the Department of Trade and Industry, the Foreign Office and the Ministry of Defence, though apparently working closely together in relation in particular to the issuing of export licences for the sale of such equipment, had quite different policy objectives. Moreover, the policy objectives changed over time with the changing circumstances of politics in the Middle East. This was clearly so, despite attempts by ministers and senior officials, including the promulgation of the so-called Howe guidelines, to clarify the government's policy. For example, during the Iran–Iraq war the DTI's policy objectives seem to have been quite clear: that export licences should be granted except in the most exceptional circumstances. The Foreign Office, however, had a much more complex set of policy objectives, based on its overall remit of maintaining Britain's diplomatic integrity. The nature of Middle East politics, involving not just the various factions in the Middle East itself but also the United States, the United Nations and, to some extent, European allies, meant that the Foreign Office was more circumspect, and much more willing than the DTI to consider refusing export licence applications. The Ministry of Defence was almost schizophrenic. On the one hand, it was (and is) a sponsor of British arms manufacturers; on the other hand, it had to bear in mind that the equipment whose sale it was promoting might be sold to a potential enemy. After the Iran–Iraq war, of course, the situation was quite different, and all the departments seem to have been driven by commercial considerations—that is bearing in mind the hostage crisis in Lebanon (in which Iran was heavily implicated), the Fatwah against Salman Rushdie, and the execution of Fazad Bazoft.

From these observations about the policy objectives of the three departments (and other observations made in the report), it could be argued that there were numerous interpretations of what the public interest required in relation to the sales of arms and defence-related equipment to Iran and Iraq, interpretations which changed over time. Basically, however, they can be condensed to just two: that the public interest would best be served by selling as much equipment as possible, because to do so would be good for British manufacturing industry; and that the public interest would best be served by selling as little equipment as possible, because selling more than absolutely necessary would be bad for British foreign relations and might, indeed, equip a potential enemy. Both could be legitimate views about how the public interest might best be served, but the actual effects of pursuing policies in line with these views would be incompatible. In addition, neither is a statement about what the public interest is, simply a view about how it might best be served.

The confusion alluded to here arose for a number of reasons. The first relates to the ambiguity of the overall policy of the government in relation to the Iran–Iraq war: that the British government would do nothing that might exacerbate or prolong hostilities, and that, in line with this policy, it would not issue licences for the export of lethal items to either party. It is quite clear from the report that despite this avowed policy of neutrality, and because of Iraq's greater potential as a market, Iraq was favoured by the British government. As early as 29 January 1981 the Overseas and Defence Committee of the Cabinet had decided that the phrase 'lethal items' should be 'interpreted in the narrowest possible terms', the 'obligations of neutrality as flexibly as possible', and that 'every opportunity should be taken to exploit Iraq's potentialities as a promising market for the sale of defence equipment' (D1.10). As Scott says, flexibility in the interpretation of publicly espoused criteria is a recurring theme in the report. Such flexibility allowed substantial sales to Iraq of defence-related equipment (D1.15). Thus, it would seem from the report that, at least in the first four years of the Iran–Iraq war, commercial considerations were the most important factors in deciding policy—though departments other than the DTI may well be forgiven for believing otherwise, as might politicians and members of the public. After all, the publicly declared policy was one of neutrality and of not supplying lethal weapons, however defined.

Unfortunately for the government, there was growing evidence that its favoured combatant in the war, Iraq, was using chemical weapons, and there was much public concern that it was so doing. Hence the introduction of the second reason for confusion. Richard Luce, Minister of State at the Foreign Office, commissioned a senior official to conduct a review of policy in relation to Iraq, the main consequence of which was the drawing up of the Howe guidelines, designed to help officials involved in the award of licences for the export of defence-related equipment and dual-use goods to Iran and Iraq. According to the oral evidence of Lord Howe (who, as Sir Geoffrey Howe, was Foreign Secretary at the time), they were also designed 'to provide a formula by reference to which Government policy could be publicly addressed and defended' (D1.76). However, it might reasonably be asked how this could be so, for, despite being circulated to departments in December 1984, and despite numerous questions in Parliament throughout 1985, they were not made fully public until 29 October 1985. Scott's view on this is very clear: the promulgation of the Howe guidelines reflected a change in policy; that change in policy should have been announced in Parliament quickly; and the main reasons why it was not so announced were related to political sensitivity and embarrassment (D1.82–88 and D1.157–58).

Howe, of course, had a quite different interpretation. His view was that it was not in the public interest to announce the guidelines, which in any case 'did not, on their own constitute government policy'. They were simply guidance to officials as to how to deal with individual cases (D1.80). The reason for the delay in making a full statement had been 'very real pressures exerted by the need to safeguard British foreign and commercial relations'. He expanded on this in his oral evidence: 'The existence of valuable trade contracts and the release to Iran of two Yarrow ships influenced the timing of the announcement. Even from a purely trade viewpoint, immediate disclosure of the guidelines, in particular guideline (ii), would have provoked criticism from our Middle Eastern allies and pressure to curb *all* exports to Iran. If the Government had felt obliged to give in to that pressure, that might in turn have exposed the government to claims from British exporters for substantial compensation and have damaged commercial relations with Iran. After the export of the two Yarrow ships, we had much less to lose' (D1.63).

The ships in question had been exported on 29 March and 5 April 1985, before parliamentary questions on 16 April, 24 April and 22 May. Howe's suggestion could not, therefore, 'explain why the guidelines were not announced in answer to [those] parliamentary questions'. In addition the 'very real pressures' referred to 'were as much present in October 1985, when the guidelines were announced, as in April or May, when they were not' (D1.157).

Why then, was the public announcement of the guidelines delayed? Scott found three main reasons. The first was that the government believed and 'feared' that a normal public announcement might suggest a more fundamental shift in policy than was intended (D1.88). The second was that there was a strong desire to avoid drawing attention to the continued supply to Iran of equipment promised under old contracts (the Yarrow ships referred to above) (D1.88). This might have offended the Saudis. The third was that public attention might have been drawn to the fact that defence related equipment had been going to Iraq and was to continue to do so: public opposition in this country might have been embarrassingly vociferous, particularly in view of the use by Iraq of chemical weapons, which had recently been confirmed (D1.159). In other words, it was political and administrative convenience and the attempt to avoid embarrassment to the government which were the driving forces behind the presentation of government policy. The barely disguised accusation is that the attempts to avoid embarrassment had led to answers being given to parliamentary questions in this period which did not comply with the principle that there is a duty on ministers to give Parliament as full information as possible about their policies and decisions and not to deceive or mislead Parliament and the public (D1.160–61).

Furthermore, the postponement of the announcement of the guidelines was also inconsistent with this principle. The reason for the announcement in late October 1985 was not the constitutional importance of the disclosure, but 'political advantage' (D1.163). This severe admonition continues: 'The obligation by ministers to be forthcoming with information in relation to parliamentary questions about their departments' activities lies at the heart of the important constitutional principle of ministerial accountability. The public interest in a full discharge of this obligation should be a constant heavy weight in the balance. Throughout the period that the inquiry has had to examine there is to be found a consistent undervaluing by government of the public interest that full information should be made available to Parliament. In circumstances where disclosure might be politically or administratively inconvenient, the balance struck by the government comes down, time and time again, against full disclosure. The decisions regarding the announcement of the Howe guidelines are an example of this tendency' (D1.165).

Similar criticisms are made throughout the remainder of the report. For example, in the section which deals with the application of the guidelines throughout the remainder of the Iran–Iraq war, Scott asserts that the answers to parliamentary questions were not consistent with the accepted obligation of ministers to be as forthcoming as possible. The main reason for withholding information had been the avoidance of domestic criticism which, for Scott, was an unacceptable reason (D2.432–34).

However, it is in relation to the way in which the Howe guidelines were dealt with after the 1988 cease fire between Iran and Iraq that Scott is most deeply critical of the activities of ministers and their officials. It is in the passages which deal with the revisions of the guidelines, and the relationships between the various ministers, departments and officials, that a reading of the Scott report reveals the third reason for the confusion in the deciding what the public interest was in relation to arms sales to Iran and Iraq. The third reason is that the circumstances under which policy was being considered after the cease fire were changing at an even faster rate than during the war itself. Matters were not helped, either, by the role of personalities, particularly the personalities of some of the individual ministers involved, notably Alan Clark and William Waldegrave, junior ministers at the Ministry of Defence and the Foreign Office respectively. Having noted that matters became more confused after the cessation of hostilities, it is, nonetheless, worth pointing out that commercial considerations were even more clearly established as the driving force behind public policy in relation to Iran and Iraq. After all, the cease fire opened up the prospect that both countries would wish to rebuild their civil industrial capabilities. This could provide lucrative opportunities for British firms.

The complications referred to above included the Middle East hostage crisis (in which Iran was heavily implicated) and the chemical warfare operations Iraq was using against its own Kurdish populations, which the British government strongly condemned. Later on, the execution of Fazad Bazoft in Iraq and the Iranian Fatwah against Salman Rushdie added yet more complications. At the time of the cease fire, however, the Foreign Office concluded that 'We need a policy that enables us to justify re-entering the defence equipment market in both countries while not opening us up to the charge that we are encouraging a resumption of hostilities' (D3.17). These comments appeared in a paper which was highly confidential, and which Howe refused to circulate, even to ministers. In a note dated 22 September 1988, from his private secretary to his junior minister, Waldegrave, it was made clear that Howe believed 'that it could look very cynical if so soon after expressing outrage over the Iraqi treatment of the Kurds we were to adopt a more flexible approach to arms sales' (D3.19). Scott found that Howe's objection was 'presentational'; 'he was prepared for the new approach to be adopted but not for it to become known' (D3.19). It was a policy which the government was to persist with.

In an attempt to begin the process of the normalisation of relations with both Iran and Iraq a meeting was held on 21 December 1988 between three junior ministers, Waldegrave at the Foreign Office, Clark at Defence and Lord Trefgarne at Trade and Industry, to discuss all the implications arising from the Gulf cease fire (D3.29). In particular, the meeting discussed the Howe guidelines and agreed that they should be modified, but in such a way that they preserved flexibility in the interpretation of the restraints on supplying defence equipment to Iran and Iraq. Letters subsequent to the meeting indicate that, in essence, the junior ministers agreed to the implementation of a more liberal policy, 'without a public announcement' as a 'temporary working premise' (D3.40). They also agreed a formulation suitable as an answer to any question about the policy, either from MPs or from foreign governments. Inquirers would receive the following reply: 'The guidelines on the export of defence equipment to Iran and Iraq are being kept under constant review, and are applied in the light of the cease fire and developments in the peace negotiations' (D3.42). In fact guideline (iii) was to be changed. The original wording was: 'We should not in future sanction new orders for any defence equipment which in our view would significantly enhance the capability of either side to prolong or exacerbate the conflict.' The new wording was: 'We should not in future sanction new orders for defence equipment which in our view would be of direct or significant assistance to either country in the conduct of offensive operations.'

As far as Scott was concerned, this meant that there had been a change in policy, even if it had been intended to be temporary. He further believed that although neither the Secretaries of State nor the Prime Minister had been informed, the new policy was consistent with the views of the Foreign Secretary. Moreover, it was clear that, because of the Kurdish problem and the possibility of adverse reactions in foreign capitals damaging British exports, senior ministers were against publicity (D3.65). Scott dismissed Waldegrave's view that the new formulation was 'no more than an interpretation' of the former guideline (iii).Waldegrave had argued that 'this flexibility of interpretation ... did not have to be announced in Parliament and in an extremely fluid and dangerous situation, it was inadvisable that it should be' (D3.97). In any case, after the Fatwah, ministers decided that the original guidelines should remain and applied 'restrictively' for Iran, 'liberally' for Iraq. This meant that the revised guideline (iii) was used in Iraq's case as 'an interpretative gloss on the original guidelines' (D3.122).

Scott regarded this interpretation as one which did not correspond with reality and as not capable 'of being sustained by serious argument'. He believed that the decisions made by ministers were 'in any ordinary use of language' an agreement to adopt a new and more liberal policy towards the sale of non-lethal defence equipment to Iraq by applying the revised formulation of guideline (iii) rather than the original (D3.128). Waldegrave and others had 'no duplicitous intention', but the flexibility claimed for the guidelines was itself 'of a duplicitous nature'. The removal from the scope of the original guideline (iii) of non-lethal defence equipment was not a flexible interpretation of the guidelines, but a decision that the guidelines would not be applied so as to restrict the sale of a certain class of defence equipment. To have described it as 'merely a flexible interpretation' was misleading (D3.124). Furthermore, to argue that there had been no change in policy because senior ministers had not approved of the revision to guideline (iii) was to fail to distinguish between substance and form, and was 'sophistry' (D3.125).

Having established to his own satisfaction that there had been a change of policy, Scott then argued that Parliament and the public ought to have been informed. This is made quite clear by a whole, and damning, chapter being devoted to 'Government Statements on Defence Sales Policy After the Cease Fire'. It deals with the letters sent in particular by Waldegrave at the Foreign Office to MPs whose constituents had raised questions about the government's policy, and with answers to parliamentary questions about that policy.

There was a total of 42 letters, 38 signed by Waldegrave and four by Howe. Almost all contained the following passage: 'British arms supplies both to Iran and Iraq continue to be governed by the strict application of guidelines which prevent the supply of lethal equipment or equipment which would significantly enhance the capacity of either side to resume hostilities. These guidelines are applied on a case by case basis' (D4.2). Most also contained the statement that: 'The government have not changed their policy on defence sales to Iraq or Iran' (D4.3). To Scott, these passages were 'not accurate'. Moreover, the inaccuracy ought to have been noted by Mr Waldegrave since he knew, 'first hand', the facts that rendered the 'no change in policy' statement untrue (D4.4 and 4.6). 'Taken overall', Waldegrave's letters were 'apt to mislead readers as to the true nature of the policy on export sales to Iraq', and Waldegrave was in a position to know that that was so. However, Scott accepted that Waldegrave 'did not intend his letters to be misleading and did not so regard them' (D4.12).

Answers to parliamentary questions were also heavily criticised. Scott believed that they failed to inform Parliament of the current state of government policy and that this failure was 'deliberate'. It was the inevitable consequence of the agreement between the three junior ministers that no publicity would be given to the decision to adopt a more liberal policy (D4.42). The 'overriding and determinative reason' for the failure to inform Parliament was quite simple: a fear of strong public opposition to the loosening of the restrictions on the supply of defence equipment to Iraq and a consequential fear that the pressure of public opposition might be detrimental to British trading interests (D4.42).

While Scott recognised that there have always been matters of public business in which it would be inappropriate to divulge information, he also believed that 'every decision taken by Ministers to withhold information from Parliament and from the public constitutes an avoidance, and sometimes an evasion, pro tanto of ministerial accountability' (D4.56). He continues that 'without the provision of full information, it was not possible for Parliament or the public to hold the executive to full account'. From this it follows 'that the withholding of information by an accountable minister should never be based on reasons of convenience or for the avoidance of political embarrassment and should always require special and strong justification' (D4.58, see also K8.5). The implication of much of the Scott report, but especially in relation to these parliamentary questions, is that the 'special and strong justification' necessary was not present. The reasons given by Howe for withholding information, throughout the period the inquiry examined, were not 'reasons of national security, nor did they relate to the operations of the security or intelligence services, nor were they analogous to disclosing proposed changes in interest or exchange rates. Lord Howe's reasons were, in the main, foreign relations reasons; a fear of adverse reactions from Washington or Riyadh at the prospect of a more favourable approach to exports to Iran; or a fear of adverse reactions from Iran if it were known that Iraq was being given more favourable treatment than itself. It is not ... in the least obvious that the foreign relations reasons identified by Lord Howe were sufficient to justify the repeated provision to Parliament and, via the letters to MPs, to members of the public, of information about Government policy that was by design incomplete and in certain respects misleading' (D4.60). Ministers had failed 'to comply with the standards set by paragraph 27 of the *Questions of Procedure for Ministers* and, more important, failed to discharge the obligations imposed by the constitutional principle of ministerial accountability'(D4.63). This is a damning conclusion.

Scott, the public interest and ethics in government

Taken at face value, the Scott report reveals that certain of the participants in the policy process under review behaved in ways which might be considered immoral by the standards of conventional morality. In particular, and to put it mildly, they made misleading statements to Parliament and the public about the true nature of government policy. For Scott, these were primarily designed to avoid political embarrassment and made because of political or administrative expediency. At least by implication, this was against the public interest and thus, according to the definition of ethics in government at the beginning of this article, may be seen as being unethical. For the ministers and officials involved, however, both the policies and their presentation were designed to protect and promote the public interest, and thus, again according to the definition of ethics in government referred to, may be seen in exactly the opposite light. Ministers believed that they were protecting Britain's commercial and diplomatic interests. This is clear from the report. Ministers and officials consistently argued that their actions were dictated by what they saw as the public interest. The various departments claim to have made decisions in this light, particularly in relation to the applications for licences for the export of defence-related equipment. It seems that these decisions were made almost always bearing in mind Britain's commercial interests. This meant on the whole a liberal interpretation of whatever the government's policy happened to be at the time. This was almost certainly the view of the DTI (and apparently always the view of Alan Clark, whichever department he happened to be in). The Foreign Office and Ministry of Defence were more ambivalent, though again it is clear from Scott that, on the whole, commercial considerations were paramount. This was especially so after the 1988 cease fire, when it appeared to be less a matter of defence-related sales than of the former combatants wishing to rebuild their civil industrial capacity.

Had it been as simple as this, the problems which bedevilled the government might not have been so intense. Nothing in politics is simple, however, certainly not in Middle East politics. First of all, of course, the sale of arms and defence-related equipment is always controversial, and never just a matter of commercial interest. It was all the more controversial in the case of Iraq because of that country's use of chemical weapons, both against Iran and against its own Kurdish populations. This became a long-standing cause of deep repugnance in Britain, and increasingly predisposed public opinion against the government's secretly favoured party. The position was only slightly ameliorated by the Iranian Fatwah against Rushdie, but made worse again by the Iraqi execution of Bazoft. Thus public opinion, always an important element in the calculations of politicians, was certainly not to be ignored in this context. However, it was not a force which made the government change its policy; rather, it was a force which made it hide its policy. Scott makes it quite clear that he believes that the fear of adverse reaction from the public played too important a part in the presentation of government policy. He also makes it clear that this is true of the government's sensitivities to the opinions of other actors in the Middle East, especially the Saudis and the Americans.

The complexity of Middle East politics is not the subject here. Suffice to say that commercial, political and diplomatic considerations must have been a very heavy burden on the British government throughout the period under review. Thus it is perhaps possible to argue that Scott, when making his comments about the avoidance of embarrassment and decisions being taken because of political and administrative convenience, was simply displaying political naivety. Might it not be the case that ministers found themselves in very difficult circumstances, took what they believed to be the 'right' decisions, in terms of the public interest, and believed that Parliament and the public more widely did not have a sufficiently sophisticated view of the world to be able to fully appreciate or understand what ministers were doing?

This is a charitable view. To some extent, it relies on the conception, expressed above, of the public interest as being many faceted. In other words, the ministers involved had particular ideas about the public interest, peculiar to their narrow perspective on public policy. They may genuinely have believed that it was served best in the ways outlined, including by the stifling of information. If so, they seem to have forgotten something which the non-politician Scott remembered and put quite clearly at the forefront of his report: in Britain we live in a parliamentary democracy. His report is replete with examples of ministers misleading Parliament and the public and of them consistently failing to meet the requirements of ministerial accountability. As he states quite baldly: 'A failure by ministers to meet the obligations of ministerial accountability by providing information about the activities of the departments, undermines . . . the democratic process.' (K8.3).

Conclusion

The Scott report makes it quite clear that there is a higher public interest than the particular concerns of the various departments or ministers. It is a public interest which is derived from parliamentary democracy. For democracy to work, ministers must be held accountable. For them to be held accountable they are under an obligation to disclose as full information as possible about their activities and the activities of their departments. In Scott's words: 'The public interest in a full discharge of this obligation should be a constant heavy weight in the balance'. To the extent that, again in Scott's words, 'In circumstances where disclosure might be politically and administratively inconvenient, the balance struck by the government [comes] down, time and time again, against full disclosure' (D1.165). In that case the government may be seen as being guilty of having behaved unethically.

Of course, the individual ministers and officials involved may not have believed themselves to have been unethical. Again, if they had a view of a public interest which is dependent on the circumstances in which particular decisions are taken, they may feel completely exonerated of the charge. Furthermore, it may not be difficult to be sympathetic to such a view. At a practical level, it is difficult for ministers and officials not to be blinded to the requirements of good government beyond their own relatively narrow concerns. The fact remains, however, that there is at least a prima facie case that throughout the period under review participants in the policy process, at least as far as it related to commercial and diplomatic relations with Iran, Iraq and other Middle Eastern countries, ignored or even undermined, the process by which ministers can be held to account. In so doing, they undermined the duty of government as a whole to protect and promote the overall public interest. The question must be, how can the practical business of daily decision-making or the everyday activities of government ministers and officials, and the questions of the public interest implied by them, be reconciled with the overall public interest in ensuring democratic accountability?

The promulgation of a code of ethics might provide a traditional answer to such a question. Unfortunately, unless it goes beyond the normal content of such a code, it is an inadequate answer. This is because such codes tend to be vague generalisations about the everyday work of the people they relate to. They tend not to be particularly helpful about what individuals should do in relation to specific acts or sets of circumstances. At the same time they do not adequately deal with wider questions, except in the most general ways. This is as true of the recently announced Civil Service Code as it is of the codes of most other professions. It is little more than a fairly conventional statement about what the public duty of civil servants is in relation to the their work and, in particular to their relationship with their ministers. In some ways it is merely a restatement of comments made in recent white papers and other public documents, including the now famous Armstrong memorandum, or in evidence to Parliamentary committees. It begins with the obvious: 'The constitutional and practical role of the civil service is, with integrity, honesty, impartiality and objectivity, to assist the duly constituted government'. It continues with other rather bland and inoffensive statements, such as 'Civil servants should conduct themselves with integrity, impartiality and honesty in their dealings with ministers and the public'. Furthermore, civil servants should 'conduct themselves in such a way as to deserve and retain the confidence of ministers and to be able to establish the same relationship with those whom they may be required to serve in . . . future.' The conduct of civil servants should be such that ministers . . . can be sure that . . . the civil service will conscientiously fulfil its duties and obligations to, and impartially assist, advise and carry out the policies of the duly constituted government.'

At face value, such clauses as these seem to be reasonable requirements to place on a civil servant, and no doubt they are adequate in most circumstances. They are of no help, however, in dealing with the question of the public interest raised above. The main reason is that they are primarily concerned with the loyalty civil servants should have to their ministers. What happens, for example, when there is a clash between the loyalty a civil servant owes to his or her minister and that owed to the public more widely or to Parliament or to the individual's sense of what is right. The clauses of the Civil Service Code referred to above suggest that there is only one possible answer: that the primary loyalty is to the minister. The Scott report is full of examples of exactly that happening. The consequence was that civil servants were merely aiding and abetting ministers in the misdemeanours Scott refers to. In so far as ministers are concerned, the clauses of the Code referred to seem simply to fortify the perception, revealed in the report and elsewhere, that the civil service is merely the tool by which ministerial policy is administered. It is certainly not a code of ethics for ministers and appears to be of no relevance to ministers at all in relation to their activities in relation to the public interest, except insofar as the Treasury and Civil Service Committee and the Office of Public Service say that the code must be read in conjunction with *Questions of Procedure for Ministers* and other public documents.

It is the relationship between ministers and their officials which is at the hub of the question of ethics in government as discussed in Britain. The current relationship, notwithstanding the promulgation of the Civil Service Code, is one in which officials are completely bound to their ministers. It may even be argued that the code has strengthened that bonding. The Code is therefore of no aid to civil servants in matters of the overall public interest when ministers actions undermine that public interest, as they seem to have done in relation to the events investigated by Scott. In so far as the bond between ministers and their officials did not prevent the overall public interest being undermined in the ways suggested by Scott, it is unhealthy. To that extent it needs to be re-examined. This is so particularly when it is realised that old safeguards against ministerial excesses seem no longer to be present. The so-called public service ethos has all but disappeared from public life, both amongst officials and amongst politicians. This has been encouraged by ministers determined to bring in private-sector values to the civil service through their management reforms. Self-interest has been encouraged by these reforms, particularly in relation to pay and conditions of service; and feelings of loyalty to the public service have been positively discouraged. Instead of being socialised into a world in which ideas of public duty were paramount, officials are now socialised into a world in which business practices are best, whatever the circumstances, and where personal ambition is exalted above all else. In such a world it can not be a surprise that officials will behave in ways by which personal objectives are put above all else. They will not question the actions of ministers because it is not in their interests to do so. Even where there is no consciousness of this attitude on the part of officials, that is how they behave because it is the acceptable way of behaving. In other words, they have become socialised into it.

This is the fault of ministers. They set the standards of public life. It is thus with ministers that the remedy must lie. However, judging by the contemptuous manner in which the criticisms in the Scott report were dealt with, and the even more contemptuous manner in which Parliament was treated, a manner which confirmed much of the tenor of the report, ministers seem primarily to be concerned with their own self-interest. Only when ministers are imbued with such an ethos will they really be able to perceive what is the public interest. Only then will they be able to fulfil the duty which T.H. Green felt lay upon government, to create the conditions in which morality shall be possible.

Truth-Telling and Power

BY ALAN DOIG*

IT IS SAID that in 1990, after the seizure at Teesport of parts of
Supergun and the first step in the controversy that led to the establishment of an inquiry under Scott, the Cabinet had to have the gun
explained to them to understand how the parts assembled and what
they were supposed to do. By 1996, shortly after its publication, the
Scott report made a somewhat surprising appearance in an article in the
British Medical Journal where it was described as the 'most detailed
account ever of the innermost workings of Whitehall', painting 'a
picture of an organisation permeated by secrecy and deceit and in thrall
to 'the interests of major industrial concerns'.[1] While the article was
largely about the influence of such concerns on government public
health policies, it was instructive that the Scott report should be seen
not only as reporting accurately on Whitehall morality in relation to its
areas of investigation but also reflecting a generic morality, applicable
to all activities in which government may be involved, from arms to
Iraq to bovine spongiform encephalopathy in cows.

How a government could move from a position of apparent ignorance
to one where deceit and influence were seen by others as integral
features of its policy-making raises important questions not only about
how ministers and governments conduct official business but also about
how they cope with fluctuations in circumstances and the demands of
competing interests. Scott was asked to hold a non-statutory inquiry
(although he was offered the powers of a Tribunal of Inquiry if he felt
he was being obstructed in the pursuit of the information he felt
germane to his work) into the export of defence and dual-use equipment
to Iraq from 1984 to 1990. In so doing, he was also asked to look at
the licensing procedures for export and to report on whether the
relevant officials and ministers operated 'in accordance with the policies
of Her Majesty's Government'(A2.2). Allowed unprecedented access to
relevant documentation, the Scott report casts a spotlight over a number
of important areas about the conduct of British politics by ministers
and their civil servants, in seeking to ascertain if ministers and officials
told the truth at those times when it may be expected that they would
(or should) and how far they sought to save face when they were
accused of not telling the truth?

Scott's concerns thus focused on two issues—the substantive scandal,

* Professor of Public Sector Management, Liverpool Business School, Liverpool John Moores University.

the breach of the law or the norm in relation to the conduct of ministers and officials, and the procedural scandal, where the 'original scandal will be extended and sustained by ... a cover-up, which is actually a whole series of second level actions that go well beyond the effort to keep the substantive scandal concealed'[2] Scott covered, firstly, whether the government altered, breached or in any way changed its own guidelines on exports to Iraq, thus misleading Parliament and the public in so doing. Secondly, he looked at whether or not ministers and officials concealed their conduct in relation to the operation of, and any changes to, the guidelines as well as, more generally, protecting themselves from allegations that might reflect on the reputation of the government and its conduct of public business.

The substantive scandal — did the government tell the truth about the guidelines?

In 1985 Geoffrey Howe announced the existence of guidelines, drawn up the previous year, on defence equipment exports to Iran and Iraq. They outlined the refusal to supply lethal weapons and the intention to 'scrutinise rigorously' all applications for export licences for the supply of defence equipment; the crucial clause concerned future approval for the export of equipment that would, in the government's view, significantly enhance the capability of either side to prolong or exacerbate the war (D1.154–165). That statement and the guidelines may have appeared to define government conduct and how it intended to deal with exports to the two countries. How they were arrived at and drafted, however, would suggest that they were neither definitive nor to be taken as well-thought-through. They were a response to media and politicians' criticism of the continuing arms trade with both sides — and especially to the Iraqi regime which was already being criticised for its internal repression. It was the product of careful internal Whitehall negotiation with one eye on Iraq as a source of lucrative contracts and one on on-going contracts to both Iraq and Iran for which compensation could be liable. Coded language such as 'future' and 'significant' underlined the discussions over the presentation, and the timing of the presentation, of the guidelines. Nevertheless, the announced guidelines were the only available record of government intent and, as such, must be seen as 'policy'. For Geoffrey Howe to claim later that the guidelines were neither policy nor absolute but 'an aspect of the management of the policy' (D1.81) was, as Scott suggested, 'no more than a play on words' as his report revealed that the policy of Her Majesty's Government in relation to exports to Iraq tended to be whatever Her Majesty's Government considered the most acceptable at a particular time, shaped by its perceptions of international constraints, the impact on trade and its relations overseas. Policy also tended to reflect existing patterns of activity as well as being influenced by changing circumstances and the likely parliamentary or public reaction. Formulation and implementation of what could be termed policy was thus affected by the issue of presentation as well as consequential reactions. Policy in relation to military and dual-use (those capable of producing items for both civil or military use) exports was defined by guidelines intended to inform procedures dealing with applications for exports. Because the government appeared to be balancing a number of issues — avoiding what it considered would be ill-informed criticism of the policy, protecting its public reputation, giving itself flexibility in terms of future policy as circumstances changed, as well making allowances of wider constituencies, such as the defence industry or overseas governments, other than those of Parliament and the public, it gave out little official information about the guidelines and their subsequent revision.

The lack of a clear statement by government on what was the policy on exports allowed it to argue later in defence of its conduct that the guidelines were not policy. Geoffrey Howe argued that the guidelines by themselves did not constitute government policy on defence sales to Iraq and Iran but that they 'constituted guidance to officials as to how they should deal with individual cases that came before them'. The policy was, he wrote in his submission to the inquiry, whatever 'allowed ministers to reach conclusions on the strength of their evaluation of competing British (interests)'; later in the same submission he claimed that the government's 'overall' policy was one of 'strict impartiality towards the Iran and Iraq conflict and in seeking a peaceful end to that conflict' (D1.80). While Scott accepted that the guidelines were not an exclusive exposition of government policy (acknowledging that policy might include existing treaty obligations as well as the statements of 'impartiality or of even-handedness'), he stated that the guidelines were represented as policy, and were a prime source or definitive statement of policy and to pretend that the guidelines were other than policy would be 'futile and unacceptable' (D1.82; D1.83).

The authority to issue guidelines derived from 1939 legislation under which successive British governments have had the legal power to demand specific products apply for export licences for specific countries. The drafting of the guidelines for applications for exports in the early 1980s involved lengthy interdepartmental negotiations over wording and intent which were intended to 'avoid being forced into exact definitions of what we were prepared to supply to either side' (D1.63 and D1.39). Government ministers were reluctant to publicly announce their existence, preferring a detailed confidential briefing 'for selected' parliamentarians and trusted representatives of the media (D1.63). At the same time both Ministry of Defence and HM Ambassador to Iraq were concerned that any announcement should not give the appearance of either drastic changes or radical departure from existing practice. Indeed, the government appeared to accept officials' advice to allow the guidelines to 'filter out' in order to minimise controversy. This failure to make any public official announcement allowed, said Scott, for the government later to be hoist with its own petard of secrecy. It was also clear that, from the beginning, any official stance of neutrality, impartiality and even-handedness would be affected by the value of trade to both countries ($2 billion in the early 1980s), an existing imbalance in arms sales toward Iraq (which were ten times the value of sales to Iran) and an awareness within government that controls over sales would need to be flexible from the onset to ensure the minimisation of damage to UK commercial and diplomatic interests. It was not surprising that a senior civil servant should note in 1984 that 'there is no principle here, just expediency' (D.20).

The Whitehall negotiations behind the guidelines, and the assumption that all exports were acceptable unless there was a sufficient reason for refusal, meant that, from the outset, the guidelines were open to interpretation or persuasion, not only from manufacturers but competing departmental interests within Whitehall. The Foreign Office was keen to emphasise to other governments that the UK position was a 'very restrictive' arms sales policy to both sides and argued that the application of the guidelines had to balance business interests against wider political and commercial concerns. The overall Ministry of Defence objective was to ensure an objective military assessment to avoid improving either side's capability but, inside the department, officials appeared to favour the interests of defence sales over the opinions of Defence Staff while not informing ministers of any divergence in opinion (D1.54). The DTI was primarily concerned with the importance of protecting 'our long term interests in Iran' (D1.77), while nurturing the growing value of the Iraqi market, and keen to maintain the necessary flexibility to pursue these objectives while protecting the effect of the guidelines on civil exports, including the sale of dual-use equipment, because its 'principal objectives are to maintain the best possible opportunities for trade with both countries ... so far as is compatible with the war. These objectives would be best served by maintaining the maximum possible flexibility in the guidelines' (D1.60). It also made the department somewhat wary of the need to highlight the policy ('an unwelcome development'). It was hardly surprising, said Scott, that disagreements continued throughout the period under review over the guidelines 'and the manner in which they might be applied' (D2.9).

The potential for ambiguity and interpretation was heightened by the practice of companies discussing export licence applications with DTI officials where, since the actual existence of the guidelines would not be revealed, the dissemination of relevant information was 'somewhat haphazard' and not an 'adequate substitute for a clear statement of the substance' (D1.150). While Scott could argue that the wording of the guidelines implied that, where there was doubt, export licences should be turned down, Paul Channon believed the reverse was true: 'In this respect', said Scott, 'the DTI view was at variance with the Foreign

Office view and at variance with the contents of Lord Howe's minute to the Prime Minister' (D1.94). The practice for implementing the guidelines, given the variations in views on their intent, also varied in terms of how far ministers were actually involved or how far they left the procedures to their civil servants; 'I would have thought', said one official of his minister who had approved the guidelines, 'that having done that he would have been content to delegate responsibility for working within those guidelines to officials within the Department' (D1.134). Finally, there were 'consistent endeavours on the part of officials and ministers to prevent being made public information that might lead to critical public debate about export licencing decisions' (D2.30) which included: a letter from a Defence Export Services Organisation official in 1986 advising a company that 'it is the wish of the British government that there should be no publicity about this sale'; a statement from an International Military Sales official that 'he was conscious of the need for a low profile' for training Iraqi officers and concealing their identity in the UK; a Middle East Desk official warning in 1988 that public knowledge about certain machine tools exports could terminate deliveries at once and that the firms should 'renounce publicity and lobbying for their own good'; and, in two cases, Richard Luce and Lord Trefgarne's assistant private secretary, advising UK companies not to give publicity to contracts.

While Scott himself accepted that 'from the formulation of the guidelines to the cease fire in August 1988 . . . it is fair, in my opinion, to conclude that government policy as publicly announced . . . was broadly consistent with policy as actually applied' (D2.427) he did express concern that: the DTI did not treat dual-use equipment as falling within the guidelines and thus rigorous scrutiny 'claimed by ministers' was not followed; impartiality and even-handedness were not always followed—an interdepartmental committee meeting in 1989 noted how 'we had already used differing interpretations for the two countries during the conflict' (D2.29) thus denying ministerial claims of 'strict impartiality'; machine tools which could 'significantly' enhance Iraq's defence capability were, albeit on the purported grounds of protecting an informant and the work of the intelligence services, allowed for export and thus were deemed to be inconsistent with the government policy; ministers were not forthcoming about the policy either by themselves or in replies to MPs, thus failing to satisfy an obligation to be as 'forthcoming as possible . . . except where important national interests require the information to be withheld' (D2. 434).

Scott was also concerned about how ministers sought retrospective justification for the failure to be forthcoming about the original guidelines. Thus Lord Howe claimed that the delay in announcing them was affected by certain contracts to Iran which, if the guidelines were publicly announced, might have resulted in international pressure to abort them, leading to claims for compensation and damage to long-term relations with Iran. Scott, however, noted that, once those contracts had been fulfilled, Howe still did not use the opportunities subsequently offered in Parliament to announce the guidelines. Howe was to justify his partial answers to MPs as 'part of a general process of informing Parliament ... in a manageable fashion', but Scott argued that ministerial answers did not comply with the *Questions of Procedure for Ministers* in giving 'as full information as possible about the policies, decisions, and actions of the Government...' (D1.160). Indeed, Scott was to accuse the government of consistently undervaluing the importance of the public interest in full disclosure, coming down 'time and time again' against it on the grounds of political and administrative convenience (D1.165).

The more controversial allegation investigated by Scott was whether the government did exercise the discretion that the legislation gave it, after 1988 and the ending of the conflict, to change the letter or spirit of the guidelines. It was clear within Whitehall that this happened. A note by a DTI official later reported: 'in December 1988 Ministry of Defence, DTI and Foreign Office ministers met to agree a revised but unpublished interpretation to the Iran/Iraqi guidelines which were becoming outdated'. Between the August 1988 cease fire and the August 1990 invasion of Kuwait, government policy on non-lethal defence and dual-case equipment was subject to alteration, in part because of changing external circumstances and in part because of competing Whitehall interests. With the Iraq market open again, manufacturers and the DTI were keen to take advantage, with both the UK and Iraq sending trade delegations to each other's country. That the government supported increasing sales, including defence equipment, to Iraq is clear from the participation of ministers in trade delegations to Iraq and how ministers and officials fought their departmental corners to extend Export Credit Guarantee Department cover (which provides insurance cover to UK exports to countries which commercial insurers consider to be too much of an insurable risk) to a greater proportion of defence sales (and to a greater proportion of such sales to Iraq). The failure to announce such increases was deemed by Scott to be inconsistent with the requirements of the *Questions of Procedures for Ministers* in response to parliamentary questions. He also rejected the DTI's claim that the proportion allocated to defence sales was to limit the amount of cover, rather than as a means of opening up cover. The claim was 'inconsistent with the facts' and the allocation was introduced with the 'main purpose' of opening up credit for defence-related products (D2.113). The government knew that there was a gap between announced policy and actual practice over the use of ECGD cover, with Scott dismissing the failure to disclose ECGD exposure on grounds of commercial confidentiality as a failure to inform the public about, and ensure ministerial accountability for, the use to which public funds were put. Such conduct he considered reprehensible in being concealed from

Parliament and the public at the same time as an impartial, even-handed defence sales policy was being officially expressed.

This trade, however, would still have been governed by the original guidelines unless changes were made to them. While ministers later denied the authority of junior colleagues to change the guidelines and claimed that, even if they did change them, they were only flexibly applying established policy 'geared to the new circumstances', the guidelines were changed. The process concerned a number of delayed decisions on defence-related goods, including machine tools, for Iraq. Between August 1988 and July 1990 discussions took place on the future of the UK's defence-related exports to both countries and the role of the guidelines in controlling those exports. Although a new policy was agreed at senior ministerial level in July 1990 (though its announcement and implementation were overtaken by the invasion of Kuwait in August that year) Scott was more interested in what had happened at junior level before that agreement. While he accepted that what was agreed was 'not put to senior ministers for approval' (D3.2), he was concerned about public ministerial comments on what policy was supposed to be in place, and whether those comments were consistent with the facts, as well as about the primacy of governments informing Parliament about what it was doing.

At junior minister and departmental level the initial approach was to develop 'a policy that enables us to justify re-entering the defence equipment market in both countries while not opening us to a charge that we are encouraging a resumption of hostilities' (D3.17). This may have meant initially not revising or removing the guidelines but interpreting them flexibly for the export of dual-use equipment and looking favourably on borderline cases. Given the public concern over the Iraqi treatment of the Kurds shortly after the end of the war this approach was not volunteered to Parliament and the public because, said Lord Howe, of 'the extremely emotional way such debates (on defence sales to Iraq) are conducted in public' and where 'the scope for misunderstanding is enormous' (D3.19).

A case-by-case flexibility, however, was insufficient for the junior DTI minister, Alan Clark, who felt that the opportunities for the UK defence industry were being 'constrained by "guidelines" whose original raison d'etre has now been removed' — that is, there was no longer any conflict to exacerbate or prolong — and that 'our policy on licensable exports' should be revised (D3.28). From draft papers and records of meetings involving Clark, Waldegrave (Foreign Office) and Trefgarne (Ministry of Defence), it is clear that 'revision' of the guidelines rather than a continuing 'flexible interpretation' (which in any case, Scott tartly pointed out, meant 'flexible application') was the objective. The outcome was a revised guideline: the main change was to revise the words in one clause where 'defence equipment designed to prolong or exacerbate the conflict' were changed to 'defence equipment which would be of direct and significant assistance to either country in the conduct of offensive operations in breach of the cease fire' (G5.20). This was agreed in February 1989 and its use as a framework for considering licences begun immediately.

A further dimension to the activities of the junior ministers in changing the guidelines came in April 1989 when Waldegrave confirmed to Clark an agreement for the differential application of the amended guidelines. Largely because the anticipated market would be greater, the guidelines would be more flexibly interpreted in respect of Iraq, which would be subject to the revised clause; Iran would remain subject to 'the existing guidelines strictly interpreted in the way that they were being used at the height of the conflict' (D3.90). All applications for exports to both countries, however, would continue to be 'scrutinised rigorously' under the unaltered clauses of the guidelines. Given a degree of concern about giving undue alarm to other Arab states over more arms for Iraq and about 'misleading encouragement to industry', however, it was agreed not to publish the changes. This desire to avoid publicity was the basis of ministerial insistence that the relaxed policy was achieved by an 'interpretation' of the existing rules rather than the substitution of a new guideline; Waldegrave later stated that 'flexibility in interpretation of the guidelines did not have to be announced in Parliament and in an extremely fluid and dangerous situation it was inadvisable that it should be' (D3.97).

The action of DTI, Foreign Office and Ministry of Defence officials and junior ministers in changing 'various aspects of export licensing practice and policy' were 'not put to senior ministers for approval' (D3.2). Indeed, senior ministers would later argue that their junior colleagues were simply reworking the existing guidelines to meet new circumstances and that records of discussions not only indicated that the junior ministers knew changes to the guidelines would require Secretary of State approval but that, in not doing so, they were demonstrating that they did not believe that what they were doing required any such approval. There were, according to Howe and Waldegrave later, a number of reasons for not telling senior ministers. These included a belief that the changes reflected Howe's earlier views on the need to liberalise the guidelines which he put in a letter to the Prime Minister in 1988 indicating the need to reformulate policies, maximise commercial opportunities, and 'use discretion within the ministerial guidelines' (D3.11–12). The changes were, in any case, 'minimal in substance and no more than minor adjustments to a continuing and unchanged policy'. If they were submitted upward, they were likely to get a testy response about being 'bothered with minor and relatively unimportant policy changes'.

Scott, however, was unconvinced. He argued that to claim the changes reflected interpretation rather than revision was 'so plainly inapposite as to be incapable of being sustained by serious argument'.

He described the agreement of the junior ministers that changed 'the criterion that would be applied to applications for licences of defence export equipment' as 'in any ordinary use of language, agreeing a change in policy'. To argue that such a change could only be a change if or when approved by senior ministers was 'sophistry'. He went on to criticise ministerial conduct in terms of public and parliamentary pronouncements, the jettisoning of even-handedness as part of government policy by April 1989 with the development of stricter implementation of the guidelines for Iran, but not Iraq. He quoted as an accurate summary a note by a senior civil servant that the guidelines had been changed, that, at the same time, their application had been relaxed, that the ministers made 'a conscious effort' not to announce what they had done and that, while what was done could argued as 'not misleading Parliament ... it may be represented as culpably failing to inform Parliament of significant change to the guidelines' (D3.115). He himself was emphatic that there was 'example after example ... of an apparent failure by ministers to discharge' their obligations under *Questions of Procedures for Ministers* to 'give Parliament, including its Select Committees, and the public as full information as possible about the policies, decisions and actions of the Government, and not to deceive or mislead Parliament and the public' (K8.1). Scott referred to the 1994 Report from the Treasury and Civil Service Select Committee and the 1995 Nolan Committee Report to emphasise the point that 'the failure by Ministers to meet the obligations of Ministerial accountability by providing information about the activities of their departments undermines, in my opinion, the democratic process' (K8.3). Specifically, Scott noted seven such failures: the deliberate non-disclosure to the House of the Howe guidelines on defence sales to Iran and Iraq; the failure to tell Parliament defence sales to Iraq were facilitated by ECGD credit cover; the failure to announce the changes to the guidelines 'to adopt a more liberal policy on defence sales to Iraq'; the failure to clarify the position of a businessman seconded to the Ministry of Defence attending a trade fair in Baghdad; and the refusal to authorise or facilitate two officials giving evidence to the Trade and Industry Select Committee hearings into the Supergun affair.

The procedural scandal — did government seek to save face over Supergun and Matrix Churchill?

In July 1989, Lord Trefgarne moved from being a junior minister at the Ministry of Defence to the equivalent post at the DTI with Alan Clark moving from the DTI to Ministry of Defence with the consequence that the balance of emphasis on the application of the guidelines among the three ministries — DTI, Foreign Office and Ministry of Defence — shifted. Clark at Ministry of Defence was much readier to challenge the refusal of licence applications by his staff than Trefgarne had been, but with an ally in Trefgarne as the new junior DTI minister where he was 'much more determined' to support exports (D3.133). Licensing was still driven by a wish to operate in favour of the applicant and the slow accumulation of intelligence on the military use of dual-use exports, such as machine tools, that might challenge that wish led to the 'equivalent to the Nelsonian use of the blind eye' (D8.11). At the same time, intelligence (and ministerial) concern about Iraq as a nuclear threat, as opposed to Iraq's development of its conventional military capability, as well as the availability of dual-use equipment from other Western countries, may have led to a lack of conviction on the need for restrictive policies with departments, especially the DTI and the Ministry of Defence, regarding 'the probability of an intended military use as insufficient to justify the refusal of export licences for the machine tools' (D8.15).

Some of that intelligence was reporting not only what was being exported but also, with the gradual impact of export controls on defence products by European countries, Iraq's role in establishing or buying 'front' companies abroad to purchase or produce material on its behalf.[3] Such intelligence was fed into the Whitehall information network but without any systematic attempt to evaluate the significance of the information, ensure it reached the right people or was put to the most effective use. The 1987 Intelligence Report—an important significant milestone in terms of information that could have alerted Whitehall about exports—was based on information from a senior executive employed by Matrix Churchill which had been part of TI Machine Tools Ltd with a history of making machine tools for munitions factories until it had been the subject of a management buy-out in a joint-venture funded by the Iraqis with the intention of developing the same machine capacity for the Iraqis. The intelligence report named a number of firms, including Matrix Churchill, who had signed contracts with the Iraqi government 'for the purchase of general purpose heavy machinery for the production of armaments in Iraq' (D2.265). The report was distributed to the DTI, Ministry of Defence and Foreign Office, where it failed to land on the right desk or was ignored (unsatisfactorily haphazard systems, unsatisfactory explanations, hit-or-miss systems were comments later made by the Scott report). The firms were called by DTI because such information might jeopardise their applications for export licences; indeed, Matrix Churchill was to tell the DTI official that some of their machine tools were being used for munitions, a remark that apparently was not acted upon. The company was also part of a delegation from the industries' representative organisation—the Machine Tool Trades Association (MTTA)—that met Alan Clark in January 1988 to express their concerns. Clark affirmed, or appeared to affirm, that 'he would support the companies in resisting revocation of their licences and in being allowed to complete their existing contracts' (D2.306) but (because 'I know what the machines are being used for; you know what the machines are being used for') suggested that, while European competitors were selling similar equipment, there was thus no reason to withhold licences but that they were advised that 'the intended use of the machines should be couched in such a manner as to emphasise the peaceful aspect to which they will be put'. Applications should stress the record of 'general engineering' usage of machine tools' and should be submitted as soon as possible in case 'bureaucratic interference occurred during any departmental and ministerial discussions'. The minister was 'giving us a nod and a wink', said one company director in a story about the meeting that was published in the *Sunday Times* in late 1990. (*Sunday Times*, 2 December 1990)

Another intelligence report with little initial impact was the 1989 Iraq Arms Manufacture paper by a Ministry of Defence armed forces member which identified the extent of Iraqi orders that would appear to suggest that they were 'building up an arms manufacturing capability' (D5.65). He identified the activities of Matrix Churchill, as well as foundries producing 'special steel for gun barrels', as part of the accumulation of technological know-how and machinery as part of 'a very significant enhancement' of that capability that could assist towards a resumption of the war with Iran. The report was not brought to ministers' attention—it 'simply fell into limbo'—because it was 'incomplete' ('inchoate' was the term used), because 'ministers were, in any event, well aware of the Iraqi procurement network' and because the real concern was with an indigenous industry for missile productions and nuclear production (D5.73). Thus, although information was available—much of it appearing in a 1990 Joint Intelligence Committee paper to ministers for an Overseas and Defence Cabinet committee meeting—Matrix Churchill licences were approved 'in the full knowledge of the procurement position as described in the JIC paper' (D5.83), partly because of the dual-use nature of their products and partly because ministers had been taking advice from officials who synthesised and focused reports to steer ministers' discussions.

Scott was to criticise both the quality and clarity of intelligence received by Whitehall as well as how Whitehall used the information. He was concerned that intelligence was packaged with other information and presented to ministers in such a way that, while not entirely accurate nor correctly interpreted, gave, on one occasion, the minister 'no alternative but to do' as officials recommended (D2.213). On another, officials did not provide the minister with all the information and thus the ability to make a decision to which he 'should have been party to' and which should have been his responsibility; the minister, said Scott, 'was, in my opinion, ill served on this occasion' (D6.103). Ironically the secret services were also critical of Whitehall's failure to listen to what it was being told as well as the use of their intelligence information to justify their treatment of Matrix Churchill. One of the service's officials described the handling of a visa application by an Iraqi procurement official connected to Matrix Churchill as a 'classic case of Whitehall wishing to have it both ways—preserve Matrix Churchill's trading relationship, and yet deny its military benefits to Iraq' (D5.15) and the Whitehall claim of protecting an intelligence source inside Matrix Churchill as 'exaggerated' and 'latched' onto to preserve 'the trading relationship' (D5.15). Indeed, it was Whitehall's lack of response to intelligence information that was to begin the road to Scott when an SIS official—whose first report on the manufacture of parts for Supergun in late 1989 had had the effect of 'throwing a brick into a puddle of treacle, a loud plop and nobody took any interest' with the consequence that 'the barrel became an issue with me because I was suffering a credibility problems with the people to whom I was addressing my reports' (F3.80)—went to HM Customs ('do we make complete fools of ourselves or do we not', they asked) and persuaded them to seize tubes intended for Supergun at Teesport. At the same time a meeting of Foreign Office, Ministry of Defence and DTI officials was convened to ensure 'all departments were aware "of the full details"' (F4.20), an interesting step in terms of the procedural aspect of the controversy; how far the government wanted to avoid an inquiry, or manage the information available to such an inquiry, into the circumstances surrounding the activities of Supergun (and later, Matrix Churchill) for fear of being accused of disregarding their own procedures and rules and thus of saying one thing in public but doing another behind the closed doors of Whitehall, of being accused of knowing that their procedures and rules were being circumvented but taking no action, and of being involved in denials or a cover up to protect itself against either or both of the accusations.

Asked to respond in Parliament about the seizures at Teesport, the government claimed that autumn 1989 was the first time it was aware Iraq was constructing a long-range gun and March 1990 the first time it learned 'in general terms of an Iraqi project to develop a long range gun' which involved two British firms, Walter Somers and Sheffield Forgemasters. A senior Conservative MP and former vice-chairman of the Party, Sir Hal Miller, stepped in to defend Walter Somers saying that he had known of the Iraq deals for two years (and had contacted the DTI, Ministry of Defence and a 'third agency' to alert them to the contracts). He added that the firm itself had been in contact with the DTI, acting 'with extreme propriety and in accordance with the British national interest'. Sir Nicholas Ridley, the DTI Secretary of State, repeated the claim that the government only recently had had knowledge 'in general terms' of the Supergun project and that the two firms had requested for licences for petro-chemical tubes—which were not necessary 'on the information available at that time'—and that, 'until a few days ago, my department had no knowledge that the goods were designed to form part of a gun' (F4.27). The claims were described by Miller as 'a direct lie', a challenge that the government did know of the project which appeared substantiated when the charges brought by HM Customs of breaking export control orders against Walter Somers' managing director, Peter Mitchell, and Christopher Crowley, a Space Research Corporation metallurgist and designer, were abruptly dropped in November 1990.

Scott's summary of the Supergun part of the controversy—in terms of the government not identifying what was being manufactured and licenced—was muddle, compounded by a failure to maintain records that would have allowed the connections to be made, by a failure of anyone to take responsibility for following up leads (neither Ministry of Defence nor DTI was 'inclined to take the matter up'), and by the conduct of the Secret Intelligence Service whose inquiry 'into the underlying facts was inadequate and its report pursuant to that investigation was apt to mislead, with the result that the senior officials who were directly involved were left unaware of the true facts, and were not in a position to brief Ministers adequately' (F4.80). In relation to the failure of the prosecution, Scott indicated that Counsel were clear that prior knowledge by DTI and Ministry of Defence—that it should have been obvious the tubes had no petro-chemical application—and the Attorney General's view on the 'realistic prospect of conviction' overrode HM Customs' concern that a failure to proceed in a case where there they believed there was evidence to show an evasion of export restrictions would deal a heavy blow 'to the credibility of enforcement in the area of export control' (J1.32). Nevertheless, Scott cleared ministers of prior knowledge of the Supergun case, reporting that Bull, the inventor, did not have any contact with UK or US intelligence services, that civil servants did not pass on what information they knew—warning signs were missed, 'something slipped down the crack' (F3.59), and possible clues 'simply fell into a chasm' (F2.85)—or the dissemination of information was held up by key individuals' failure to appreciate the value or importance of that information, and that Sir Hal Miller did not speak to the intelligence services in 1988 ('memory fades over time', said Scott).

It was clear that HM Customs felt very strongly about the decision, both in terms of its role—'to be seen to be determined to make sanctions effective' (J1.38)—and the potential waste of time and resources already invested in its other inquiries which included that of Matrix Churchill, begun one month before the seizure at Teesport. From the onset HM Customs were aware of possible reservations in Whitehall over the Matrix Churchill case but were prepared to continue. This prompted a prescient warning from a DTI official to one of his ministers about any public dissection of decisions on licences and possible worsening trade relations with Iraq: 'the dirty washing liable to emerge from the action proposed by HM Customs will add to the problems posed by the gun. For DTI the timing is extraordinarily embarrassing . . .' (G2.16). The embarrassment was compounded by the attention the media had been paying to the Iraqi arms trade since the seizure of the tubes at Teesport and the row with Miller. They not only uncovered the details of the UK firm Astra and its links with Supergun, and the role of Iraqi front companies based in the UK, but also other military deals with Iraq (training for Iraqi pilots, protective clothing, tests to build missiles, radar units, ammunition-making machines, rocket propellant, battle-field radios, and plant to make missile and tank parts) involving major British firms at a time when Iraq was making threats against Kuwait. These made for a series of highly-negative images for the government, and suspicions about government conduct over exports to Iraq, as the Matrix Churchill trial approached.

As HM Customs inquiries continued, so the reaction in Whitehall was not to seek to stop the prosecution but to prepare to present its previous actions the best possible light, to limit access to sensitive personnel or material and to do the minimum required, to avoid being accused of obstruction or a cover-up. Thus relevant documents, such as the November 1987 Intelligence report, were not handed to HM Customs investigators, either because the departments did not put themselves out to assist or because HM Customs were not clear in specifying what they were looking for ('a failure at all levels', said Scott). In the case of the Trade and Industry Committee inquiry, set up in April 1990 into whether or not government knew about the Supergun project for longer than Ridley had claimed and which had already suffered a set back when Hal Miller refused to attend because, he said, he was only interested in ensuring Walter Somers and its directors were not prosecuted ('I was never interested in showing up government policy'), it was denied access to a number of officials. Two were 'forbidden' to attend on ministerial instruction because they were due to be prosecution witnesses at a criminal trial and ministers refused access to two others on the grounds that they had retired.

The basis for this was the Memorandum of Guidance for officials appearing before select committees which states that officials appear on behalf of ministers; thus it is 'customary' for a Minister to select the official to appear on his or her behalf. If the committee wanted an official not nominated by the minister, the committee could still order the official's attendance; even in such cases, 'the official remains subject to Ministerial instructions as to how to answer questions'. In the case of the Trade and Industry Committee, senior civil servants believed that the two retired officials did not have access to departmental papers and thus their appearance 'would be inappropriate and unproductive'; the latters' private addresses were also withheld so as not 'to facilitate access' to them. When called before Scott, one senior civil servant said that retirement meant that, 'under the conventions that apply to the relationship between select committees and government departments', former officials were no longer responsible to Ministers and 'could not therefore give official evidence on behalf of a minister'. To give them access to papers and let them give evidence would be allowing them 'to give full evidence' about a department's actions 'without being responsible to Ministers for their evidence'. This, apparently, 'would have been inconsistent with the established conventions'. Despite further claims by senior civil servants that they were accountable for the actions of their predecessors as though they were their own, and that select committees 'are essentially in the business of calling the continuing executive to account' (F4.62), Scott thought the reasons for non-attendance unhelpful, an 'unnecessary obstacle' and 'a failure to comply fully with the obligations of accountability owed to Parliament'.

Of more concern to ministers, Whitehall and HM Customs, however, were the likely comments of a minister, Alan Clark, in respect of the Machine Tools Technology Association meeting, particularly if Clark had told the manufacturers to 'cloud the truth' and press on with lucrative Iraqi contracts. 'If there is an element of truth to this it would not be prudent for us to proceed. The political repercussions could be serious' (G5.16) noted HM Customs, criticised by Scott for not checking what Clark actually said (it obtained a copy of the minutes and were aware that it was 'open to misinterpretation') and what his audience thought he was telling them. Not unnaturally the government was also keen to know what Clark would say but Clark denied to the Prime Minister that he was advising MTTA members to conceal military use of their products. Rather, he claimed that he was suggesting downgrading the specification of machine tools so 'they could not be used for military purposes' and having the civilian use emphasised.

Whitehall, however, knew what Clark was doing. A gathering of various Permanent Secretaries and the Head of the Civil Service to discuss the *Sunday Times* article noted the 'damaging' paragraph in the internal record, the encouragement to false representation, the official 'nod and work' and the need to 'brazen beyond that'. This last phrase was something the DTI Permanent Secretary thought later 'he had not used' (G5.43) but which, Butler told Scott, 'had not necessarily been wrong, but had been ambiguous and had been misinterpreted' (G5.43). Although the chairman of HM Customs was also present at the same meeting, he did not pass on this concern. In the event it would probably have had less weight than the interview his Investigation Division officers had with Clark in July 1991, which led them to believe that any attempt by the defence to argue that government either encouraged or knew what the firm was doing had, from Clark's version of the meeting, no substance. Over 12 months later, in the *Sunday Telegraph* in August 1992, Clark was reported as saying he 'had tipped off' machine tool manufacturers on how to frame their applications to get round the guidelines because be thought the guidelines were tiresome and intrusive, because his job was to maximise exports and because the longer the war went on the better (G8.1). By telephone (he refused another interview) Clark reiterated his earlier interview with HM Customs officers, describing the newspaper claims as 'balls' and advice on how to complete license applications as 'improper' behaviour by a minister.

Clark's protestations were buttressed by steps taken to protect other material on the decision-making processes in Whitehall as a private matter, including those documents felt too sensitive—such as those related to the security services, advice to ministers, internal dealings of the Crown—and for which a Public Interest Immunity certificate would be issued to indicate their unavailability on the grounds that it would not be in the public interest to have such information in the public domain. Ministers are supposed to read the certificates and the related documents and form their own view as to their admissibility either because of the contents or the category ('class') to which they belong. Ministers are also supposed to be aware that certificated documents may still be called for by a judge for the latter to decide if the interests of justice overrode the immunity claimed by the certificate. How far these details were explained to each minister is unclear but there were divergences in interpretation; Baker wanted to bar one official's evidence; Clarke, as the succeeding Home Secretary, was happy to recommend the reverse); Garel-Jones believed he was not being asked to 'consider the merit of any particular document' while both he and Rifkind believed they had no discretion other than to sign a certificate for certain categories of documents. Heseltine was ordered to sign his (limited) certificate, but was not informed that it was open to him to agree to disclosure, by the Attorney General who himself had not 'read any of the documents that it was proposed the Certificate should protect' (G13.76). Furthermore, the Attorney General did not think it was his duty to ensure consistency as to 'what documents were included in the classes described in the certificate', while further documents were later added to those seen by two ministers without their being told and being able to give an opinion on immunity.

The contradictions over the certificates were compounded by the trial judge's ruling that some should be disclosed. Asked if they wanted to drop the prosecution rather than face disclosure, 'none of the departments regarded its PII class claims as of sufficient importance to justify an attempt to halt the prosecution rather than submit to disclosure' (G14.30), but what they contained provided the defence with material on which to examine ministerial witnesses about the guidelines and licence applications. The first into the witness box was Alan Clark who described what he said at the meeting with the Machine Tools Technologies Association as being 'economical with the actualité', explaining that he was inviting companies to highlight a peaceful use for their machine tools even though it was, at least so long as the war lasted, very unlikely they would be put to such a use. The impact of his evidence was compounded by his use of the term 'Whitehall cosmetics' to describe the need to keep the records ambiguous by avoiding the mention of any military use. It was on that revelation—that a company was being prosecuted for following what they interpreted as ministerial advice ('by implication' as Clark put it)—that the trial collapsed amid media and parliamentary uproar in November 1992.

The apparent possibility of governmental double standards and behind-the-scenes manipulation, and the inevitable calls for an inquiry, emerged from media attention devoted to the previously classified documents released to the defence during the trial. These talked of 'the falling guillotine' of a 1988 UN arms embargo on machine tool exports, of changes to the Howe guidelines in 1988, of ministers seeking to conceal evidence, of 'the dirty washing' that the Matrix Churchill trial had added to the 'problems' caused by the Supergun investigation. Dominating the headlines, however, were media suggestions that the Cabinet may have endorsed 'a secret policy change' over arms sales to Iraq. Since the current Prime Minister had been the Chancellor of the Exchequer at that time, this caused a furore over the possible complicity of current ministers in the controversy and immediately prompted John Major to set up the Scott inquiry.

While seen as a breathing space for an embattled Prime Minister, the continuing flow of documents clearly showed a Whitehall which had known that decisions on the export of dual-use machine tools was at variance with official policy, thus attracting media allegations of collusion, hypocrisy and deceit which focused on the possibility that the government may have been willing to allow Matrix Churchill executives to be jailed rather than reveal inconsistencies between policy and practice and despite the help one of them had given the secret services. The furore was kept in the public arena by a number of related events which included: the collapse of another trial for similar reasons, attempts at justification for their actions by Clark, the Attorney General and other ministers, suggestions in released classified documents that their disclosure to the Matrix Churchill lawyers faced 'strong resistance' from some ministers, allegations that the cabinet 'secretly altered' the Howe guidelines but that civil servants kept the changes secret 'in compliance with ministerial wishes', and allegations that Whitehall knew that the reasons for approving the Matrix Churchill export licences were questionable but could 'produce a convincing line if questioned in public'.

This divergence between what the media claimed government was doing and the government's insistence on honourable conduct in the face of difficult circumstances continued during the inquiry's hearings and its delayed publication. Both the government and Whitehall sought to avoid any sense that any variation between its official or public stance and its practice was deliberate or premeditated. Thus ministerial witnesses such as Ken Clarke argued that he was 'right' to sign PII certificates while William Waldegrave accepted that 'false impressions' may have been given and 'wrong decisions' taken but that these were done 'against the background of what actually, in the long term, was in the best interests for Britain'. Sir Robin Butler reported that a meeting had been held following the *Sunday Times* report on the MTTA meeting to decide what to do about Alan Clark because he had not followed 'an agreed HM Government view'. David Mellor professed that he did not see intelligence reports but argued that, in any case, these were not 'the word of God' (Alan Clark also accused the intelligence services of 'obsessional possessiveness, while Howe described their reports as 'not even straws in the wind, they are cornflakes in the wind'). Mellor thought it impossible to say whether the information would have made any difference and would have been 'astonished if there was a deliberate attempt to conceal'. The former DTI official responsible for licensing exports said he was more concerned with antiques and artworks than with defence sales because the former 'tended to involve large expensive things owned by rich and powerful people'; a colleague blamed the 'intense and unrelenting pressure of work' for errors in processing applications and the failure to alert ministers to areas of concern (including, in the case of one application, the failure to turn over a page of the relevant report).

Geoffrey Howe used his written evidence to attack the inquiry framework, in particular the failure to alert witness to lines of questioning in advance, to allow the right of representation by a lawyer and the right to cross-examination, in what appeared to be the first visible expression of the concern by ministers and Whitehall at the range and depth of the inquiry's questioning. Criticism of the inquiry continued when Sir Robin Butler complained of 'wild allegations and prejudging of issues in media reports', and Richard Luce criticised the inquiry's lack of 'any experience of international affairs or parliamentary matters' as a 'fundamental mistake'. The drafting of the report was marked by media warnings of whispering campaigns and attempts at damage limitation by the government. These increased as the report's publication was delayed and as government realised that reactions to the immediate impact of its findings were crucial. The mechanics of who would receive the report and in what order was itself the subject of intense rows and finally arranged in a way that allowed government 'to have a reaction on an informed basis'. Scott himself reacted sharply to both the 'strong representations' of government over publication and to the interviews Hurd and Howe were giving on what the latter described as the 'burning, smouldering sense of injustice' of those who could be criticised in the forthcoming report. Scott described Howe's belief in the right of representation and cross-examination as something that would have turned the hearings into 'a circus both in the Roman sense and in the Bertram Mills sense'.

Much of the media speculation centred on those most likely to be criticised in the report and how far the government would distance itself from any Scott might condemn unreservedly or criticise. The key lay in whether the report contained a 'killer phrase' that could condemn a minister or whether Scott simply offered opinions and facts without judgement or censure. The two ministers considered to be the most vulnerable were the Attorney General and Waldegrave. The latter's position was worsened by the leaking in February 1996 of the part of the draft report pertaining to him which emphasised Scott's view (as it did in the final report) that statements in letters signed by the minister in 1989 while at the Foreign Office were 'not accurate' and 'not true'; that for him to argue another statement was true was not 'remotely arguable'; and that written evidence to the inquiry claiming that a further statement was an accurate account of government policy, 'was not' (D4.1–D4.16). Conversely, Howe took the opportunity shortly before the publication of the report to launch a broad-ranging pre-publication attack on the inquiry procedures, Scott's personal approach to the inquiry ('a disposition to challenge convention, to defy precedent, to present issues in black-and-white terms has been matched by tenacious enthusiasm for his own views'), and the 'gap of non-comprehension between the solitary Scott and the real world' over the uses of constitutional confidentiality and the need to ignore the report's conclusions (*Spectator*, 27 January 1996). Howe's views were ably supported by at least one other minister: Garel-Jones not only supported his 'thoughtful and measured critique of Scott' but also condemned the activities of the media and Scott.

A more muted line was taken on the release of the report which did lack the executive summary underlining the major criticisms (the 'lack of a telling sound-bite'). Scott himself, moreover, was to accept at a press conference that, to say there was no conspiracy or no cover-up, was a fair summary of his findings. The government immediately launched an image management campaign to give the impression that it had been acquitted, an approach that was to prompt a sharp retort from Scott that 'any soundbite answer, any summary one-line answer is bound to be a distortion of what I have taken care to express in the report'. Nevertheless the launch of the report, its detail and denseness, and its ability to qualify its own criticisms (Waldegrave's conduct was accepted as not intending to mislead, nor to be seen as insincere, since he had acted as he did because 'he did not regard the agreement he had reached with his fellow ministers as having constituted a change in policy' (D4.6) gave the initial impression less of conspiracy and cover-up than of cock-up and confusion. The report also added little new significant information, or insight, than had been available in the documents disclosed at the collapse of the Matrix Churchill trial and thus gave the opposition parties and the media little new ammunition with which to attack the government or put it on the defensive in the period up to the parliamentary debate on the report. Indeed, the government response, no doubt influenced by the fact that Tory backbenchers did not feel the report an issue which appeared politically significant to their constituency parties, was to argue that the report did not represent ministers as acting with duplicitous intent. The Prime Minister immediately issued his full support for the two ministers most under threat and the Conservative Central Office issued a detailed briefing note to allow easy rebuttals of possible hostile questioning. Between publication of the report and the parliamentary debate, the Prime Minister let it be known he was considering 'very seriously' reforms to the 'shortcomings' and 'mistakes' identified in the report, while Waldegrave accepted that 'of course there were things that went wrong' but these amounted neither to conspiracy nor to deceit. Lyall argued that, while he and Scott may differ on the use of PII certificates, the report neither questioned his integrity nor suggested that he was involved in a conspiracy to send innocent men to prison.

This management of the government's image survived the critical onslaught of the broadsheets (most of which devoted several pages to the report's publication) as well as the inability of the opposition parties to formulate an effective set of charges on the basis of the report, and meant that, when the debate on the report took place at the end of February 1996, the government was less concerned with rebutting opposition criticism than with keeping its own party majority together. This it achieved by offering a number of 'reforms', including a parliamentary inquiry into ministerial accountability by the Public Service Committee; a review of the convention restricting parliamentary questions about arms sales; greater supervision of HM Customs prosecutions; a review by another parliamentary committee (Intelligence and Security Oversight) on sharing intelligence between departments; a review of the use of PII certificates; and a review of export licensing powers. Further concessions were offered during the debate to Conservative backbench critics on the government's intentions to act on PII certificates, open government and ministerial responsibilities: it achieved a majority of one.

Conclusion

To call arming the Iraqis, or the possibility of allowing Matrix Churchill directors to face the possibility of going to jail, a government conspiracy was, on the basis of the Scott report, somewhat strong; it also presupposes a degree of coherent, coordinated and ongoing decision-making within government and Whitehall that was simply not there. Scott himself was critical of the position of HM Customs as an 'independent' prosecuting authority which may be 'an important tenet of our unwritten constitution' but one which, according to Scott, failed to take account of the fact that 'Ministers may have a legitimate contribution to make to decisions as to the allocation of finite resources, whether of manpower or of money, to the investigation and prosecution of particular classes of cases' (C3.8). Furthermore Scott could find no evidence of government interference (or deliberate non-interference) in the events leading up to the Matrix Churchill trial. Indeed, given that at the outset a senior official at the DTI warned Nicholas Ridley that Iraq was 'already very huffy' about attempts to break up its arms procurement activities, and that a move against Matrix Churchill 'will only add to the problem', and given that Ridley himself then wrote to the Prime Minister in June 1990 'that he could see no prospect of any improvement in the position (in relation to trade relations with Iraq) while investigations into possible breaches of export controls continue' (G2.21), it would have been at this point, and to the government's advantage, to intervene to avoiding having a trial. Rather than criticise HM Customs, therefore, Scott (and the government) could well have pointed to the limits on interference by government of the prosecution process, particularly when in the hands of agencies which, slightly, prize their professional autonomy.[4]

On the other hand, once the trial was inevitable, it is also clear that attempts were made at damage limitation. In this context, seeking to put the best possible light on past conduct and seeking to minimise criticism of ongoing activities, Scott was highly critical of what he saw as the abuse of process and procedure to protect government activities from the disruption of parliamentary comment and the damage of public criticism. It is clear from the Scott report that the government sought a duplicitous approach to their 'policy' on arms sales, publicly asserting standards that were not being matched within Whitehall as ministers and officials interpreted and then changed the guidelines to best take advantage of changing circumstances before attempting to deny any divergence between presentation and implementation of that policy in the face of public criticism. In seeking who was responsible for this, Scott made continuous reference to the *Questions of Procedure for Ministers* which plainly states that 'each minister is responsible to Parliament for the conduct of his or her department, and for the actions carried out by the department in pursuit of government policies or in the discharge of responsibilities laid upon him or her as a minister. Ministers are accountable to Parliament, in the sense that they have a duty to explain in Parliament the exercise of their powers and duties and to give an account to Parliament of what is done by them in their capacity as ministers or by their departments. This includes the duty to give Parliament, including its select committees, and the public as full information as possible about the policies, decisions and actions of the government, and not to deceive or mislead Parliament and the public' (para. 27). Nevertheless, Scott was ambivalent about what comprised ministerial accountability and what comprised ministerial responsibility. Senior civil servants argued that the former is the unavoidable constitutional requirement but need not 'include blame accepted by a minister unless he or she has some personal responsibility or personal involvement because of the complexity of government and the inevitable need for ministerial delegation of responsibilities to and reliance on the advice of officials' (K8.15). Scott accepted the distinction so long as the information was available to allow Parliament and the public to judge the absence of involvement or where 'responsibility for what has occurred ought to be placed'. Scott's acceptance of this conditionality to ministerial responsibility does not, as his report does not generally, thus resolve the issue of why ministers did what they did, and whether they were wrong in so doing. It could be argued that the root of the matter was one of political prevarication or pragmatism where the inadequacies of the administration of the 'policy' reflected a reluctance by ministers to address decisively issues that were subject to change and to establish firm means at a senior level to address differing on-going interests over export controls which were, consequently, 'only as effective as the government of the day intends them to be' with trade the crux of the matter: 'indeed, fears about and a desire to imitate the French pragmatism regarding the export of arms and related products often seemed a central concern of government policy in this area'.[5]

The failure of political decisiveness or will led to confusion or at least to a vacuum where a tendency to determine priorities may be driven by existing departmental imperatives, aided and abetted by an ineffectual system of parliamentary accountability and a tendency for senior ministers to keep away from pragmatic decisions made by junior ministers who, just as the Machine Tool Technologies Association representatives took Clark's hints, knew what was expected of them: 'those on the inside would argue that 'realpolitik' always takes precedence over ethical considerations in international affairs. They would point to Britain's strategic interest in Gulf stability, to export earnings, employment and Britain's technological base, and to the equally two-faced behaviour of Britain's trade rivals as justification for the cover-up policy'.[6] Such practice is not new (or restricted to one party), nor is that of presenting political pragmatism in the best possible constitutional light. Where the official facade and attempts at face-saving went wrong was the unfortunate conduct of a self-righteous Alan Clark who may have been described by Howe as a 'walking definition of recklessness', 'almost at pains to provoke us' and someone who 'couldn't see an apple cart without wanting to overturn it' but who thought the guidelines so 'elastically drafted' as to make them 'fair game' for wide interpretation—and particularly to support almost any decision ministers chose to take on exports to Iraq—and who made no secret of this at crucial (and somewhat unpredictable) moments.

Such pragmatism was not one espoused by ministers in their evidence to Scott as the basis for conducting government business yet it was Waldegrave who later told the Treasury and Civil Service Committee in March 1994 that 'much of government activity is much more like playing poker than playing chess; you don't put all your cards up at one time'. Both he and the Head of the Civil Service told the Committee that on rare occasions ministers may have to mislead the House; on other occasions they may have to give 'an accurate but incomplete answer'. This may be how all governments see the business of politics and may explain why they tried to argue, as in this case, that they did indeed operate 'in accordance with the policies of HM Government' in terms of the drafting, use and amendments of the guidelines. Nevertheless, such conduct is not conduct about which the government was prepared to tell the truth, preferring to seek to save face by insisting on the integrity of their policies and their behaviour that thus embroiled them in an inquiry that revealed only too clearly the intertwining of the substantive and procedural scandals that, but for one vote, may well have led to the fall of the government.

1   *British Medical Journal*, 24 February 1996.
2   A. Markovits and M. Silverstein, 'Power and Process in Liberal Democracies', in A. Markovits and M. Silverstein (eds), *The Politics of Scandal* (Homes and Meier, 1988), p. viii.
3   J. Sweeney, *Trading With The Enemy* (Pan, 1993); K.R. Timmerman, The Death Lobby, (Bantam, 1992); Trade and Industry Committee, Second Report. *Exports to Iraq: Project Babylon and Long Range Guns*, HC 86, 1991–92.
4   See A. Doig and M. Levi, 'Delinquance Economique et Justice Penale: Le Cas du Royaume-Uni', *Deviance et Société, 1996/3, pp. 247–59*.
5   M. Phythian and W. Little, 'Administering Britain's Arms Trade', *Public Administration*, 1993, p. 266.
6   M. Phythian and W. Little, 'Parliament and Arms Sales', *Parliamentary Affairs*, 1993, p. 305.

Freedom of Information

BY PATRICK BIRKINSHAW*

'DO YOU really mean that the politicians will decide whether they want to run a political theatre ... or whether we have a participatory democracy where we can discuss and debate issues in advance. M. Connarty MP (HC 84, 1995–96). I do not see any conflict ... between a certain amount of theatre and a participating democracy.' Sir T. Burns. (Ibid.) It was inevitable that the aftermath of the Scott report would produce widespread claims that a Freedom of Information Act would have prevented the scandal taking place. Such an Act, or equivalent laws allow individuals a presumptive right of access to government—held documents generally, enforceable by judicial or tribunal order and subject to clearly defined exemptions and exclusions.[1] Freedom of information is often part of a legislative framework providing for open government, so that in the USA, for instance, laws open up the meetings of government agencies and their advisory committees to the public, as well as opening up administrative processes to public scrutiny and participation. In his report Scott himself addresses the question of export licensing in the United States and its relationship to freedom of information requirements, noting how such matters are exempt from the US legislation, though whether they are conclusively exempt may be determined by a federal court. Although certain information relating to arms export(s) was regarded as exempt, relevant information on exports to Iraq was provided to a US congressional subcommittee inquiring into defence exports to Iraq under threat of sub poena (D4.59). This included details on licensing decisions, end-users and as much 'cumulative data' as possible, information of a kind denied to Parliament.

In his evidence to the Commons Public Service Committee's investigation of ministerial accountability and responsibility, Sir Richard appears to have become a convert to the freedom of information cause (HC 313, 1995–96). Quite simply, we shall never know whether a Freedom of Information Act would have prevented the Matrix Churchill episode. By itself, it probably would not have done so. What Matrix Churchill has shown, however, is that we have precious few safeguards where high-handed elements in government seek to suppress evidence and information. If ministers wish to lie to Parliament, there is very little Parliament can do to establish what has happened—probably very little that any

* Professor of Law, University of Hull.

Parliament can do if the executive is intent on lying to it. Adequate institutional restraints are not in place to prevent similar abuses in future. The lesson of Scott for any future government may be that there should never again be such an inquiry with such sweeping powers of investigation. If John Major does not regret its appointment, his party certainly does. Nor can anyone be firm in their faith that a change of government will bring a different attitude to the holding of such inquiries in the future—it is interesting that the person widely spoken of as the next Lord Chancellor in a Labour government forcefully suggested in 1996 that the new era of an expanded judicial review, and outspoken extra judicial criticism of government by judges, should be reined in lest the judges undermine their office,[2] a prospect which the Conservative Lord Chancellor, Lord Mackay, foresaw if the European Convention on Human Rights was incorporated into British law. The opposition parties have promised constitutional reform which would bring with it freedom of information. This would be welcome, but it must be appreciated that there is a culture of secrecy in the British government which even a change of government and the introduction of freedom of information laws would still take many years to eradicate. The recommendations of the Nolan Committee reports on *Standards in Public Life* (Cm 2850 and 3270) have done much to emphasise the importance of openness in official decision-making and of giving informed reasons for decisions. It has highlighted the need for appropriate degrees of accountability for public action and for integrity, as well as directing its attention more recently to 'whistle-blowing' in the public interest.

Why is there a culture of secrecy in British government? At the root of it probably lies a sense of compliance and one's place in society which do not encourage participation in government or challenge of its decisions. An acceptance of the Crown behind the government—the tradition, conservatism and allure that the symbol still represents and the fact that it is a convenient cover for matters constitutional—does not encourage an inquisitive approach on the part of citizens/subjects. As Sir Stephen Sedley has reminded us, the Crown allows for an obscurity in so many crucial constitutional and legal practices which prevents clearer definition being given to matters of governmental duty or right.[3] This is not to say that things are perfect elsewhere but very few comparably developed democratic states allow government such complete protection against claims for information by citizens or legislatures. Nonetheless, the events revealed by Matrix Churchill were encouraged by a form of government which is closely allied to Crown prerogative and a governmental system that has not been fully constitutionalised. Or rather, perhaps, a constitution which places maximum emphasis upon senses of tradition, propriety and good form but which is notable for an absence of legal restraint and legal mechanisms to police its higher orders: in other words, the absence of a written constitution and a constitutional court.

Scott gave authoritative support for the view that in the face of an uncompromising executive, Parliament is effectively powerless. For over six years it had been misinformed and deceived. It lacked the means to verify the accuracy of the information with which it was provided. Provision of information to Parliament that is accurate and reliable is the cornerstone of accountability of ministers to Parliament, Scott declared in his evidence to the Public Service Committee. This should be supported by a Commissioner, a servant of Parliament, who would have power to inspect and rule on cases where information was held back on public interest grounds, with powers to punish for contempt in the case of non-compliance. Such a development would require legislation, given that at present all such powers are exercised by the House on report from committees. On the floor of the House—save in very rare moods of resentment—the government controls the agenda. As a safeguard Scott has recommended that the duty on ministers should be statutory and judicially enforceable. The Public Service Committee has recommended changes to reinforce the position of Parliament but not in terms which go as far as Scott's suggestions (HC 313, 1995–6 and for the government reply HC 67, 1996–7). There is no doubt that the position of Parliament needs strengthening, but this is not an argument against the provision of freedom of information laws to enable the citizen to know what government is up to and to help them participate in government where they are so minded.

On various fronts the Government is facing irresistible demands for open government and freedom of information legislation. First of all, such laws have emerged in most comparable democratic countries. Secondly, it is assuming an ever increasing European dimension particularly through the EU, but also through the influence of the Court of Human Rights of the European Convention on Human Rights. Thirdly, there is the development of the World Wide Web and the Internet which is carrying more and more governmental information, much of it chosen by government but increasingly a response to freedom of information laws, with details on their operation. Growing internal pressure and change in public opinion have also resulted in significant advances in the open government movement and reform of official secrecy laws. A statute allows access to the documents of local authorities and provides for open government there—and several other public bodies. Finally, widespread evidence, including that from the Select Committee on the Parliamentary Commissioner for Administration, suggests that a Freedom of Information Act improves decision making by ministers and civil servants and ensures informed public debate on the issues of the day. In Australia, it had resulted in 'greater public participation in policy debate' even after proposals had reached the Cabinet (HC 84, 1995–6).

Various attempts have been made to reform secrecy laws and introduce access to information laws in Britain. Secrecy laws were reformed in 1989 with the repeal of the Official Secrets Act 1911, section 2, and this was accompanied by a statute putting MI5 and its activities on to a statutory basis. In 1994, MI6 and GCHQ were similarly placed on to a statutory footing and a special parliamentary committee was established to investigate non-operational aspects of the work of the security and intelligence services.

From 1992 the government operated under a policy of greater openness and made a conscious decision to make more information available about its operations. This followed the Citizen's Charter initiative of the Prime Minister. The names of the heads of MI5 and MI6 were published along with the names of Cabinet committees and *Questions of Procedure for Ministers* — the official code of practice for ministers in office (it says a lot about excessive secrecy that such a document should have been confidential before). There followed the 1993 White Paper on *Open Government and Access to Information* (Cm 2290) which spelt out plans to provide information to individuals, originally on the same basis as MPs and parliamentary questions, a model which — possibly given the embarrassment to be caused by the impending Scott report and the misleading responses to MPs — was abandoned by the time of the Code of Practice on Open Government which took effect from April 1994. A further development was the transfer of Mr Waldegrave from his position as minister with responsibility for open government under the Citizen's Charter initiative to the Ministry of Agriculture, Fisheries and Food — again no doubt with an eye on impending publication and criticism in the report. The White Paper also promised a complete revision of practice on publication of public records, as well as a revision of all statutory prohibitions on disclosing information, most of which provided some form of criminal punishment and which made repeal of section 2 of the Official Secrets Act less relevant in terms of encouraging openness. Progress on this review had been very slow. Further undertakings were given to provide a right of access to personal information about themselves to individuals and a right of access to information concerning health and safety. These two undertakings were to be given statutory support, but more than three years after the publication of the White Paper no such statutes have graced the statute book, although in the case of personal information an EU Directive has to be implemented by 1998 and contains many features of a privacy protection law.

The Code on Openness

The 1994 Code on open government is a truly remarkable document. It is an administrative code and not a legal provision; it therefore creates no legal rights or duties which are enforceable through the courts, although the possibility of legal challenge by way of judicial review may be present (e.g. for a breach of legitimate expectation). It does not give access to documents but to information which is filleted by officials, and this is subject to exemptions which take up four and a half pages of the nine-page code; the information to which access will be given covers one page. Exemptions cover 15 items where release would cause or risk serious harm or damage to e.g. defence and security, internal discussion and advice, law enforcement and legal proceedings, effective management of the economy and public services, commercial confidences. Personal privacy is protected against unwarranted invasions. In some cases no harm need be proved. Immigration and nationality information was effectively excluded and other exclusions relate to the operation of the Parliamentary Commissioner for Administration Act. Disclosure of information which would breach parliamentary privilege may also be withheld.

The Code on access said information of the following kind would be published automatically (subject to exemptions) by departments and agencies under the jurisdiction of the Parliamentary Ombudsman and the Northern Ireland Ombudsman: the facts and analysis of facts considered by government to be relevant and important in framing major policies, materials concerning departments' 'dealings with the public' (i.e. rules and regulations and internal guidance affecting the public; reasons for decisions, and information on public services'. The following information would be released by departments covered by the Code upon request and subject to exemptions: 'information relating to their policies, actions and decisions and other matters related to their areas of responsibility'.

No enforcement mechanism was provided by way of courts or tribunals. However, the Ombudsman has expressed the view that the onus is on the bodies covered by the Code to justify their refusal and not on applicants to justify their request. The government relied upon the Ombudsman who would simply investigate complaints against bodies alleged to have breached the Code and the undertaking given by government to provide information. He cannot enforce the Code but negotiates a settlement which is invariably accepted. In the case of reluctance, the matter may be referred to the Select Committee on the Parliamentary Commissioner (no information complaints have yet been so referred). The Committee has taken evidence on the operation of the Code and has made a series of forceful recommendations. Before examining these, something may be said about the extra-statutory or extra-code concessions which the Ombudsman seems to have extracted from the government and on the evidence of the impact of the Code on one department, the Treasury. It should be noted that the Code does not allow access to information held by central government as such, but to information held by bodies covered by the Parliamentary Ombudsman's statute. Most ministries and all executive agencies are covered and a large number of non-departmental bodies are also included, but some (e.g. the Cabinet Office, the PM's private office and the Bank of England) are not. Many functions of government are not within the

Ombudsman's jurisdiction and access to information complaints on these cannot be the subject of investigations. Ministers may also place an embargo on the Ombudsman handing over information to third parties. An assurance has nevertheless been given by the Prime Minister that 'the Ombudsman has it in his hands to hand information over' (HC 88, 1995–96), and this has been taken to imply an extra-statutory concession not to interfere with this (comforting, perhaps, but not law).

The Ombudsman has been vigilant to point out—and here he has drawn on undertakings in the Code—that even where an exemption has been claimed by a relevant body on the ground that disclosure will cause harm, he nonetheless has a discretionary power to overrule that body's refusal to hand over information where he believes it is in the greater good for information to be disclosed. The government remains committed to the application of this test 'where appropriate'. He has persuaded departments to hand over documents and not just information in response to requests. On the whole the Ombudsman has assumed a combative role and, apart from a couple of cases, his investigations have not been resisted. He had to desist in his investigation into a complaint concerning personal files held by MI5. When the Home Office claimed that the Parliamentary Commissioner Act 1967 barred his investigation on the ground of 'national security', he did manage to extract an undertaking that he would have access to such documents where they were relevant for a complaint investigation but he was not entitled to investigate operational matters of MI5. Complaints, however, have been very few, as have requests under the Code.[4] In spite of numerous and notorious cases involving the Child Support Agency, only four requests had been made for information under the Code to that agency. Publicity for the Code seemed abysmally low and in evidence before the select committee it was stated that only £100,000 was set aside for that purpose, that the Department of the Environment had spent only £170 and that the Revenue Adjudicator had not seen the publication for 'front-line staff' *The Ombudsman in Your Files*. It does appear somewhat desultory.

The response of different departments and agencies to the Code was mixed. After a year some had not provided necessary statistics. Like other departments, the Treasury had produced its own guidance on the Code, which it undertook to disclose to the select committee. The Treasury had, however, provided interesting evidence of the impact of the Code on its practices in relation to release of information, following a complaint about delay in responding to a request from a member of the public for a report about financial malpractice in the civil service, as well as the Ombudsman's interest in the delay in the publication of a Treasury report on *Maladministration and Remedies* which followed a critical investigation and report by the select committee on that subject.

According to the Permanent Secretary at the Treasury, 'The culture change, I think, is to get people into a frame of mind where you start thinking about [disclosure] at an earlier point, not waiting until you are challenged about the document that you have prepared for a different purpose. I think we will see gradually that this will become second nature to people' (HC 84, 1995–96, Q.357). But his evidence may also give support to those who argue that freedom of information will produce anodyne documents which do not reveal the real decision-making process. The department has, however, pioneered some valuable practices including the publication of the minutes of the monthly meetings between the Chancellor and the Governor of the Bank of England. Much of its material is placed on the Internet and in 1995 it dealt with 55,000 requests for information 'in the first two to three hours' after the budget. The following from the Permanent Secretary on greater openness in policy formulation offers a positive view of the longer term effects of the Code: 'The way I see this going is to disclose more of the background debate options and arguments about issues when a decision has been made. What at this stage I cannot see is that the process of the method of decisions being reached in a debate, the ping-pong that takes place in terms of the debate reaching a decision, should be readily disclosed. Once having reached a decision there is a lot to be said for setting out the other options that were discussed and what the advantages and disadvantages were.'

Many commentators are in agreement that the Code is a big advance on previous practice, and a code has also been produced for the NHS, to be policed by the Health Service Commissioner. Local authorities have produced their own codes, non-acceptance and non-compliance with which may well amount to maladministration. This is a withdrawal from the commitment in the 1993 White Paper for a code produced by central government to be policed by the Local Government Ombudsman. But the Code on access is not a freedom of information statute and this has been promised as one of the first measures that an incoming Labour government would enact. It would be a part of wider constitutional reform. The Labour proposals would qualify some of the exemptions, allow a defence of public interest disclosure, extend the range of documents to which access would be allowed (including personal records) and provide for challenge to refusals before a tribunal which would have power to enforce its decisions. Proposals also include repeal of the Official Secrets Act 1989 and provision of a public interest defence to prosecutions where information was leaked contrary to a legal prohibition but in the public interest.

The Select Committee on the Parliamentary Commissioner has conducted its own review of the Code and has found it to be 'a valuable and important contribution to more open government'. It made significant recommendations for reform, including the introduction of a statute on access to information and a right of access to documents as well as to information. It believed that each body covered by the Code should produce guidance on procedures, including internal appeals or higher review in the case of initial refusal to disclose, and charges. It did not recommend the establishment of an enforcement agency, either courts or tribunals, apart from the Ombudsman, so in effect there would be no 'enforcement' in the strict sense, but it would keep the position under review. In the internal advice exemption there should be a clear separation between factual analysis and research on the one hand, which should be disclosed, and 'sensitive policy advice' on the other. The exemption covering 'unreliable information' should be removed: one may ask whether it is unreliable because of a faulty factual basis which the government ought to have known about and whether this should not be publicly available. The guidance, the committee recommended, should include a section on the need to consider the possible release of internal discussion after the relevant decision has been taken. It also recommended greater expenditure on publicity and monitoring of the operation of the code. A thorough revision of the jurisdiction of the Ombudsman was recommended and if any evidence of non-compliance was forthcoming the question of enforcement powers would be reviewed.

The government have replied to the committee but have held in reserve, possibly for a later reply to the Public Service Committee, responses to various important recommendations. These include the question of access to Cabinet papers, the question of whether the harm test applies to 'internal discussion' concerning such papers, whether there should be access to documents and not information, whether there should be a Freedom of Information Act, the desirability of a clear separation of factual analysis and research from sensitive policy advice, and release of more internal discussion after decisions have been taken. It did accept that fees should not be used to make a profit and commercial requesters would not be charged a different rate from private citizens unless departments wished to charge for 'services reflecting the commercial value of certain information'. It accepted many of the committee's recommendations which did not impact on ministerial responsibility (and see HC 75, 1996–7).

The committee and the Conservative government clearly wish to maintain the position of Parliament as the body to which ministers are responsible, and providing enforcement powers to other bodies will, it is assumed, undermine this position. Giving the Code a statutory basis would make a profound difference, sending out a message that the government is serious in its access to information policies. Would a Labour government press ahead with its proposed reforms? Major differences between the committee and the Labour position include a judicial form of enforcement and a public interest defence against disclosure of official secrets. This last point ties in with a 'whistle-blowers' charter. Other factors which are not addressed include the absence of legal provisions which consciously seek to open up the meetings of governmental bodies.

In terms of open government it is clear that the new regulatory regimes which have been spawned by privatisation programmes have been accompanied by serious legitimisation crises because of a lack of openness in the manner in which they have operated. This has been a criticism by consumers and by the regulated industries. OFTEL has responded by engaging in more open meetings with interest groups to assist in policy discussions. Looking around more widely, it is clear that the vast gamut of advisory committees that advise government departments are not subject to provisions such as those to be found in the Federal Advisory Committee Act of the USA which allows not only public attendance at their meetings but also provides safeguards to prevent packing of membership by interest groups.

Public interest defence and whistle-blower's charter

The law currently provides little support for conscientious employees who leak information to the media or others about the wrongdoings of their employers from a public interest motive. A public interest defence may apply under the law of confidentiality, but it is far from certain that there would be rights against unlawful dismissal provided there is compliance with other formalities. Civil servants are expected to ventilate grievances through official channels, although Nolan in his first report urged the government to extend such protection. In a range of circumstances, conventions, but more usually the law, allow a variety of officials or individuals to disclose information of wrongdoing to those in an official or semi-official capacity. Again it was revealed in Nolan's investigation that the departmental Accounting Officer was to be allowed to report misgivings about expenditure to the Comptroller and Auditor General and the Public Accounts Committee in a wider range of circumstances. But generally, the employee is poorly if not disastrously placed after disclosure. Who will employ a sneak?

The European dimension

An increasingly important part of the freedom of information debate has been the European dimension. First, because of a growing awareness of the alienation of EU citizens from the institutions of the Union. Secondly, because of the lack of information provided in a timely fashion by ministers, the Council and the Commission on EU affairs to national parliaments. This EU dimension naturally enough had no place in Scott's report, but it will assume a growing domestic significance on the debate surrounding openness, transparency and the EU and must be assessed in a paper addressing future prospects and developments.

In December 1993 and February 1994 the Council and Commission respectively made decisions on public access to documents.[5] These followed the Declaration on the Right of Access to Information in the Maastricht Treaty and various Council and Commission statements. The Decisions set out the time limits for responses, fees and details for reading documents. The Decisions are operative as from the 1 January 1994 for the Council and 15 February 1994 for the Commission and a joint code was published in December 1993.[6] This states that steps shall be taken to implement these principles by 1 January 1994—there was some slippage in the case of the Commission but nothing turns on the discrepancy. Relevant departments of the General Secretariat of the Council shall endeavour to find a 'fair solution' where applications relate to 'very large documents' (sic) meaning voluminous files.

Applications must be sent in writing to the Council (Secretary General) for Council documents or relevant Commission Department, HQ or Commission Offices in Member States or Delegations in non-Member States. Applications, which must be made in a sufficiently precise manner, should contain information which allows the requested document(s) to be identified and further details may be requested from the applicant. The right is conferred on the 'public'; it is not restricted to citizens of the European Union .

The 1993 code allows access to 'documents'—and is not restricted to information as in the case of the British code on access to information. This term covers any medium containing existing data held by the Council or Commission. The Council is to have regard to its rules of procedure, particularly Article 22, which states that detailed arrangements shall be adopted on access 'disclosure of which is without serious or prejudicial consequences'. The Decision does not say to whom or for what. Although the Council's deliberations are covered by 'the obligation of professional secrecy' this is subject to Article 7(5) which allows for the publication of the record of votes in certain circumstances.

Most of the meetings of the Council are closed to the public, although a limited number are transmitted by audio-visual means.[7]

The code stipulates that 'Where the document held by an institution (i.e. Council or Commission) was written by a natural or legal person, a Member State, another Community institution or body of any other national or international body, the application must be sent direct to the author.' Presumably the latter make the decision. What if they adopt, as some states do, a persistent practice of refusal? How could these decisions be enforced? Would Article 5 of the Treaty of Rome be of use to applicants? This provides that Member States must take all appropriate measures to ensure the fulfilment of Treaty obligations. Or would the decisions be directly enforceable through the domestic courts of Member States in the case of documents originating from a Member State? The preamble to the decision of the Council says the provisions are applicable to any document held by the Council: 'excluding documents written by a person, body or institution outside the Council'. Could one obtain documents from the national systems where they were 'written'?

Communications between the British government and international bodies, and information entrusted in confidence to other states or international organisations are protected areas under the Official Secrets Act 1989. In the case of the British Parliamentary Ombudsman his governing statute prevents him investigating a complaint relating to 'Action taken in matters certified by a Secretary of State or other Minister of the Crown to affect relations or dealings between the Government of the UK and any other Government or any international organisation of States or Governments'. A difference of opinion has arisen between the Council and Sweden—and other Member States— concerning Council documents and their liberal disclosure by the Swedish authorities, a disclosure that was far more liberal than the Council's.[8] The British Parliamentary Ombudsman has already investigated some information complaints which have an EC dimension.

Restrictions may be placed on the commercial exploitation of released documents. Relevant departments have to inform applicants within one month whether the application has been approved or whether they advise rejection. Unsuccessful applicants are advised that they are given one month to seek a 'confirmatory application' i.e. an internal review of that decision. Where the request is made, institutions are given a further month from its submission to make their decision. Where the outcome is a denial of access, that decision must be given to the applicant in writing 'as soon as possible' and must state the grounds of the decision and the opportunities for redress—judicial or ombudsman.

The EU Ombudsman had by April 1996 received several complaints concerning lack of transparency and one concerning a refusal by the Council (No. 110) to disclose minutes of its meetings (see below). The EU Ombudsman was appointed in July 1995 to investigate complaints against Community institutions excluding the courts. This latter case proved inadmissible because judicial proceedings had commenced but the other cases were admissible. To date there were no recorded findings of maladministration in information complaints. When the EU Ombudsman was being established, the Council was minded to refuse access to classified documents from Member States in the possession of the Council or Commission. The powers of the Ombudsman now to investigate and obtain documents are quite considerable and Community institutions have to facilitate access to files and furnish him with what he wants (OJ L 113/15, 4 May 1994, Article 3(2) and (3)). Those institutions also have to give access to documents originating in a Member State although there are provisos covering secret information. The governing rules of the EU Ombudsman require Member States to provide him with information upon request unless protected by secrecy. This request is made via the Permanent Representatives of the Member States to the European Communities. States may provide secret information on the basis that it is not divulged to others. This corresponds with Article 5 of the Treaty of Rome and could presumably be enforced by the Commission where pressure by the European Parliament was unproductive.

The decisions and code are silent about access to personal information by the data subjects although nothing would appear to indicate it was not covered by the code subject to exemptions. The Directive from the Council and Parliament of 1995 (OJEC L 281/31, 23 November 1995) will apply to personal data held electronically and manually and will necessitate amendment to our domestic law on data protection. It does not apply to community institutions.

Exemptions

There are exemptions to access. These include mandatory exemptions where disclosure could undermine the protection of the public interest including public security, monetary stability, court proceedings, inspections and investigations; the protection of the individual and privacy; the protection of industrial and commercial secrecy; the Community's financial interests; the protection of confidentiality as requested by the natural or legal persons or Member State legislature that supplied the information. The Commission, however, has provided guidance on communications and 'open dialogue' with special interest groups in which it states that classification of information as confidential or secret by secondary sources will be respected. The interest groups will effectively be the sole judges of 'confidentiality' of their own information (COM (93) 258).

Access may be refused in order to protect the institution's interest in the confidentiality of its proceedings. This would imply a discretionary exemption (see below). The Code was to be implemented by 1 January 1994 and is to be reviewed by January 1996. As of May 1996, the review had not taken place, but an 'update' is soon to be published which will introduce minor changes. According to information from the Commission, it appeared that the internal review behind the update will not be published.

The code has already been the subject of litigation before the lower European Union court, the Court of First Instance.[9] The *Carvel* case involved an English reporter who sought access to Council documents including preparatory reports, the attendance and voting records and/or the minutes of specified meetings of the Council of Ministers for Justice and for Agriculture. He relied upon the code and Council decision. The Council originally released certain documents, which it subsequently claimed were released as the consequence of an administrative error. It refused access to other documents because they related to matters of deliberation in the Council and were covered by the confidentiality provisions in the Decision under Article 4(2) and the Code. They would also breach the confidentiality provisions of its own Rules of Procedure. The applicants brought an application in the Court of First Instance seeking an annulment of the Council's decision on the basis that it amounted to a blanket refusal to release information and that the Council had not exercised its discretion and balanced all relevant considerations in making its judgment. The Danish and Dutch governments testified that no such considerations or balancing had taken place before the decision to refuse access. It was clear from the terms of the 1993 decision that the Council must balance the interests of the applicants and their own interests in confidentiality of proceedings before making the decision and this had not been done. The reason why confidentiality was required included the fact that members of the Council wish to feel free to move away from their nationally mandated positions to reach agreement with other members: 'compromise and negotiation [are] vital to the adoption of Community legislation'. This process would be jeopardised if parties were mindful that their positions could be made public. An attempt to get the Court of First Instance to order production to it of a report by the Council's Legal Service on the widespread use of Statements by national representatives to gain special exemptions from EC legislation failed (*The Economist*, 16 September 1995).

The court found for the applicant in so far as the discretion had not been exercised observing that the exercise of discretion under Article 5(1) cannot defeat rights under the decision on access. The court declined to make any wider ruling on access rights to Council documents. Subsequently, on 2 October 1995, the Council adopted a code of practice on Public Access to the Minutes and Statements in the Minutes of the Council Acting as Legislator (PRES/95/271, 2 October 1995). While this code seeks to give greater access to statements and the minutes, it is still subject to a large amount of discretion.

The limited range of the code

There would appear to be problems concerning the precise application of the 1993 code, as bodies other than the Council and Commission would not appear to be covered. What, for instance, is the position of the European Council, the Political Committee under the second pillar and the Common Foreign and Security Policy secretariat,[10] the coordinating committee under the third pillar, the Social Affairs Committee, the Committee of the Regions and other bodies established under the 1992 Maastricht Treaty? A large catalogue of bodies does not appear to be covered by the code and decisions. In the Spring of 1996, the EU Ombudsman launched an investigation on his own initiative into the access to information practices of Community bodies not covered by the code, e.g. the European Investment Bank, European Monetary Institute and the committees listed above. The results should make interesting reading.

The European Parliament is not covered by the code on access. It is developing its powers in the Treaty and is using informal powers to make it more like a traditional legislative assembly with powers of oversight and supervision over the executive and to give it a greater role in exacting accountability from the Commission and Council. These include the creation of the EU Ombudsman, questioning newly appointed Commissioners, a right of petition to the European Parliament by EU citizens and a right to appoint committees of inquiry to investigate alleged maladministration and illegality in the implementation of Community law. It also has rights to be consulted and ask questions about the second and third pillars of the EU.

Parliamentary review of EC policy and legislation

From the point of view of national parliaments of Member States there has been considerable disquiet expressed over the inability of parliaments to examine their ministers on the basis of sufficient information and with sufficient time before the proposals go to the Council from the Commission. And in the UK there has been considerable hostility to the extension of Qualified Majority Voting and away from unanimous votes in the Council on legislative proposals. The *Carvel* litigation exposed the 'off the record' deals done between ministers in the Council so as not only to defeat the mandate of a national parliament but also to produce de facto concessions the legality of which must be questionable. From a British perspective, this is seen as undermining the position of the Westminster Parliament. In Britain both Houses have select committees to scrutinise Community measures and policies. The House of Commons has a Committee covering European Legislation and the House of Lords a Committee on the European Communities. The remit of the Lords Committee is wider and it may examine intergovernmental pillars although it has found information under title V—the Common Foreign and Security Policy—exiguous. The Commons Committee is not formerly allowed to address the merits of legislative proposals, but it does ask questions which indirectly address the merits of proposals. The Declaration on the role of national parliaments in the Maastricht Treaty (No. 13) has been treated as a dead letter by all concerned and Declaration 14 on the Conference of National Parliaments has been a waste of time—at least in the eyes of the House of Commons Foreign Affairs Committee (HC 642-I, 1992–93).

The real problem facing national legislatures and the European Parliament is how the right balance is struck between their respective roles in supervising the EU legislative and executive processes.[11]

There is a widespread criticism of a lack of timely and complete information from the Commission and Council to national parliaments on legislative proposals and also a shortfall of information on the second and third pillars. The House of Commons Home and Foreign Affairs committees do receive filleted information on these pillars as does the House of Lords committee; the Commons European legislation committee does not. Serious thought must be given to the incorporation in a revised Treaty of duties upon the Council and Commission to provide information as a legal duty to national parliaments on the legislative programme and on the second and third pillars in the case of the Council and its related bodies.

Conclusion

Openness and freedom of information legislation are becoming European affairs and not simply domestic ones. They should become global. Scott's report focused our attention on Parliament's right to be informed to facilitate accountable government. His subsequent statements have said almost as much about a Freedom of Information Act. These two rights should not be seen as mutually exclusive — the latter undermining the former as has frequently been suggested by British governments. The two are complementary: the one involving an effective legislature, the other an informed and involved citizenry better able to understand and participate in government decision-making. If the EU is to be accepted as fully legitimate in Britain, these developments are as crucial for the EU and its institutions and their relationship to national institutions as they are for our domestic institutions.

In Britain the 1994 Code on access should be elevated to statutory form and should set a minimum standard of openness not a maximum. The recommendations of the Select Committee on the Parliamentary Commissioner for Administration should be implemented, though my preference would be for an enforcement mechanism above the Ombudsman. Departments should publish all disclosures of information under the code which previously would not have been published, a serious commitment to publish the provisions and use the Internet should be forthcoming. There must be a legislative framework for open government and public meetings. A law of sorts exists for local government and a variety of other public bodies. Greater consistency in principle is now required. I have set out the arguments why a whistle-blower's charter is required.

On the EU front Treaty revisions are needed to allow a right of access by national parliaments to Commission and Council information and to that of their various satellite bodies. There should also be a Treaty right to documents for individuals though the right may not be coextensive with that of Parliament or more appropriately its committees. What is suitable for a parliamentary committee in closed session may not be suitable for a citizen. But the right in both cases should be no more restrictive than is absolutely necessary.

To repeat, would the introducing of a Freedom of Information Act and open government have prevented Matrix Churchill from occurring? Probably not. But it would have made the task of concealment that much more difficult. And in a culture of openness it would have made the ultimate revelation that more damning.

1   P. Birkinshaw, *Freedom of Information*, (2nd edn. Butterworths, 1996).
2   Lord Irvine of Lairg 'Judges and Decision-Makers: The Theory and Practice of *Wednesbury* Review', *Public Law*, 1996, 59.

3 Sir Stephen Sedley 'The Sound of Silence: Constitutional Law without a Constitution', *Law Quarterly Review,* 1994, 270.

4 Seventy-two complaints by the end of 1995. In 1995 there were 1353 'code requests' to departments and agencies with 114 refusals: *1995 Report on the Code of Practice on Access to Government Information.*

5 Commission Decision 93/730/EC, OJ L 340/41 (31 December 1993) and Council Decision 93/731/EC, OJ L 340/43. A Communication from the Commission listed those European and other countries where rights of access to government information generally existed and not just rights to personal information: OJ 1993, C 156, p. 5.

6 OJ L 1993 340/41.

7 Since February 1993, 28 meetings of the Council, including those on general affairs were opened up, OJEC, C 79/22, 18 March 1996.

8 This involved Council papers relating to Europol and the very different responses to requests from Swedish reporters by the Swedish government and the EU Council.

9 *Carvel v EU Council* [1996] All ER (EC) 53. See OJEC C 213/22 on publication of votes in relation to Council Directives.

10 See *A Partnership of Nations*, Cm 3181 (1996) p. 30 on government suggestion involving these bodies and intergovernmental proposals concerning defence under the Western European Union.

11 See P. Birkinshaw and D. Ashiagbor, *Common Market Law Review*, 1996, 499, and W. van Gerven, 'Toward a Coherent Constitutional System within the European Union', *European Public Law*, 1996, 81, and the Commons European Legislation Committee *Role of National Parliaments in the European Union*, HC 51, xxvii, 1995–96.

Judges as Trouble-Shooters

BY BRIAN THOMPSON

THE preceding chapters have taken us through various aspects of government illuminated by the Scott report. In this concluding one, we look at the lessons which may be learnt from the inquiry on the subject of using judges to investigate politically sensitive issues.

Why judicial inquiries?

Ministers and their advisers are more likely to make the political assessment that an event is so important as to merit the appointment of a judge to conduct an investigation if it involves serious injury. This encompasses major accidents arising from all modes of transport (including maritime pollution incidents in which wildlife and the physical environment are affected, e.g. the Braer, off the Shetlands), public (dis)order (e.g. Brixton riots, the Dunblane shootings), or incidents in which a political, or especially a governmental, 'life' or reputation is threatened (e.g. Profumo, the Crown Agents). The definition of governmental not only includes ministers and their officials, but also other areas of what one may loosely term the public sector. In common with more core governmental activities, there must be public concern about these other public sector actions. Thus, for example, the action of the Cleveland Social Services authority in placing into care a large number of children who had been identified by hospital paediatricians as having suffered sexual abuse, led to complaints by the families which were taken up by the local MP. His campaigning played a part in the government's decision to instigate an inquiry by the judge, Dame Elizabeth Butler-Sloss.

The craft of a judge sitting in a civil trial involves the writing of a judgment in which the relevant facts are recounted, the legal issues are identified, the law is interpreted and applied with a statement of the reasons which led to the decision. In both the criminal and civil law the process is adversarial, with the judge, for the main part, relying upon the opposing parties to present their own arguments and to probe those of their opponent. The judge is left to decide which arguments are the stronger. So far as fact finding is concerned, where there is a material difference between the parties' versions, the test to be applied is the balance of probabilities. In a criminal trial the jury are the judges of fact and the burden of proof applied here is that of beyond a reasonable doubt.

Inquiries, however, are not given to judges simply because of the fit between their professional skills and the technical requirements of the tasks. Lawyers could be, and are, entrusted with various types of inquiry, e.g. the Clapham rail accident, investigations under the Companies Acts. Judges are appointed because they bring to such inquiries the symbolic qualities of independence and impartiality. They confer legitimacy by showing that the matter is being taken seriously and that it has been taken out of the political arena. Of course, even if it were true to say that judges are apolitical, the decision to commission them is intensely and inevitably political. The general perception is that the judges, who are independent of government and impartial in their courts, carry this with them when moved to other tasks. Perhaps one may say that the judges offer transferable symbolism in addition to transferable skills.

Scott examined

Judges then can be expected to be able to marshal facts and arguments, from which they can draw conclusions and present this in a readable judgment or report. A common criticism of Scott's report is that it is not reader-friendly. This charge seems to have been based on its length and absence of a summary. The report is long because Scott carefully recounted the history of the events he was asked to investigate. The style is not difficult and there is a liberal use of headings and sub-headings which should guide most readers. In a soundbite culture the absence of a brief presentation of the issues is apparently a drawback.

Another point which was made was that Scott did not come to any conclusions. Such a view is palpably false. It might, however, be based on the critical assessments Scott made of two ministers, Waldegrave and Lyell and on the fact that they survived the critique indicated that it was not sufficiently serious or clear. To put it another way, the report did not contain any killer quotes. If we take first Scott's treatment of Waldegrave over the modification of the Howe guidelines, it is worth reproducing the relevant passage in full. 'Mr Waldegrave knew, first hand, the facts that, in my opinion, rendered the "no change in policy" statement untrue. I accept that, when he signed these letters, he did not regard the agreement he had reached with other ministers as having constituted a change in policy towards Iraq. In his evidence to the inquiry, he strenuously and consistently asserted his belief, in the face of a volume of, to my mind, overwhelming evidence to the contrary, that policy on defence sales had, indeed, remained unchanged. I did not receive the impression of any insincerity on his part in giving me the evidence he did. But it is clear, in my opinion, that policy on defence sales to Iraq did not remain unchanged' (D4.6). This is surely a clear criticism but it would seem that the government's news management operation was successful. It got its message out before others had a chance to read the original. Scott's words were therefore read in the light of the governmental spin, and so the sting was drawn.

Scott's criticism of Waldegrave had in a draft version, been leaked. This may have built up the expectation of the final version, so the fact that Scott found Waldegrave to be sincere diminished the finding that an objective view would lead one to conclude that the policy had changed. Why did Scott include his assessment that Waldegrave was sincere in his protestations made to the inquiry? Perhaps it was because it was regarded as being fair to him given that criticism of him had been leaked. More likely, it is that Waldegrave's view was part of the evidence and so had to be presented. A reading of the paragraph made without knowing the government's gloss would be far less charitable to Waldegrave.

Turning to the other ministerial survivor of Scott's censure, the Attorney General, he evaded the criticism of his responsibility for the failure to honour an undertaking given Heseltine to ensure that the trial judge was informed, through prosecuting counsel, of his reservations about the Public Interest Immunity certificate he had signed. This was achieved by responding, instead, to Scott's finding of fault with his interpretation of the current law on PII, where he could point to other judicial opinion which supported him.

Sir Nicholas had suggested in his evidence to Scott that he was constitutionally but not personally responsible. This passage from the report records and refutes the Attorney General's defence: 'I accept the general statement of practice made by the Attorney General in these passages from his evidence. And I accept the genuineness of his belief that he was personally as opposed to constitutionally blameless for the inadequacy of the instructions sent to Mr Moses. But I do not accept that he was not personally at fault. The issues that had been raised by Mr Heseltine's stand on the PII certificate did not fall into the category of the mundane, routine run of the mill issues that could properly be left to be dealt with by officials at the Treasury Solicitor's department without the Attorney General's supervision. Mr Heseltine had taken his stand, not as a result of any legal analysis which he was not equipped to make, but as a result of an apprehension that justice might not be done if the documents were withheld from the defendants. Such an apprehension on the part of a senior minister, charged, as is the government as a whole, with the taking of decisions regarding the maintenance of national security and the promotion of the national interest, raised very serious issues, constitutional and legal, as to the role of PII certificates in criminal cases. If the responsible minister does not regard the withholding of the documents from the defence as being in the public interest, what is the function of the PII certificate that he has, so it is said, a duty to sign? Is it proper for counsel to inform the judge that the minister believes that the documents should be disclosed to the defence? What is the position if another minister believes that his department's documents, not distinguishable in character, should not be disclosed to the defence? These are difficult questions. The answers are not obvious either in principle or on authority. I would not have expected Mr Heseltine, a non-lawyer, to have articulated them. But I would have expected the Attorney General to have done so. I would have expected him to recognise that important constitutional and legal issues were raised by Mr Heseltine's stand and to have ensured that Mr Moses, whose responsibility was to place the issues fairly before the court, was adequately instructed so that he could discharge that responsibility. So far as the preparation of Mr Moses' brief and the instructions to Mr Moses were concerned, there was in my opinion, an absence of the personal involvement by the Attorney General that Mr Heseltine's stance and its implications had made necessary' (G13.125). Presumably the complaint against this passage is that it is too long. Yet surely one can be in no doubt of Scott's views that the Sir Nicholas was at fault.

Larded throughout the report Scott makes judgements and assigns responsibility and blame: on the inadequacy of the manner in which the 1990 regularising statute was dealt with allowing export control orders to be made without any parliamentary supervision (C1.108–11); on failures in the assessment and distribution of intelligence (e.g. D2.287); on various aspects of the investigation and preparation of the prosecution of Matrix Churchill (G18.12). Scott does indict people but he does it carefully after considering arguments for and against.

Lessons of the report

The report was published during a tense period in the relationship between the judiciary and the executive. Some of this has been detailed by Diana Woodhouse.[1] Briefly, the executive has had a bad time in the courts, losing several cases of judicial review. The Home Secretary has been the minister most frequently found to have acted unlawfully, e.g. in relation to decisions on sentencing and asylum/deportation. In addition to defeats in the domestic courts, the government has also lost in the European Court of Human Rights and the Court of Justice of the European Communities. The Home Secretary might be forgiven for thinking that he was particularly under fire from judges as his proposals for the reform of sentencing have been subjected to strong criticism by Lord Taylor and his successor as Lord Chief Justice, Lord Bingham. Some sections of the press have responded to the government's reverses by criticising the judges, and either through malice or ignorance, misrepresenting their position and accusing them of almost being an alternative government.[2] Scott, as we have seen, was criticised by Lord Howe for his procedure and his decision not to have a specialist assessor, which prompted him to defend his decisions. Scott gave the usual press conference on the publication of his report but then disappeared to Ireland for some fox-hunting. He had recorded some television programmes which were broadcast just before publication. Clearly there was interest in the report and its author. Subsequently, he went round the country giving lectures, usually at universities, where he developed his views on PII, freedom of information and ministerial accountability.[3] This was somewhat unusual. Judges have given lectures at university law schools but this flurry of activity gave the impression of not only a lecture tour, but also a campaign to promote his views. One of the first things that Lord Mackay did upon his appointment as Lord Chancellor was to relax the Kilmuir rules and leave individual judges to decide for themselves whether they would take opportunities to talk with the media. By commissioning Scott the government thrust him into the public eye; Lord Howe and others kept him there by attacking him and he responded with his lectures.

So Scott appeared to be another cannon in the judicial artillery participating in their bombardment of the government. Does this context tell us anything about the use of the judiciary as trouble-shooters? Does the resort to judges in sensitive political circumstances, which seeks to use their legitimising function, run the risk of diminishing this asset? Is there a danger that the judges' reputation for impartiality will be tarnished when they operate as political trouble-shooters, so that when they return to their courts they will not be regarded as unbiased?

The danger of an adverse public perception of the judiciary is perhaps more likely to arise in the field of criminal justice in general, and particularly over sentencing. The Home Secretary and his opposition shadow may well have caught the public mood, reflecting it in their proposals to increase the punitive elements of the system, whereas the judiciary appear to be softer on crime. There is a structural issue here: how can we ensure that the judiciary as a relevant professional group can contribute to the policy debate but not impair their role to implement the law? It would be retrograde and undemocratic to allow the judiciary's views to be expressed in confidence, but perhaps news conferences following on after party conferences are too confrontational, too overtly political. Of course this may be a result of the Home Secretary's personal style and that the Lord Chief Justices have felt that they have had no alternative to the very public and political presentation of their views. A change in personnel might reduce what appears to be a relationship tinged with antipathy.

I would argue that there are other factors which will lead to the judges deciding cases which have an inherently political character. This derives from a process which might be called constitution creep. Gradually the judges are acquiring jobs which are clearly those of constitutional courts in other countries. The development of the law relating to European Union is such that the House of Lords has held that it could strike down legislation as being incompatible with our obligations under European law. If the European Convention on Human Rights were to be incorporated into British law this would mean that our courts would be entitled to strike down legislation which infringed those rights. In the first situation the increase in judicial power derives from Parliament as it enacted the European Communities Act 1972, and in the second a statute would be required to allow the judges to take into account the European Convention on Human Rights. So the European dimension to our constitutional arrangements is gradually eroding the traditional doctrine of parliamentary sovereignty which held that the ultimate source of law was Parliament and that its statutes prevailed over all other legal norms.

If a Scottish Parliament is established, then the UK takes on a more federal character and the Law Lords would presumably be given the jurisdiction to rule on conflicts between the legislatures in Westminster and Edinburgh over their respective powers. Such disputes are political and there is great potential for disappointment with, and anger at, the judges and their decisions.

In these circumstances I think that we would have to take the separation of powers much more seriously.[4] What is the justification for permitting the members of the final court of appeal to be members of one of the chambers of the legislature? We may then want to consider how the judges can retain legitimacy if they will be striking down legislation, and this may mean some sort of judicial appointments commission. I think it unlikely that we would move towards Senate confirmation hearings, although I see nothing wrong with the candidates for the most senior judicial appointments being put through their paces by a Commons select committee.

Now it could be that the current stage in the relationship between the judiciary and the executive is a transitory one and that hostilities will cease, or at least diminish. If it is the case that the period of activism in the field of judicial review is related to a perception by the judges that Parliament is not performing its scrutinising role adequately, then this might change if Parliament reasserted itself. There is a feeling in some quarters that we are moving to a kind of judicial supremacism, and the writings of some judges, it is felt, hint at the idea of fundamental law which is superior to Parliament. Lord Irvine, the Shadow Lord Chancellor, has fired a warning shot reasserting the traditional doctrine of the sovereignty of Parliament.[5]

If the supposition is correct that the relationship between the judiciary and the other two branches of government will continue to be tense, what does this mean for any future inquiries into political scandals conducted by judges? Well, it is likely that they will continue because of the need for a person who can generate confidence that there will not be a cover-up. Politicians are simply not trusted to be able to do this sort of work themselves. Yet the outcome is absolutely dependent upon them. Whilst it is the government which initiates, draws up the terms of reference and makes the initial response, it is Parliament which will dispose. If MPs wish it, there will be casualties. If you have a body of mixed membership, like the Nolan Committee, with a majority of outsiders, a few politicians and a judge chairing it, it is not clear that its report will be likely to be acceptable both to the public and to Parliament. Certainly, it is clear that for many MPs it was the public reaction to the Nolan report that ensured it was not rejected out of hand.

A properly resourced judicial inquiry, with cooperation, can get to the bottom of things, but the judge does have to exercise some caution. If culprits are found, then, as appeared to be the position with Scott, the judge can not be the direct political assassin. The role is that of the provider of the ammunition with which others shoot. I suggest that there was nothing wrong with the Scott report in the sense of providing ammunition; it was just that there was not the political will to ensure that there were casualties either through volunteered or coerced resignation.

The lesson seems to have been learnt that there should be a time limit on the duration of an inquiry. The Nolan Committee was charged with producing its first report within six months. This will have a bearing on the report. Scott took a long time but did a thorough job: instead of being overwhelmed by the Whitehall tactic of deluging him with files, he thrived and mastered the material. However, since it was part of the record, he had to include it in the report which made it indigestible to much of the public. Speed, however, may mean a more superficial inquiry.

We may seem to have to have strayed from the initial consideration of judges as trouble-shooters into other matters. Scott has shown us that when the stakes are high, judicial investigators will not have an easy task. The general relationship between the judiciary and the other branches of government is currently one of political tension, and that is likely to continue. The judiciary's relationship with the public is unlikely to be adversely affected by these sorts of inquiries, as it will not trust anyone else to do them. The threat to the judiciary's relationship with the public comes from the judges' own forays into the political arena over topics which are regarded as important by the public like criminal justice. The Scott episode is a useful prompt to remind us that while the primary focus was on the failings of the executive and legislative branches of government, we should not neglect but keep under review the 'least dangerous branch' as Alexander Bickel termed the US Supreme Court.

1   'Politicians and the Judiciary: a Changing Relationship', *Parliamentary Affairs*, 1995, 401; and 'Politicians and the Judges: A Conflict of Interest', *Parliamentary Affairs*, 1996, 423.

2   See A. Le Sueur 'The Judicial Review Debate', *Government and Opposition*, 1996, 31, 8, arguing that it is a political strategy to engage the judges.

3   For three of his lectures see 'Ministerial Accountability' and 'The Acceptable and Unacceptable Use of Public Interest Immunity' both in *Public Law*, 1996, 410, 427; and 'The Use of Public Interest Immunity Claims in Criminal Cases' in the electronic law journal *Web Journal of Current Legal Issues* at <http://www.ncl.ac.uk/~nlawww/1996/issue2/scott2/html>.

4   See R. Stevens, 'Judges, Politics and the Confusing Role of the Judiciary', The Hardwicke Building Lecture, 21 May 1996.

5   See Stevens op. cit. who refers to lectures by Sir John Laws, 'Is the High Court the Guardian of Fundamental Constitutional Rights', *Public Law*, 1993, 59; and 'Law and Democracy' *Public Law*, 1995, 72 and by Lord Woolf , 'Droit Public—English Style', *Public Law*, 1995, 57. For an article by Lord Irvine in which he is concerned about developments in judicial review see 'Judges and Decision-Makers: The Theory and Practice of *Wednesbury* Review', *Public Law*, 1996, 59.

INDEX